RELIGION IN
PUBLIC AND
PRIVATE LIFE

RELIGION IN
PUBLIC AND
PRIVATE LIFE

CLARKE E. COCHRAN

ROUTLEDGE New York and London

Published in 1990 by

Routledge
An imprint of Routledge, Chapman and Hall, Inc.
29 West 35 Street
New York, NY 10001

Published in Great Britain by

Routledge
11 New Fetter Lane
London EC4P 4EE

Library of Congress Cataloging in Publication Data

Cochran, Clarke E.
    Religion in public and private life / Clarke E. Cochran.
      p.   cm.
    Includes bibliographical references.
    ISBN 0-415-90247-9—ISBN 0-415-90283-5 (pbk.) :
    1. United States—Religion. 2. United States—Religious life and customs. 3. Religion and sociology—United States. 4. Religion and politics—United States. I. Title.
BL2525.C62 1990
306.6'0973—dc20   89-70102

To
David, Katherine, Lee, and Margaret

Contents

Preface

This book assesses religion's private and public qualities. Because religion manifests itself in character, narratives, and institutions, it intersects the conventional distinction between private and public life. More precisely, religion suffuses private life, yet is itself a public thing. Other institutions also inhabit this territory, and religion's relation to public and private is not singular. But there are unique qualities about religion that enable it to make distinct contributions to public and private life and, therefore, to politics. At the same time, politics has something to teach religion.

This topic, put this way, is particularly important because some of our pivotal political, social, and moral controversies involve precisely the question of where to draw the line (or whether to draw it) between what is properly a private, individual concern and a public concern. This question arises, for example, in relation to abortion, prayer in public schools, child care, and provision of health and welfare services. Religious groups have said a good deal on these topics, and what they have said has become contentious in the public arena. Defining the proper role of such groups depends on understanding what is properly public and what private, and on the placement of religion with respect to those categories.

The connection between religion and politics exhibits tension, at least partly because public and private life strain against one another. Each pushes against and challenges the other. The following reflections illustrate this tension. Private life is the occasion for contact with transcendence through truth, trust, or mystery. Religion is particularly attuned to this contact. Yet transcendence is frightening, and supportive others (a public) help the person to bear it. Private life also may be the occasion for delusion; it needs correction from the public. The same public that supports must also challenge, so the relation between private and public always will be touched with tension. Similarly, there are public episodes of transcendence and delusion. The former are incomplete without private appropriation, while the latter can be challenged by individual, private witness (as in the emperor's new clothes).

From another angle, the political virtue of justice reveals the tension between private and public life, for it calls for transforming private interests into common goods. The public–private relationship must be political and dynamic, if private interest is to be transformed and if public goods are to be prevented from slipping into private hands. Change and transformation require pushing, pulling, and tugging. The private pulls against other private interests and against the public, while public strains against private. It is inaccurate to say that public and private are opposed, for each transforms the other. Each needs the other; their struggle entwines them.

Religion is a constant reminder of the unity of public and private life, but also of the boundary between them. Private and public life need each other, but they are different realms. The validity and the distinctive character of each contributes to a healthy society. Religion affirms the public–private distinction, but also the unity that lies beneath that distinction.

As a system of belief, behavior, and emotion relating to a reality beyond human control or achievement, religion suggests to the sensitive participant in culture just what is at stake in public–private controversies. Culture is first of all public; its beliefs, customs, traditions, stories, and emotions are the common possession of citizens who need share no significant private life. Culture's material and spiritual goods attract and (perhaps often) repel, just because they are part of a deeply ingrained heritage.

Because religion warns that culture is not divine, it insinuates the tension between culture and something higher than culture. Religion is linked to culture and frequently coopted by it, but the inherent dynamic of religion's orientation to a transcendent source of being independent of human control opens the path toward cultural conflict. As much as culture takes upon itself divine color, it cannot hide its human roots.

Though the tension between the divine and the mundane sometimes manifests itself as stress between private and public life, the individual person, where the competing attractions of culture and the sacred intersect, is the locus of tension. The perspective of religion reveals the person as a field of cross-cutting tensions between the divine and culture in private and public life.

Because it influences moral virtue and individual well-being, religion can powerfully assist the state by inculcating and nourishing a moral foundation for culture. Yet this role is easily misunderstood and often converted into either theocracy or civil religion. I criticize these concepts as false resolutions of the tension between religion and politics. I criticize as well the concept of separation of church and state as an account of the proper relation between religion and politics.

Although I have stressed the intersection of religion and public life, religion nevertheless fundamentally reminds us of the limits of politics and of the nonequivalence of politics and public life. We must remember that religion points resolutely to life beyond politics. It reminds us that public problems and their solutions are not entirely political. Indeed, the distinctive contribution of religion to public and private life, to individuals and to culture, is to refer them to what is beyond politics. I discuss some of these things also—

sin, evil, death, tragedy, forgiveness, promise, and trust—and how they appear on the border between public and private life.

From one point of view these reflections concern the legitimacy of religion's involvement in politics. At the same time, they concern the legitimacy of politics itself. Political legitimacy today is problematic because the boundaries of public and private life are confused. Giving the state the right to intervene in certain areas of life—reproduction, say, or moral education—disturbs those who regard these as private matters and pleases those who regard them as public issues. Some regard the appearance of religion on the political scene as timely, for it promises the moral and cultural legitimacy needed by modern politics. Others, however, though recognizing that religion in the past has addressed the question of political legitimacy, regard this behavior as improper in a secular society. Therefore, they assign religion to the private realm, precluding it from touching public legitimacy. The problem thus presented resolves itself to this: on what grounds does religion, particularly in the form of a church, legitimately concern itself with politics, and on what ground does politics legitimately concern itself with fundamental issues of morality?

The following chapters provide a complex answer to this question. Addressing both the public–private distinction and the religion–politics distinction, they operate on several levels at once. The complexity of this operation, however, is necessary if the legitimacy of religion's interaction with politics is to be fully developed. I shall keep as clear as possible the levels that each part of the book considers. But I ask the reader's indulgence in advance for inevitable shifts in level as I discuss each dimension in as many aspects as possible.

The distinctive contribution of this book is not so much the originality of its particular ideas, but the ways in which it joins ideas not previously associated. Specifically, it connects ideas about the meaning of public and private life to the recently renewed interest in virtue, character, and narrative. It then applies the resulting synthesis to the most important problems of religion and politics.

Earlier versions of parts of this book have appeared in other places. Some of the ideas of chapter 1 first appeared in "Public/Private, Secular/Sacred: A Context for Understanding the Church/State Debate," *Journal of Church and State*, 29 (Winter 1987), pp. 113–125. Part of chapter 6 appeared as "The Radical Gospel and Christian Prudence," in *The Ethical Dimension of Political Life*, ed. Francis Canavan (Durham, NC: Duke University Press, 1983). An early version of sections of chapter 8 appeared as "The Dynamics of Tension: Normative Dimensions of Religion and Politics," *Journal of Political Science*, 16 (Spring 1988), pp. 14–23. This was reprinted in C. Dunn, ed., *Religion in American Politics* (Washington: Congressional Quarterly Press, Inc., 1988.) I am most grateful for permission to use these materials here.

A book on private and public life inescapably incurs debts both private and public. These are a joy to discharge. My family supported the conception, writing, and rewriting with both real and feigned interest at the right times. My gratitude is the shape of our life together. Mary Louise and Bill Boniface furnished the quiet of Carry Over Farm at a crucial stage.

Financial and material support came from Texas Tech University in the form of a Faculty Development Leave during 1986–87 and from the Earhart Foundation as a Fellowship Research Grant during the same period. I am deeply grateful for their confidence in me. I wish also to thank the staffs of the libraries of the University of Maryland and Georgetown University, where most of the research was done. I appreciate the opportunity during my stay in Washington, D.C., to be part of the monthly breakfasts of the Association for Public Justice and the monthly Georgetown University Colloquium in Social and Political Theory. The stimulation they afforded permeates the entire work.

I am grateful to Bruce Douglass for arranging a course on religion and politics at Georgetown during the spring of 1987. My thanks go also to the students in that course—Kate Bertini, Rich Burke, Tim Giere, Dale Kuehne, and Deborah Wallace—on whom I first experimented with these ideas. I learned much from the comments and suggestions made by the students in my graduate seminar at Texas Tech, who discussed a somewhat more refined version: Travis Billings, Wade Cowan, Sean Flynn, Marsha Guffey, Y. K. Hui, Seon Hee Kwon, Tim Walker, Jim Walters, Meng Zheng Wen, Duffy Wilkes, and James Yancey. I owe a special debt to colleagues who read and made valuable suggestions on all or part of the manuscript at different stages. Thanks to: Bruce Douglass, Booth Fowler, Jim Glass, Carey McWilliams, Neal Riemer, Jim Skillen, and Glenn Tinder. Jay Wilson and the editorial staff at Routledge have worked hard to improve what I sent them.

1
Religion in Tension: Paradoxes of Public and Private Life

> No distinction essential to a discussion of
> religion and the church offers greater obsta-
> cles to clarity than that suggested by the two
> sets of terms *sacred, religious, churchly*, etc.,
> on the one hand, and *secular, profane,*
> *worldly*, etc., on the other.
> —Sydney E. Ahlstrom, *A Religious*
> *History of the American People*

Prayer is the metaphor of religion. Nothing captures the religious impulse better than the attitude of piety and dependence embodied in prayerful communication between believer and God. The postures of prayer—kneeling, upraised hands, bowed head—graphically represent religion. Privacy and prayer go together. "But when you pray, go to your private room and, when you have shut your door, pray to your Father who is in that secret place" (Matt. 6:6). Jesus' admonition links privacy and God. Religion seems primarily to concern private life. It is a path for deepening the meaning of private life.

This account, however, is only half the story. Religion is also a public thing. "Go, therefore, and make disciples of all the nations" (Matt. 28:19). Proselytization and conversion are also models of religion. Notice that the command is to convert nations, not individuals. Conversion happens publicly and has public effects, for new religious forces have cultural consequences.

Thus prayer and conversion, two essential religious phenomena, reveal a tension between public and private life. Indeed, the dilemma is even deeper, for prayer and conversion themselves are both private and public. The individual prays in secret, in her private room, but also with others in congregations and public buildings. Nations are converted, but so, obviously, are individuals—and often for quite private reasons. Religion in its most elemental character displays both public and private qualities.

This phenomenon is not uniquely Christian. Judaism describes a religion, but also a culture and an ethnic heritage. Roman religion embraced both household and public gods. Islam accommodates holy wars and Sufi mysticism. Even the relatively "apolitical" religions of the East such as Buddhism and Hinduism define entire cultures, including private and public life.

Despite the clear way religion transcends any sharp public-private dichotomy, contemporary liberal thought posits an equally problematic distinction regarding religion, that between church and state. By contemporary liberal thought, I refer to the ideological commitment to the central significance of individual freedom and the protection and advancement of that freedom through state action. Because freedom is endangered by established power and privilege, liberalism fought to protect religious freedom from established churches, relying in the American context on the idea of separation of church and state. The differentiation of church and state mirrors the contrast between sacred and secular, spiritual and temporal, holy and profane. Church involves faith, worship, and the salvation of souls. Politics, power, and policy concern the secular world. When the church enters that world, it oversteps its limits.

I shall argue that these conventional distinctions are fundamentally flawed. It is not my part to present a cultural history or a comparative cultural analysis of public and private life or religion and politics, but it is certainly fitting to remark that the conventional distinctions between secular and sacred just recounted are particularly Western. Indeed, they are especially characteristic of the modern West. Yet it is increasingly the case that the reality of modern Western life cannot conform to these widely accepted distinctions, and they have little bearing in the rest of the world.

The conventional distinction between church and state, sacred and secular, is rooted in the more fundamental contrast between public and private. Conventionally and, I shall argue, erroneously, the sacred, attentive to the individual soul and its relation to transcendence, is perceived as involving private things proper to the individual alone. In contrast, the secular is the realm of public affairs, where persons are mutually concerned with their life together. Church–Sacred–Private. State–Secular–Public. These parallel distinctions lie deep within our culture and our ideology. Of them, the most fundamental is public–private.

I intend ultimately to show that this dichotomy is untenable, at least in the forms in which it normally appears. Indeed, the focal affirmation of this book is that religion brings a vital dynamic to political life, that religious experience has a legitimate political dimension. Moreover, politics has a special relation to religious life. In this chapter, I wish to show how the distinction appears in our customary thought and discussion, how recent politics and policy reveal its weakness, and how it must be transcended.

I shall first illustrate the roots of the distinction in liberalism and in American religious and political life, including how religion itself has succumbed to the dichotomizing forces. I shall indicate also the genuine historical value of the distinction. Second, I shall illustrate how the rise of religious politics and contemporary church–state debates have clouded the conventional distinction. Third, I shall argue that current policy issues cannot be resolved if the dichotomy is preserved. The clouding is primarily due, not to new religious fervor, but to features of contemporary policy issues and conflicts that cast doubt on the distinction itself. These issues reveal the inseparability of public and private life.

The three tasks set above for this chapter prepare the ground for the argument of the book that public and private life, though possessing distinctive features, are not radically separate. The features distinctive to each define permeable spheres of life. These spheres intersect, forming regions of overlap and border territories. These metaphors must not be taken too literally. The concepts of private and public life are not to be reified. They are concepts used to mark out identifiable, but inseparable areas of human life, individual and social.

The limitations of private life are partially remedied by public. Conversely, the strengths of private life balance the limitations of public. Like all borders, that of public and private reflects elements of harmony and tension. Because religion is one of the most significant forces on the public-private border, its interaction with politics reveals in a special way the consonance and strain characteristic of the public-private border. This chapter, and the book as a whole, explore in parallel fashion public and private life, religion and politics on the public-private border, and the dynamic tensions produced by the mixture.

Public-private: Liberalism and American Culture

Michael Walzer contends that liberalism's principal achievement, characteristic, and problem is the "art of separation":

> Liberal theorists preached and practiced an art of separation. They drew
> lines, marked off different realms, and created the sociopolitical map with
> which we are still familiar. . . . Liberalism is a world of walls, and each one
> creates a new liberty.[1]

One such wall divides public from private life. The public realm, to be sure, is necessarily related to the private, but its relation is that of the police officer to the houses of a neighborhood. He is to protect them, not to peep into them.

Though there are different strands within liberalism and different kinds of liberals, they share, I believe, a common commitment to an individualist conception of value, to the centrality of freedom as autonomy, and to fair procedures and the rule of law.[2] What I am concerned with are the tendencies of this central core of individualism, autonomy, proceduralism, and rationality. These produce a strong commitment to privacy and to the separation of public and private life (in one form or another) within all varieties of liberalism.

Clearly, within liberalism, the content of the public and private realms changes over time. At one time, private agreement determined wages and working conditions. Later, public law comprehensively regulated them. At one time, law regulated abortion in the interest of public health and morality. Later, it became the private choice of the pregnant woman. Indeed, it is possible to write the history of liberalism as the story of changing ideas and practices of liberty. But the essential separation of public and private, and the contribution it makes to liberty, remains relatively stable. Liberal theory and American practice attempt to follow the art of separation by developing clear and consistent principles governing, for example, search and seizure, public disclosure of private finances, private prayer in public schools, and censorship of sexually explicit materials.

The lines shift, but the search for straight and clear ones continues, for the protection and enhancement of human development and of fundamental human rights demands an area of privacy in which the individual person makes choices and determines a direction for life. Moreover, conversely, the public realm must be protected from the attempt to impose private choices in religion, philosophy, and personal morality. Free individuals and a free society require considerable space for privacy with clearly defined boundaries and a public arena safe from private passions.

This book challenges the cleavage of public from private life, not the distinction between them. Development of institutions to protect individual liberty from the depredations of public institutions has been the great achievement of liberal politics, as has the development of institutional protection of public liberty from warring private belief. My criticism of various manifestations of the public–private split does not denigrate these achievements. It may be too much to say that liberalism's art of separation is total. First-amendment freedoms, for example, were certainly designed to protect public speech and the public uses of the freedoms of press and association.

Nevertheless, the bifurcation of these realms goes too far in contemporary liberal thought. The defense of and uses of freedom of speech, for example, have shifted in this century from a public to a private emphasis. The now common synonym "freedom of expression" for freedom of speech nicely captures the shift.

Separation of public and private, combined with the changing content of each, has created bizarre situations in ordinary life. Religion is still, according to the dominant conventions, essentially private. As such, it is too controversial and contentious to be portrayed or described, let alone evaluated, in, for example, television shows or public school textbooks. TV series characters rarely go to church, pray, or talk about religion. As recent highly publicized court cases have shown, elementary and secondary school textbooks, in deference to private religious sensibilities, hardly mention religion in American history, politics, and culture—that is, in American public life. Yet these same shows and texts devote considerable attention to the now public and controversial issues of abortion, contraception, teen sex, and homosexuality, topics until recently considered private.

Confusion about the boundaries between public and private life has been charted by analysts of popular culture for some time. Particularly telling have been Christopher Lasch's discussion of the narcissistic personality, in which the boundaries of private self and public world are dissolved, and Philip Rieff's account of how the therapeutic impulse defines a culture in which the personal becomes political.[3] The most explicit consideration of public and private in this literature, however, is the work of the sociologist Robert N. Bellah and his colleagues.[4]

Habits of the Heart attempts to understand American culture, including American politics, from the inside; that is, from the hearts of individuals as they attempt to articulate their understanding of public and private life in the cultural language available to them. *Habits of the Heart* focuses on what the authors believe to be the most significant manifestations of the sharp separation of public and private life in American culture. They explore these manifestations through interviews with "representative" Americans about their private lives of self-identity, love and marriage, work, and therapy, as well as their public lives of civic involvement, activism, citizenship and politics, and religion.

Bellah and his coauthors discover four languages of self and society in American culture: utilitarian individualism, expressive individualism, the republican tradition, and the biblical tradition. They argue that the individualist traditions have overwhelmed the republican and biblical, resulting in truncated political and social dialogue and emaciated individual life. Living culture requires argument among healthy, competing traditions. If one is dominant, culture loses its vitality, and individuals develop constricted identities, able to express only a few of their deepest longings. Contemporary culture, the authors argue, is dominated by the language of individualism (an uneasy amalgam of both individualistic strands) and value relativism. Though a second language of community (having elements of the republican and biblical traditions) percolates below the surface in their respondents' talk, it is too weak to balance the controlling individualism. Those interviewed tend to interpret even their public activities in individualistic terms. In their own commentary the authors advocate communitarian ideas, images, and symbols. In American life religion is often a refuge from the liberal world of rationalism and skepticism and from individualistic, competitive liberal political and economic life. Precisely because it is a refuge, it avoids public challenge to liberalism.[5]

As revealing as it is of how individualistic language pervades American culture, *Habits of the Heart* ultimately fails to fashion a communal alternative. It contains evocations of community, but does not achieve theoretical depth about community or its interaction with character and virtue. Moreover, the authors' recommendations for speaking to fragmented individualism appeal only briefly and vaguely to vestiges of the biblical and republican traditions, to the ecology movement and ideas of integration, and to social movements (yet to be created) to transform the social, economic, and work worlds. How these are connected to community—and, indeed, the meaning of community itself—is unspecified.

The ideas and practices discussed by Bellah and his colleagues should sound familiar, for a good deal of American political life, particularly constitutional law, has involved drawing and redrawing boundaries between individual and community, private and public. Influenced by American culture and by long-term Western secularization, American religion has also largely accepted its relegation to the private realm. The distinction between public and private in liberal political ideology has been paralleled by a theological distinction that largely kept conservative religion out of politics and allowed liberal religion in, but only on what seemed to be political not religious terms.

Liberal and conservative Christian theology part company on, among other things, the question of whether salvation is public or private.[6] Does redemption come to the individual through a community of believers mediated by public signs and rituals such as liturgy and sacraments? Or does salvation depend only on a personal, private relationship between God and the individual believer? The dominant answer, particularly in the Protestant tradition that has so shaped all American religion, is to affirm the latter, but both answers can be found.

Note the different political implications of these positions. If salvation is public, then direct action for social reform can be justified, as in the abolition, civil rights, and anti-war movements. If, however, salvation is private, then only changing individual hearts through conversion will change society for the better. Evangelical and fundamentalist religion, with its conservative view of salvation, paradoxically reinforces liberal social institutions separating public from private, secular from sacred, state from church. The evangelical-fundamentalist commitment is to the centrality of the *private* decision to accept Christ as *personal* Lord and Savior. And His salvation is principally from a life of personal sin and degradation, not of social sin!

It might well be objected at this point that I have emphasized evangelical Protestant religion at the expense of the far more communal traditions of

Catholicism and Judaism. I have, but for a reason. The reason simply is that up until recently, even Jews and Catholics have tended to adopt the private role of religion—with the exception of commitment to certain particular public policy positions. Doing so was one way of being accepted in the dominant Protestant culture. While there is certainly a tradition of more public and communal ideas of salvation in American religion, perhaps especially in Judaism and Catholicism, the dominant strain is an individualized, privatized Protestantism, to which even Jews and Catholics are not immune. Paradoxically, our civil religion requires that our deepest private religious commitments be kept to ourselves so as to give "no offense" to those of differing private beliefs.[7] It seems then perfectly reasonable for American private life to have become increasingly religious in the 1970s and 1980s as public life became increasingly secular. The paradox, of course, is that the most "private" of the religious groups, the evangelicals and fundamentalists, have gone very "public" in the last decade. This fact suggests how problematic is the public–private distinction in both culture and theology.

The separations are not as tidy as I have described nor have they ever been. But it is important to stress the public–private separation in liberal theory and American culture, and to acknowledge its value for civic peace and stability, before showing how clouded it has become and how it must be revised. For the history of religious persecution (and its contemporary horror) teach that justice and human dignity require that religious belief be protected from public coercion and that public space be protected from the violence not rarely engendered by religious passion. The liberal separation of public and private may be flawed, but a dented and battered shield has proved better than none at all in protecting American culture from the excesses of uncivil religions and political ideologies.

Defining Religion

I have frequently mentioned religion without giving it precise meaning. As a vast range of experiences may be considered religious from some perspectives, in order for my argument to attain sharp focus it must identify a more specific range of experience. I shall be rash in defining religion, giving what I hope are good reasons for my definition, but not disputing equally good definitions found in the vast literatures of theology, anthropology, philosophy of religion, sociology of religion, or the history of political theory. I do not contend that mine is a fundamentally better definition than others, only that it is better for my purposes. I do not mean that it best advances my particular arguments, but that it best reveals the private and public sides of religion and their political implications.

I shall adopt the definition employed by Peter L. Benson and Dorothy L. Williams for a purpose quite different from mine.[8] Their definition, designed for interviews with political actors, takes the mainly substantive and exclusive orientation I need, while incorporating some functional and inclusive elements, thus avoiding important traps that I shall describe below. Benson and Williams define religion in the following way:

> *Religion* (at the individual level) is the cognitions (values, beliefs, thoughts), affect (feelings, attitudes), and behaviors involved in apprehending and responding to a reality (a supernatural being or beings, force, energy, principle, absolute consciousness) that is affirmed to exist.[9]

Benson and Williams further specify that this reality must transcend human control and that it is ultimate reality, in the sense of standing behind, sustaining, or holding together the diverse phenomena of the world.

This definition has the advantage of explicitly including all of the dimensions of religion and all of the essential qualities of religion. Though it may seem to give primacy of place to belief and transcendence, the definition also explicitly requires values, thoughts, feelings, attitudes, and behaviors. Religion requires that all these dimensions be present in relation to a transcendent object. Something that only fulfills an individual need to believe, for example, would not qualify.

The definition clearly includes theistic religions such as Islam, Judaism, Roman Catholicism, and Methodism. But it also includes such nontheistic religions as Pantheism, Theravada Buddhism, and Theosophy. These religions do not have personal gods, but they do recognize a reality transcending the human and the natural physical world, and such religions make various claims about the nature of that reality. Yet the definition excludes systems that are philosophical or ideological, such as Marxism, science, humanism, and psychoanalytic theory, without denying that these have religious dimensions and perform religious functions for many persons. Such systems, however, make no claims about or in some cases deny the existence of transcendent reality.

So religion for my purposes must refer to a reality beyond the human level. And it must include dimensions of cognition, emotion, and action, that is, it cannot be simply personal belief or simply routinized behavior alone, even if these seem to refer to ultimate reality. All three dimensions must be present. When I speak of religion in the following pages, it will be with this understanding. The definition of Benson and Williams, however,focuses on the individual person, which is appropriate for their research. But religion at the border between private and public life fixes my attention. Therefore, I shall employ the Benson and Williams definition with particular attention to culturally manifested beliefs, cognition, affects, and behaviors. This treatment will allow me to address individual religiosity without privileging it. At the same time, the warnings against a narrow focus on institutional religion and the provision for individual religiosity will allow me to avoid blessing only institutional religions.

Religion, in the sense I employ here, is an orientation to the transcendent, to what its adherents believe to be beyond them (indeed, beyond any human control or dependence) in being, worth, power, and dignity. Therefore, religion provides an orientation for faith and commitment, for trust and loyalty to a center of meaning. And it generates various loosely or tightly knit particular principles governing action, including social, political, economic, moral, and cultural principles. Religion contributes to identity, for adherents define themselves—in part, at least—by their relationship to the reality beyond them. In the same way, religion provides a sense of place in the order of being and, therefore, a sense of meaning and a foundation for relations with fellow believers. Religion normally manifests itself socially in ritual, symbol, tradition, ceremony, and collective action.

Different definitions of religion are appropriate for different investigations. My definition requires justification relative to other possibilities. There are a number of well-known distinctions and difficulties associated with defining religion.[10] Definitions may be substantive or functional. The former focus on the sacred realm and capture what "looks" most like religion, but they miss important religious aspects of other phenomena captured by functional definitions. For example, substantive definitions look for belief in a god or gods, for a clerical class, for church buildings, and the like. The presence of enough of these elements means the presence of religion. Functional definitions, on the other hand, emphasize the role that such elements play in individual or social life. As these roles, or functions, are more important than the particular structures that produce them, functional definitions look for the areas of life that produce religious effects, rather than for specific structures of belief or action. If a political ideology, for example, supplies ultimate meaning for its adherents, then it is religious, whether or not it makes reference to supreme beings.

Definitions may also be inclusive or exclusive. Inclusive definitions allow incorporation of any experience or phenomenon at the individual or social level that performs religious functions, even if the person or group concerned does not recognize or consider it as religious. Psychological constructs, ideological movements, or cultural values could all be included within religion if these helped create individual or group identity and meaning. Exclusive definitions, on the other hand, require that religious phenomena be intentionally directed toward the supernatural as a way of performing certain functions. Exclusive definitions have the virtue of precision, but may miss important religious manifestations, while inclusive definitions have the danger of losing focus.

As my purpose is not sociological, I am not concerned with all possible religious phenomena. Therefore, a relatively exclusive and substantive definition is most helpful for my purposes, for it keeps the discussion focused, resisting the temptation to let religion wander far afield. So many things can with some reason claim to be religious or quasi-religious, from feelings of individual well-being to majestic panoramas and political ideologies, that disciplined discussion requires fairly precise definitions.

Therefore, I opt for a substantive and exclusive definition of religion, requiring beliefs and behaviors intentionally oriented toward a sacred or transcendent realm different from and surpassing mundane existence. Religion is not philosophy or individual belief. Though these possess some of the same functions as religion, it would unduly broaden the discussion to include philosophical systems or purely individual belief as religion. Religion must make, for my purposes, some reference to a sacred or transcendent reality.

The definition, however, needs some functional and inclusive elements, for I want to avoid some common traps. The first trap is that of defining religion institutionally. Religion in this trap becomes synonymous with church, the organized side of the sacred. Although such a focus more precisely delimits the investigation, it fatally reduces religion to its public manifestations and excludes a good deal of sacred experience, cutting it down to a common institutional denominator. The institutional concept of religion is misleading for another reason. Such a notion makes it difficult, even definitionally illegitimate, to discuss apart from the churches religion's challenge to politics or religion's dangers. If institutional religion possesses a monopoly, what do we do with the idea of civil religion or with public, noninstitutional expressions of religion such as those found in Abraham Lincoln's rhetoric?

The second trap is like the first. Substantive and exclusive definitions tend to focus discussion on the forms of religion most prominent in Western civilization and even on particularly Christian religions, for these are the most institutionalized and the most clearly oriented toward a distinction between the sacred and the profane. The institutional definition of religion prejudices the concept toward well-organized, even hierarchical, religions. Many Eastern religions have questionable claims to being religions, if we adopt too inclusive a definition. Though I am dealing primarily with the American experience of religion and politics in this book, I intend its applicability to be broader. That is, because my definition of religion is at least partially inclusive, and because institutions of public and private life occur in all cultures, the relation of religion to public and private that I propose is not exclusively American. My arguments in this book, though illustrated primarily from an American context, are generally applicable. Focusing on highly institutionalized forms of religion would be unduly restrictive and dangerously ethnocentric.

There is another trap in defining or discussing religion. This is to focus on one dimension alone. Religion is experiential, ideological, ritualistic, and intellectual. It is reductionist to call it a belief system or a ritual system, thereby identifying it with only one dimension. Although such identification may have the advantage of clarity, it misses important parts of reality. One prominent manifestation of this trap is to focus on religious "needs." For example, one might contend that every person has a need for affirmation from a source beyond his individual life, or that every society needs transcendent legitimation. Religion, then, is whatever satisfies this need.

In this view the individual aspects of religion become identified with a supposed universal, personal (or sometimes social) need satisfied by religious belief. This view fails to do justice to the historical variability of individual needs and religious institutions, and it ignores other, equally valid, dimensions of religion, such as belief and behavior. Though I shall speak of inner life and the ways in which religion relates to it, religion is not equivalent to or primarily a function of inner life or its "needs." The real issue, for my purposes, is the religious aspect of the location of the individual in society or, more precisely, of the border between private and public life.

The Clouding of Distinctions

The distinction between priestly and prophetic religion might constitute another objection to my argument about public and private within American religion. The proper distinction, this objection runs, is not between public and private salvation, but between the priestly dimension of religion, which unites the individual to God, and the prophetic, which calls the community to account before God. Priestly religion is private; prophetic religion public. This distinction, originally found in the Hebrew Bible, is indeed a legitimate strand running through many religions. It certainly has its American counterparts. The distinction, however, is too clean. Priestly religion is public as well as private, particularly in the original biblical context. The priest offered sacrifice for the whole community, and the words of the prophet could be addressed to specific individuals. Therefore, the priestly-prophetic distinction does not help us to find clear lines of separation between public and private life in a theological context.

Recent church-state debates, however, and the rise of religious politics, especially the new religious right, further disrupt any clarity of separation. The new religious right provokes negative reaction in large part because in both style and content its politics muddle the boundaries between public and private. The new religious right reveals how fragile, and ultimately untenable, are the conventional, tidy distinctions.

Jimmy Carter presaged this phenomenon. While his policies adhered to the liberal separation of church and state, his evangelical style unsettled many liberals. Similarly, the style of evangelicals and fundamentalists on the Right makes private belief explicitly the centerpiece of public policy. Disdaining to separate religious and secular life, they violate the open, tolerant, permissive, inoffensive American "religion of civility."[11] The emotional style of private salvation spills onto the public stage, disrupting its elaborate rituals of accommodation and toleration. As in the period of the Great Awakening, intensely personal, private religious experience begins to have profound public consequences.[12] Border guards standing watch over the line between public and private raise the alarm as much for potential as actual incursion. The new religious right "wants to enter the public arena making public claims on the basis of private truths," a possibility more disturbing than any substantive claims.[13]

Moreover, it is not only the religious right that has rediscovered the public dimension of private belief. All theology is now more ready to challenge traditional sacred-secular distinctions.[14] Liberation theology is only the most obvious example on the Left. Thus the separation of private and public is challenged by changes in religious life. But it would be a mistake to see the challenge as coming primarily from renewed religious fervor, thus blaming it all on Jerry Falwell. Beyond such reasons are policy conflicts and issues that inherently cast doubt on the viability of the standard American expression of the distinction. The argument of this section is that the conventional distinction between public and private is itself incoherent in both religion and politics, and technological, political, and policy developments are making this more and more clear to liberal and conservative, secular and religious groups. There is a meaning to the language of public and private, but it is not the standard meaning.

Tocqueville's discussion of religion provides a clue. Tocqueville defends the separation of church and state. Such separation protects religion from state domination, he contends; moreover, it benefits the state because a flourishing religion supplies the moral foundation for liberty and equality. A striking passage reflects this perspective:

> I have remarked that the members of the American clergy in general, without even excepting those who do not admit religious liberty, are all in favour of civil freedom; but they do not support any particular political system. They keep aloof from parties, and from public affairs. In the United States religion exercises but little influence upon the laws, and upon the details of public opinion; but it directs the manners of the community, and by regulating domestic life, it regulates the state.[15]

Tocqueville certainly exaggerates the aloofness of religion. Ministers were active in the Revolution and in the abolition movement, for example. Prohibitionism also was strongly religious. And these are only the major examples. But, compared to eighteenth- and nineteenth-century Europe, Tocqueville's point about the general detachment and nonpartisan stance of the clergy is well taken. Aloofness from secular affairs and involvement in domestic life, however, depend on the state's reciprocal aloofness from the private, domestic sphere. Today, however, government has (necessarily) entered deeply into domestic life, and citizens look to government to protect their private interests. Religion in response has entered public life.

This point may be reinforced by some striking recent examples of how public and private intersect and mingle. I want to draw particularly from issues of reproduction, sexuality, and family life, without suggesting that these are the only issues of religion and politics or the only areas of intersection. But they do illustrate quickly and clearly the incoherence of a sharp public-private distinction in contemporary politics.

Reproduction

What could be more private than making babies? *Prima facie*, the decision to conceive and conception itself are (private) matters for a husband and wife. But consider the possibilities for conception in the late twentieth century: sexual intercourse; artificial insemination; artificial insemination by donor; *in vitro* fertilization; surrogate mothers. In some of these procedures a single man or woman might decide to have a child with no normal participation by a member of the opposite sex, surely the ultimate in privacy!

Notice that these newly devised technologies of reproduction involve moral issues on which religion and "private" morality clearly and legitimately have a voice. Yet they are also issues that require law and public regulation for many sorts of reasons: legal permissibility of the procedures; protection of the rights of all the parties involved (parents, surrogates, donors, physicians); informed consent; licensing of qualified medical personnel; and the question of public funding for the procedures themselves and for research and development. The recent "Baby M" case demonstrates the necessity of laws governing new procedures of conception. Methods of alternate conception move reproduction from the privacy of the marriage bed to the public arena. Is not the private marriage bed itself created by the public institution of marriage?

Is abortion best grasped politically and legally as a private matter between a woman and her physician or as a public question of justice for unborn children? Should abortion (if permitted) be financed by private or by public funds? As "pro-life" advocates today argue, the slavery controversy of the nineteenth-century was built on the ultimate impossibility of considering the slave simply a piece of private property. Likewise, the private realm cannot contain the dynamics of abortion.

Sexuality

Sexual relations take place in the privacy of the home; yet for thousands of years they have been closely regulated by religious practices and codes of ethics, both private and public. Sexuality has been a prominent issue on the public agenda in the 1980s, as the following topics illustrate: local ordinances forbidding discrimination against homosexuals; the constitutionality of sodomy laws; sex education in the public schools; AIDS; federal funding for family planning and contraceptive services; pornography. Pornography after all fixates on the public display of private parts. Is it most appropriately considered a matter of private taste or public morality and decency? Would mandatory AIDS testing be an invasion of privacy or an essential public-health measure?

Family

The changes in reproduction and sexuality just alluded to reflect and affect basic family values and structures, which are also undergoing change for other reasons. While the family is the locus of domestic, private life, it is also *par excellence* a public institution. One of the fundamental sources of private rights, it is charged with essential public responsibilities, such as child-rearing and property transmittal. Moreover, recent changes in family life (especially gender roles, divorce, and illegitimacy) have profoundly affected such public policy issues as: economic stability, child care, child abuse, crime rates, poverty and welfare, women's rights, and health care.

To the new religious right the decay of the traditional family symbolizes the decay of a nation that has deserted God. Prayer in the public schools becomes a symbolic rallying cry for worry about the family and its effect on the nation. Though prayer is among the most private activities, it has many public forms. Prayer in the public schools becomes a public affirmation of the nation's intention to return to traditional ways in both public and private life. That the public school should be such a rallying point is ironic, as education as a *public* requirement and responsibility is only somewhat more than a hundred years old in this country. And the recent growth of home schools and fundamentalist schools illustrates the difficulty of determining whether education is clearly a private or a public right and responsibility.[16]

The critical point is that these divisive social issues have entered into and profoundly affected both religious and political consciousness. Questions of reproduction, sexuality, and family life have troubled the courts, legislatures, and presidential campaigns. These same issues exercise the religious imagination as well, and not only in recent years. As I have suggested, religious codes have regulated reproduction, sex, and family for thousands of years. Now the political and cultural implications of these issues have taken on importance in the churches. Such issues make very evident the tensions on the borders of both public and private life and of religion and politics.

Conclusions

American church-state debates and issues of religion and politics can be fully understood only in the context of the separation of public and private life in liberal political theory and American politics. Yet the emergence of religious politics has clouded the distinction between public and private, as has the emergence of public policy questions concerning reproduction, sexuality, the role of women, and the development of the modern state. These issues cast grave doubt on our received understanding of the separation of public from private life. Therefore, they cast grave doubt on our understanding of religion and politics.

The distinction between public and private is crucial to liberalism because it is a foundational concept in liberal society. The absence of a distinction between public and private life is one defining characteristic of totalitarianism and of other nonliberal schools of political thought and practice. Liberalism attempts to resolve policy questions of sexuality, reproduction, family life, and euthanasia by establishing areas of protected private rights for individual persons or families.

Liberalism, then, is committed to an equilibrium between the public and private spheres of life. Contemporary social and cultural disequilibrium, however, will preclude restoration of balance unless more integral conceptions of individual and society can replace the predominantly individualistic assumptions of liberal political theory. Moreover, no clarity about fundamental policy questions is possible until the relation between public and private life can be clarified. In addition, as the meaning of public and private become more uncertain, fundamental liberal values such as public interest, participation, individual rights, and privacy become more difficult to defend.[17]

My focus will be on the public–private distinction itself and its coherence. Recent works in the history of political theory and in liberalism refer to this distinction and even advocate locating issues on one or the other side of it, but they largely take the meaning of these terms for granted, assuming an eternal fixity about the public and private realms. But this is just what is questionable. What does make something private or public, and are there clear boundaries between them? As long as we adhere to traditional categories of public and private, the idea of separation of church and state will dominate our thinking about religion and politics. And we shall fail to understand the more profound place of religion in political life.

The previous arguments clearly set a task for political philosophy. The nature of public and private life must be examined so that the distinction may be reformulated or, quite possibly, transcended. Such a task demands investigation of the foundations of both personal character and of community and the ways in which they depend on both public space and private intimacy. The task demands as well examination of the ways in which religion is fundamentally both private and public.

The temptation is to treat the distinction between public and private as fixed. Yet the boundaries may be dependent upon circumstances, with no fixed, essential distinction possible. Easy answers to the boundary question will not do. Rather, the boundary must be seen as a border with its particular tensions and difficulties. Life on this border is not easy, but it is not impossible either. Rather, its own special rewards and hardships must be described and appreciated.

How do we determine when some particular thing is appropriately treated as public and when as private? Most things, even if there is a fixed boundary in some areas, are neither simply one nor the other; therefore, we need principles to determine how to treat them in concrete situations. Witness the policy examples of abortion, family, gender, and education. The social world blends both private and public. That the same phenomenon can sometimes properly be public and sometimes private suggests that these are overlapping spheres of life. Their dynamic interaction with religion is the focus of this book.

Faith, whether Christian, Jewish, Islamic, or Hindu, has never fit nicely into either category. Obviously, faith possesses many attributes of privacy and demands a large measure of freedom from public interference. But just as clearly, faith manifests both public dimensions of worship, creed, and ethical directive. Religion is located at the crossroads of public and private; therefore, it is deeply involved in the policy questions of our time.

Because it sits at the private-public crossroads, religion has political effects. For example, the notion of civil religion, as propounded by some of its advocates, suggests that a stable political society requires a strong measure of public faith. What is the evidence for this contention? Is it in fact true? And, if so, what is and should be the relationship between the public faith of a society and its private faiths? Merely to say that religion has public dimensions is not therefore to conclude that it must or should function as a cultural legitimator.

The principal danger is the desire for harmony, the desire to wrap all phenomena and concepts into one neat package without loose ends. Indeed, separating public and private, politics and religion, is an effort to assure harmony by quarantine. I have argued that this solution is not possible. Though there may be occasions for harmony, life on the border is one of tension. We should beware of easy harmonizations. Indeed, we shall discover in the following chapters that there is no fixed solution, no smooth dovetail between public and private (or religion and politics). But neither need there be war between them. The solution lies in learning to live in and to appreciate the tension between the disparate attractions of public and private life, between their often competing claims. Simple solutions like civil religion, secularization, and separation of church and state will not do.

There is a new fascination with integration in contemporary political philosophy. By this I mean a concern to connect different aspects of life, emphasizing development from one stage of life to another, and recognizing communal bonds. I have in mind the new communitarian literature represented by thinkers such as Michael Sandel and Michael Walzer, the turn to scriptural interpretation by political scientists such as Walzer and Aaron Wildavsky, the revival of Aristotelian perspectives and narrative concerns represented by Alasdair MacIntyre, and the new attention to first principles and ethical naturalism represented by Hadley Arkes and J. Budziszewski.[18]

Even liberalism, the great practitioner of the art of separation, has begun to search and discover within itself a reconciliation of individuality and community, private and public life. The fragmentation of politics and culture in contemporary society has demanded of liberalism renewed attention to such matters.[19] Naturalism, scripture, community, and narrative weave together individual and social, fact and value, public and private, theory and practice, personal qualities and the real world. The narrative turn weaves together past and present, thoughts, feeling, and actions, and the human, natural, and (perhaps) supernatural worlds, focusing on character and the traditions that link it to community.

There is a great deal to be said for this movement, and I have said some of it. But the tragic dimension of human life makes it plain that we cannot have all the good things, that even goods sometimes conflict, and that personal character resists total absorption in community. Public and private, though not separate, are different aspects of life. The following chapters explore this difference and the role religion plays in conserving it.

Religion is both like and unlike other institutions and experiences. Religion weaves its way through private and public life. Yet religion carries marks that distinguish it from other phenomena, and these marks press conspicuously upon the private and public worlds.

Not the least reason for making this claim is that religion itself generates distinctive features of public and private life. Even without an historical or cross-cultural examination, it is clear that different religions (and the same religions at different times) produce different evaluations of the relative importance of public and private life. A religion such as Judaism, which emphasizes the history of a people and collective responsibility, is attuned to the public effects of individual action and provides structures for public participation—for example, through ritual—in the deepest religious experiences. The formative effect of such structures and experiences has political influences as well. Even more, Judaism offers the origins of a covenantal conception of political order. Yet such faith also has specific consequences for the private realm as well, as the religious significance of the family in Judaism illustrates.

To take another example, the implications of viewing salvation primarily in terms of the individual or primarily in terms of the community of believers are substantial for family life, individual behavior, political participation, and public policy. The ways in which this belief is expressed in theology, prayer, worship, and the social structures of the faithful have an impact on the pattern and evaluation of private and public life among the faithful. The differences between Catholics and evangelicals in the United States, for example, stem substantially from such factors.

Moreover, as the social organization of the faithful is public from the perspective of the individual believer, the religious realm itself is a forum for public participation when that realm is constituted by structures open to many or most of the members. Tocqueville reflected in these terms on the salutary effects of American religion in educating democracy.[20] Public participation within the church teaches skills that may be transferable to the state. Yet this is not always the case, and religion's relation to the political realm is certainly not uniform. It is equally possible, and historically the case within certain periods in Christianity, for example, that the stress placed on individual salvation or on the community of believers impugned the political realm.

Moreover, the historical development of some religions makes them far more amenable to alliance with the public world than with the private. Islam, for example, originating as it does in alliance with a political and military force of tremendous energy, remains today a most public faith. This does not mean, of course, that it rules out the existence of private life, only that the fusion of faith and political power is more "natural" in Islam than in Buddhism, for example.

I have used the images of border and tension to describe the connection between private and public life and between religion and politics. I want at this point to be especially clear about the implications of these images and, therefore, about various dimensions of the relationship between public and private life.

Borders define territories over which polities rule. Territories expand and contract over time. Thus, the areas of life principally governed by the structures of the private realm change from time to time, even though its defining characteristics do not. The public realm operates similarly. Public and private life are not universal ontological categories. Unfortunately, we make the same mistakes in theory as in politics. We mistake the territory for the polity itself. Neither the United States nor Saudi Arabia, say, is simply territory within current geographical boundaries, though these are inseparable from the nation and enter into its identity. Rather, each nation is best defined by its distinctive principles and structures of government and power and by the

particular way of life of its people. I realize that the matter is more complicated than this, and that there are well-known identity paradoxes first considered by Aristotle. But I intend the analogy to clarify the relation between
public and private, not to serve as a subject in its own right.

With respect to public and private the analogy establishes that it is a
mistake totally to identify public and private with particular territories, that
is, substantive areas of life such as ruling, sexuality, family, religion, or
productive labor. Doing so leads to the erroneous conclusion that, as there
is no universal or constant territory of either public or private life, public
and private are therefore simply terms of convenience with no fixed meaning
or—an equally erroneous conclusion—that one is simply a subcategory of
the other. Rather, we must realize that there are stable characteristics to the
two terms and that they represent different aspects of life, although the
substantive areas they govern (some more fittingly than others) vary from
time to time and from culture to culture.

All this is to say that public and private life are distinct concepts. What
about their borders? Borders both divide and attach. National boundaries
separate one state from another, but also establish a relationship between
them. Mexico has an option whether to establish a relationship with Zambia,
but it has no choice about the United States. These two countries must
develop a connection. This relation will establish what goes on at the border
and what crosses the border, legally and illegally. Will the border be tranquil
or tense, militarized or demilitarized, open, fenced, or walled? Think of
various national borders. Such examples suggest the range of possibilities.
There will always be commerce across borders. Sometimes the commerce is
free, open, large-scale, and mainly legal. Sometimes it is highly regulated,
minimal, and principally contraband. But borders always present two sorts
of questions: how tense are things at the border? and what kinds of commerce
in persons and things cross that border?

Put this in terms of public and private life. The first question establishes
whether their relationship is primarily tense, antagonistic, or harmonious.
The commerce relation specifies the conditions under which certain matters
can pass from public to private, and vice versa, as well as the conditions
under which private life can intervene in public, and vice versa.

The temptation of a study such as this is to want the public–private border
to be harmonious and tidy, to have clear definitions of the edges of each
form of life and definite specifications of the limits of each, and to indicate
definitively what may cross and under what conditions. Clear rules initiate,
it is thought, peace and harmony. There is, however, another possibility: the
peace and harmony of the grave.

If the metaphor of the border is misleading, it may be helpful to imagine
the border not as a line, but as the common area defined by two partially
overlapping spheres. These are the spheres of public and of private life. The

space defined by their overlapping is rich with possibilities. All kinds of institutions and social structures exist at least partially in this space—family, economic enterprise, social clubs, hobby associations, and religion. The ways they live in this space vary historically and culturally.

As all of these structures occupy this border territory, all will find a place in the pages that follow. But these pages are most concerned with religion's place in this domain and with how it touches the political activity of the public sphere.

2

Private Life

Private faces in public places
Are wiser and nicer
Than public faces in private places.
—W. H. Auden

There is a strong tendency to treat public and private as phenomena of inclusion and exclusion. In this dichotomy the public becomes the realm of inclusion, in which many persons have rights to space, information, resources, and so forth.[1] Persons in the public realm have the right to be included in the activities affecting the entire society generally and themselves particularly. Conversely, the private realm is one of exclusion. In private the individual person or group may exclude others from interaction, from information, resources, and space. In other words, the person or group controls access. The primary experience may be seen either as a right against society (the liberal emphasis) or as deprivation from the more inclusive public experience (the participatory democracy emphasis), but it is the same phenomenon. Although there is truth to this account of public and private, it is a limited truth.

Barrington Moore's examination of primitive societies leads him to the conclusion that, though in some societies it seems "very nearly the case" that there is nothing to correspond to American notions of privacy, the desire for privacy in some regard appears universal. Privacy and rights to privacy, however, develop only as the public develops, as societies become more complex and organized. Other research on primitive cultures also suggests that there is something universal about privacy and its relation to publicity.[2]

Yet to show that the desire, at least occasionally, to exclude others from some areas of one's life is universal is not to prove that the public-private distinction as we know it in modern Western society is universal. It is likely that not all cultures have it. This is Martin Krygier's finding after considering the public law, private law distinction in "stateless" societies.[3]

To recognize, however, that the conventional Western private-public distinction is not universal, is not to argue against a distinction between public and private and its importance even in primitive societies. Indeed, Krygier's

21

verdict reinforces the importance of the *relationship* between public and private. It appears that the desire for some area of privacy is culturally universal, but that the occasions for that desire are not. Moreover, the realization of the desire (that is, the existence of private life) is dependent on an at least quasi-public sphere. What is significant is that there is a foundation for private life in the basic need to have (at least occasionally) a place and time of one's own and that this desire is socially structured. The suggestion that structures for realizing the desire are dependent upon a public realm also suggests that, as much as we might wish to divorce public from private, they are symbiotic.[4]

The tensions between public and private can be fully explicated only if the notion of exclusion from access is balanced by an inclusive element in private life. In short, the very fact of tension between private and public suggests that they cannot be seen apart from one another. While the desire for privacy may be universal, the public realm determines the social structures required to realize the desire. Hence, the public facilitates the private at the very time its own oppressiveness puts it in tension with the private.

This chapter makes two claims. First, though the private sphere is often defined by exclusion, private life also discloses an inclusive character, which gives purpose to private life, providing it with the impetus to break out of the closed world of the self. Moreover, the private world's inclusivity overlaps with the public sphere. Second, religion is the best indicator of the unity of the inclusive and exclusive sides of private life. Though religion is deeply connected to the fundamental qualities of the private sphere, it cannot be simply a private matter. Because inclusivity draws the private into connection with the public, religion too becomes part of the public sphere.

Privacy and Private Life

Privacy signals the clearest tension between public and private life. The term "private life" itself carries little emotional baggage. Its definition may spark debate, but not passionate disagreement. Politically it carries even less charge. Privacy, on the other hand, immediately suggests rights and the exclusion of the public (or part of it) from areas of private life. Yet private life and privacy are not coextensive. The life of the family, for example, is normally considered private, but the right to privacy within the family is more limited than the life of the family. When it is "out in public," a family is still living its life, but its privacy claims are much diminished. The public also can demand of families information about the health and income of members and can even remove children under certain circumstances. On the other hand, a judge may have a claim to privacy in her "private chambers." A certain right to privacy pertains even to her conduct of public business.

Thus, although privacy and private life are closely related, they are certainly not equivalent.

Privacy is politically highly charged; emotional and ideological issues such as abortion, pornography, and drug testing evoke the claim of a moral or legal right to protect an area of life from public scrutiny; that is, they evoke privacy claims.

Given this fact, it is not surprising to find an overwhelming philosophical, political, and legal literature on privacy and the right to privacy.[5] Privacy strongly implies the differentiation of self from others and the exclusion of others from, or at least control of others' access to, important parts of one's life. Though privacy is highly valued in modern culture, approval is not unqualified. The excluded often do not appreciate the privacy claim and resent their separation. After all, if he has nothing to hide (read: if he weren't trying to be so high and mighty), why won't he talk to us? Moreover, privacy may be viewed as a political threat to the community, an opportunity for subversion. Or privacy may prove a cultural threat to common values by creating new, or at least different, values. Fear and resentment conspire to arouse the public against privacy.

The public might be right. Rights to privacy are very useful to spies, traitors, thieves, and liars. Yet privacy also is valued for protection of the person and of intimate relations from the destructive prying of outsiders, especially the state. The privacy literature is rife both with accounts of contemporary technological and political threats to privacy and with doubts about the efficacy of the concept at all.

I want to avoid most of this literature and most of these controversies. The debates are often ingrown and parochial; discussions of threats to privacy are repetitive; emotions run high. The more neutral ground of private life should prove firmer. Once we have a purchase on it and a sense of its textures, we shall be in a better position to handle privacy. For privacy is a derivative concept from private life. It witnesses the need to protect and nurture private life. Because privacy involves claims about the right to a private life, private life has first title to theoretical attention.

There is another reason to put privacy aside temporarily. Privacy discussions often focus on unusual circumstances or difficult moral issues, for example, the right to abortion, wiretapping in racketeering investigations, and centralized computer data banks. Because of the social value of special talent and exceptional achievement, attention converges on hard cases and threats to privacy. Yet ordinary days characterize most of private life. To turn attention quickly to privacy and its admittedly important issues is to miss the weight of the common activities of private life. Children close their doors to study or listen to music; parents feed, cloth, teach, and discipline their children without outside interference; individuals pray or decline to pray without public repercussions. What is the shape and significance of these forms of ordinary private life? What is their bearing on public life?

Privacy applies to both individuals and groups. Just as individual persons have rights to privacy, groups have rights to control access to information and to other aspects of their lives. A family might seek private space for itself collectively, through a vacation in an isolated cottage. Or an individual family member might seek a room of her own. Although family life is private, it has public characteristics from the point of view of the individual family member. This chapter will move back and forth between individual and group private life.

Characteristics of Private Life

Definition of Private Life

One thing must be clear. With private as with public, meanings change rapidly. Matters considered private in one culture may not be in another; matters considered private at one time in a particular culture do not remain so at all times. We need not go as far as Tracy Strong, who contends that there is no constant part of an individual that is essentially private, to recognize that generalization about private life is very difficult. Michael Walzer, for example, points out that "in Europe during the Middle Ages, the care of souls was public, the care of bodies private. Today, in most European countries, the situation is reversed."[6] This observation possesses significance for religion as well as for the variability of public and private. Religion appears private in this chapter, but Walzer's remark shows that it is not essentially so. Its public character appears in the following chapter. Thus, it is misleading to define private life by listing certain domains of life as essentially private, for example, religion, family, sexual intercourse, and excretion. At this point, we must be satisfied with rough generalizations about the qualitative differences that make areas of life private rather than public.

The phrase "rather than public" suggests the most basic and common sense of private, its contrast with public. Indeed, some of the oldest senses of the word have connotations of loss, taking away, or absence associated with not being public, meanings the words "privation" and "deprivation" retain today.[7] These emphasized the exclusivity of the private. Their original etymology is from the Latin *privatus*, meaning withdrawn from public life, deprived of office, or peculiar to oneself, and this word is itself derived from *privare*, meaning to bereave or to deprive. In general, the *Oxford English Dictionary* takes the meaning of "private" to be "opposite of public." Thus a private person is one not holding public office. The military rank of private designates a common soldier, one without rank or distinction. Private can mean concealed or secret, that is, kept from public view or knowledge, and its meaning includes those things not open to the public or to public view as in private parts, private property, private meeting, private home.[8] Thus, private things are those belonging or pertaining to particular individuals or groups rather than to the public as a whole. The sense of physical separation is enhanced in somewhat archaic, but still telling, uses of "private" with respect to places or persons in the sense of retired (or retiring), secluded, and unfrequented. For example, "He is a very private person."

Even though the similar word "privilege" has a different etymology, there is room with respect to "private" for positive connotations, particularly as modern individualism develops. For things and places not open to the public are privileged. Prerogative of access, not deprivation, becomes the distinctive mark of the private realm. Inclusion in a special group is impossible without excluding outsiders. Although the original and dominant meaning of private relates to exclusion from public, the term necessarily encompasses those included.

The senses of individual versus public, of exclusion (and to some extent of inclusion), of hidden and open are captured in van Gunsteren's summary of the conventional contrast between public and private[9]:

Public	*Private*
free access	restricted access
authority and law	power and love
artificial, human construct	naturally given
impersonality	intimacy, privacy
bureaucracy	initiative, creativity
politics, decisions for collectivities	free exchange among individuals
outer	inner
body	mind

Note that positive connotations tend to fall into the private column, a reversal of the etymological origins and another confirmation of the variability in these concepts.

These general considerations and contrasts, however, do not move us very far toward a precise understanding of private life. Some definitions of privacy, however, have the potential to clarify the more general term, private. Michael Weinstein, for example, points out that "shorn of theoretical interpretation, privacy appears in consciousness as a condition of voluntary limitation of communication to or from certain others, in a situation, with respect to specified information, for the purpose of conducting an activity in pursuit of a perceived good."[10] Applied to private life, this definition includes the contrast with public, for the private is voluntary (though, pace Weinstein, it may be possible in some instances for genuine private life to emerge even in situations of involuntary exclusion) limitation of contact with others with respect to certain information. This limitation points up the exclusionary side of private life. The family, for example, is private with respect to the state, for it voluntarily limits disclosure of many aspects of its life, keeping them secret, hidden, or isolated from the state's agents. Yet Weinstein's definition also suggests an inclusive side of private life in the reference to pursuit of a perceived good. The family withdraws in order to expand the possibilities of family life, to achieve goods that would be impossible if its activities were open to the gaze of the public.

Limited access does mean control or exclusion. But intimacy, solitude, anonymity, and reserve are inclusive, for they are ways of being in which personal goods such as thinking, deciding, and praying are pursued, in which personhood is developed. Looking at private life as both exclusion and inclusion helps to make sense of J. Roland Pennock's finding that various discussions of privacy (and this is applicable to private life as well) seem to involve two different dimensions: autonomy and control of access to information. Some authors stress the former, others the latter.[11] The former stresses the activities of private life, the freedom of the self to develop its own ways, to make its own choices. The latter entails exclusion of others from specified areas of life.

This division in the literature of privacy suggests nothing so much as the similar split in the literature of freedom between positive and negative understandings, "freedom to" and "freedom from." Though partisans of each do fierce battle, one implies the other. Freedom is meaningless unless it is freedom from some restrictions in order to pursue or to choose among some range of goods.[12] The ability to choose certain ends signifies that one is free from restrictions on choosing them. Just as freedom involves two inseparable dimensions, private life involves two complementary phenomena. To define the excluded is to specify the included. Actively to grant some persons a right to participate is to define who is not welcome. This perspective works even in the most private area of life, solitude. Here everyone else is excluded except the individual person. Even though no one else is included, the point of seeking solitude is to include in one's life parts of oneself denied a hearing on other occasions.

I have not traveled very far on the road to understanding private life. I have argued that private life cannot be defined by certain forms or domains of life (family, for example). Rather, it should be defined by qualities of exclusion and inclusion. I have given preliminary clarification to what I mean by the ideas of exclusion and inclusion. And I have made the case that both are necessary parts of private life. Next I hope to show that this truth is more than trivial. It is more than true by definition, an objection to which my discussion is so far open. Rather, each dimension makes a separate and distinct contribution to the qualities of private life and to the totality of personal and political good. First, however, I want to show how religion is intimately associated with private life. As modern culture characteristically considers religion a private matter, the discussion need not be protracted.

Religion and Private Conscience

It seems natural in contemporary society to look first for religion in the private realm. And so shall we; for whatever else religion is, it resides in the believer's character and private conscience. This is doubly so in the West, for the Christianity that came to dominate the religious life of Western culture challenged the primacy of politics.[13] This challenge was particularly significant, for in the classical city public life, though often honored in the breach, took pride of place. By appealing to the virtues of simple, daily life and by opening the lives of ordinary people to direct contact with God, Christianity exalted the private realm's eminence.

This feature of Christianity especially troubled Arendt, who argued that private virtues endanger the public realm.[14] Once private life becomes primary, individuals are tempted to allow collective life to be made; that is, administered by others, which places it in the realm of fabrication rather than action. Turned over to experts, the public realm loses its distinctive character, as the former citizens can gorge themselves on private consumption.

Arendt argued that public life is needed to fight the private world's powerful attractions of comfort and satiation. Until Christianity burst into the classical world with evangelistic fervor, the evident vulgarity of the private world kept the best minds from embracing it. The appearance of Christianity, however, posed a real problem, for it presented the possibility of an administered society (hence, no need for politics) designed to liberate individuals not for vulgar, material consumption, but for prayer, contemplation, and worldlessness. Here was a private ideal attractive to the most exalted minds and spirits, while still offering salvation to the most ordinary peasant or artisan.

The validity of Arendt's insight turns on the nature of love, the highest Christian virtue. Whether Christianity is worldless or worldly, private or public, turns on whether love moves beyond public action, as Arendt believed, or constitutes public action *par excellence*, respecting persons and creating a new world between them. But one need not fully accept Arendt's interpretation of Christianity to see the problem, a problem not limited to Christianity. Any religion promising individual salvation based on personal action or faith can bypass the public. Though such religions might acknowledge its importance for preserving prosperity, stability, and peace, the public realm possesses no intrinsic value. Therefore, it can be left to the administration of kings, bureaucrats, prelates, or presidents, while individual believers work out their own salvation.

One may deplore this situation, as does Arendt, or applaud it. The point here is not to evaluate this feature of religion, but to draw attention to it. For religion, especially religion in the West and in America, is clearly a phenomenon of private life.

Moreover, religion's focus on the soul of the individual believer suggests a deep and private grounding of character and virtue. The qualities most prized by religions are frequently those of character or soul—for example, patience, faith, detachment, ahimsa, tranquility.

The origins of individual character and virtue are mysteries.[15] Participation in religion's public ceremonies is insufficient to explain why a person turns out this way instead of that. There is a unique side of character, a singular mix of virtues and vices, that, despite similarities within a religious tradition, marks each believer as original. Religion is irreducibly private.

The role of confession keenly points to the centrality of private conscience and the context of intimacy. Not all religions have institutionalized self-disclosure of failings, sins, and vices. But many do, formally or informally. Though one thinks of the Catholic ritual disclosure of sins to a priest as confession, similar practices appear in many forms. It may occur in counseling, in a congregational setting, in intimate sharing among friends. In whatever way it happens, however, confession points to the contexts of private life—intimacy, trust, family, friendship.[16] Conscience and character, deeply connected to religious faith in believers, need confession, and confession must have the protection of private life, so that public roles can continue.

Exclusion and Private Life

Why are the following appropriately private: sexual intercourse, a family's discussion of its vacation plans, a children's soccer coach discussing with a player the player's tendency to cry on the field, and an artist's unfinished canvas? Note that all of these may on occasion have public sides, when, for example, the intercourse involves coercion; the vacation plans affect employers; persecution by other team members causes the tears; the artist invites general comment on the canvas. The practices of particular cultures may also contrive to make all of these things, or at least certain aspects of them, regularly public. Normally, however, in American culture each of these matters is considered primarily private and may even involve rights to exclude others from participation or from observation. Here is the sense of private as exclusion, as opposite of public. The private is defined by its hiddenness from public view, by its removal from public concern and scrutiny, by control of access and resources. But what makes such matters as the examples above appropriately private in this sense? What is it about them that, for the most part and in this culture, excludes the public? Answering these questions requires exploring a number of dimensions of exclusion: the personal, secrecy, shame, imperfection, and mystery. It is these qualities that define the exclusive dimension of the private sphere.

Personal versus Impersonal

Some things are personal, no one else's proper concern. "Mind your own business" expresses this well. But what makes something a particular person's business? One answer avers that the private-public line separates the personal from the impersonal. A family's vacation plans involve the personal dynamics of the family members, each family's particular relationships between parent and child, child and child, and spouse and spouse. To subject discussions of dates, places, and activities to outside view is to make the planning impersonal, to study it as part of the sociology of leisure, perhaps, or to subject it to the blandishments of tourist agencies.

Some areas of life must be set apart from the public, because the public is necessarily largely impersonal, especially in modern society. Setting personal areas of life apart from the public protects them from the invasion of impersonality, in which the intimate areas of individual and family life lose their singularity and are molded to fit the bureaucratic requirements of government and business. Though disclosure of personal matters can contribute to personal development, disclosing them in an impersonal setting deforms the personal instead of enriching it. As John R. Silber has said, "Complete disclosure . . . may be fulfilling, redemptive, and enlarging only when it is disclosure before a person of very special qualities in an atmosphere of utter trust."[17] The impersonality of modern society explains much of the concern for privacy in America. Protecting private life shelters the personal from the impersonal forces of contemporary business, culture, and politics. Thus, at one level, making personal matters private requires no justification except that they are personal. Personal intimacy may be overridden by other moral considerations, but it creates a presumption for private life that justifies exclusion of all or part of the public.

The connection of religion with these features of the personal is evident. "My faith is my personal business" is a common sort of phrase, and it manifests a basic truth. Whatever one's faith or lack of faith is, it is one's own. Whatever else it exists to do, religion intends to make the transcendent approachable, to link it to the deepest recesses of the person's heart. This does not mean that the transcendent becomes familiar. This is hardly the case in many religions, and virtually all religions maintain some distance between the divine and the believer. Nevertheless, the public can be thought of as impersonal, but religion cannot. Formal, yes; but not impersonal.

Secrecy

The private is often the secret. The personal is frequently hidden. Some religions have secret rites of initiation, for example, puberty rites or the

Eleusinian Mysteries, designed to bring individuals into contact with the transcendent. Erotic love involves confidences and secret assignations. Sexual intercourse is hidden from view. There are, of course, many kinds of secrets, from elopement plans to blueprints for military systems. Secrecy involves all levels from the person to the entire society.[18] The private and the secret are not the same, but they are related, and private life often entails specific, deliberate attempts to conceal.

Suspicion of the private often proceeds from this quality. Private life allows hiding many things, some of which would best be revealed. Lies, fraud, deceit, hypocrisy, and deceptions of all kinds depend on secrecy. Though personal matters counsel privacy, they also facilitate deceits that depend on concealment. Private life "provides the cover under which most human wrongdoing takes place, and then it protects the guilty from taking responsibility for their transgressions once committed."[19] Private life has its grim side, nowhere more nasty than here. The hidden is suspect. Protection of the home from police searches allows evidence of vicious crimes to be hidden or destroyed—hence, the frequent criticisms of the exclusionary rule in American constitutional law. Corruption, malfeasance, and dangerous policies may be concealed by reasons of state security. Personal friendships are broken by secrets. Suspicion of secrecy spills over into private life. Private life includes secrets that are personal and familial, the secrets of a friendship, and the secrets of a business partnership. The accusatory question, "What have you got to hide?" is as effective in private life as in public.

Secrecy facilitates deceit. But it also facilitates goodness, at both important and trivial levels. "There is such a thing as an innocent secret. Those who believe that only the guilty have anything to hide . . . deserve to go through life without ever receiving birthday surprises."[20] Secrets, the ultimate exclusion, foster personal and social good. Pleasant surprises must be kept hidden. The secret words lovers speak to one another reinforce their attachment. It even conduces to the good to hide less than noble things. Some personal faults, if revealed, could ruin a marriage or a friendship. Ordinary social intercourse requires that we keep to ourselves many of our impressions, opinions, and assessments. The secret dimension of private life makes routine, peaceful, and mutually beneficial interaction possible, though at the very real cost of allowing concealment of many damaging deceits and the escape of many guilty parties. Secrets, despite their double nature, are the stuff of private life.

Shame

Private life also comprises the exclusion of the public for reasons of shame and guilt. This dimension is closely related to secrecy. Many secrets involve guilt and shame for past actions.[21] We are ashamed when our guilt appears in public. The face we try to present publicly is, if not perfect, at least calculated to be acceptable, either to the whole public or to a certain group. But this public face is not the whole self; it is a self with "makeup" to cover the blemishes and to highlight the strong features. Some people are afraid to be seen in public without cosmetics. All of us are ashamed to be seen without our psychic cosmetics. We think and do so many rotten things; we fail to do so many fine things. These truths are part of our lives, individual and collective (e.g., secrets bringing shame on an entire family), and we keep them private because of the guilt and shame they produce.

Public disclosure, then, is not the only cause of shame. We can also feel ashamed of ourselves privately, internally. Conscience's internal publication of guilt breeds shame. So shame involves the private part of a person or group that he or it does not want known. Unlike secrecy, which may concern good or innocent matters, shame refers to an ugly part (at least a part perceived as ugly) that the person wishes to hide, often even from himself. The existence of a gap between who the person is and who he aspires or wishes to be (or to be seen to be) generates guilt. The greater the gap (or the more central the aspiration) the greater the shame and guilt.

Shame need not reflect moral guilt. A person may be ashamed of some bodily feature, a large nose or a misshapen leg, for example. Indeed, the sense of shame is nearly universally associated with certain physical functions of coition and excretion common to all human beings.

Religion plays an important role with respect to guilt, shame, and imperfection. First, it reveals them, sensitizing believers to parts of their lives they would rather ignore or suppress. Shame often reflects moral guilt, and religion plays a major role in revealing such guilt to the individual and to others. Second, religion supplies various ways of managing these less-than-comfortable aspects of life. It provides rationalizations, excuses, justifications, healing, forgiveness, punishment, redemption. Different religions furnish different mechanisms for dealing with these qualities, and some religions provide alternative mechanisms at different times. But because a relation with the sacred encompasses the human qualities of shame, guilt, imperfection, and the secret stories of the self, religion must afford a way of understanding and coping with them, of integrating them within identity, but also of overcoming them. Of course, religion may also help create the sense of guilt, shame, and imperfection, and one may deplore this. Nevertheless, begetting them still manifests the intimate relation between religion and private life. Note also that many of these ideas make their way via religion from the private to the public realm. Forgiveness, reparation, and rationalization of guilt, for example, have their public counterparts.

I do not propose here further to analyze the roots of shame or to classify the kinds of shame. My purpose is only to point out that it constitutes a crucial dimension of both religion and private life, one with both positive and negative features. Because each person has thoughts, actions, and desires as well as physical features and bodily necessities causing shame, private life, and particularly religion, facilitates social interaction by carefully controlling the circumstances and the persons to whom these aspects of the self are revealed. Because private life controls their disclosure, we can forget them in the ordinary course of life. Were it not subject to such control, the sense of shame would overwhelm many ordinary and useful feelings, interfering with daily life, both individual and collective. Private life frees persons to act and react without debilitating fear that their guilt must become public and that they will, by acting, thinking, or desiring, commit some further sin that must inevitably become public. Because guilt can be kept private, the sense of shame is not overpowering. On the other hand, because ugliness *may* become public, shame puts a check on the worst inclinations. The most secret recesses of private life still, therefore, have public echoes.

But privacy with respect to guilt and shame carries a grave danger. To keep guilt inside is to risk being consumed by it. To be ashamed of oneself and to present a public face of calm and composure is to risk fragmentation of self. Such insights are as old as psychiatry, indeed as old as penitential and confessional practices in religion. Held within, guilt and shame may generalize beyond specific faults to disgust with the self as a whole. Shame transmutes into fear of self and particularly of close relations with others, lest they discover the shameful self. Taken to its extreme, this fear, derived from a generalized shame, breeds the desperate need to live exclusively in a private world.

Imperfection

Another reason for excluding the public from the private world is that world's imperfection.[22] An artist may legitimately wish to conceal or at least hold back from the public an unfinished work, even though he is in no way ashamed of it. It is simply unfinished and not ready for public view. To make it public, he judges, may be to mislead the public about his art or about this piece; or the public might misjudge him or the piece were they to see it in its imperfection. (There can be some shame in this kind of situation. A person *may* feel guilty or ashamed about imperfection.)

We need time to work on our imperfect self-representations before displaying them publicly. Premature public display can interrupt the improvement program. I may wish to lose some weight before buying a new bathing suit and visiting the beach. So we reasonably regard as private certain parts of ourselves and certain things we are in the midst of doing. Of course, this withholding is not always appropriate. The employee may not refuse to reveal unfinished work when the employer reasonably inquires about the progress of a project.

Mystery

I have suggested in the preceding sections that private life as exclusion is related to weakness and incompletion as well as to the achievement of the good. The dimensions of private life discussed in these sections principally involve exclusion. Secrecy, the personal, shame and guilt, and imperfection compel withdrawing some parts of life from public scrutiny. These parts may be admirable or shameful, good or bad, but they are legitimately private. That they are private, not public, is conducive to human development, but it is also an opportunity for evil to flourish.

This mystery of private life is the final dimension of privacy as exclusion. The relation of personal to impersonal and of personal to other persons, the deceit and the pleasant surprise that both depend on secrecy, the alternation of guilt and forgiveness, and of imperfection becoming perfection point to the mystery of the individual person. A person is always a mystery to others, for much of his life is private, but the person is also a mystery to himself. A private life, some private time and space away from others, is necessary to explore that mystery.

Private life is thus bounded by those parts of life excluded from public view for reasons of personal need, secrecy, shame, imperfection, and mystery. These reasons take on different shapes and refer to different elements in different cultures, but there seem to be such reasons and areas of life in all cultures. Religion too is intimately bound up with mystery, secrecy, and the personal, as well as with the other exclusive dimensions of private life.

I have already alluded to the mystery of character and personality, and mystery forms a principal element of exclusivity. Life's greatest mystery is death, but suffering and joy are only slightly less mysterious. We ask, and we look to religion to answer, the meaning of death. We wonder why we deserve suffering, or whence comes this wholly unexpected joy, and how can it be retained? Though we may reject the answers religions give to these questions, they are questions that involve transcendence and that religion is most often called to answer. They are as well the side of religion to which attachments are most deeply formed if the answers seem satisfactory.

We cannot understand ourselves, discover our talents and our weaknesses, define our hopes and our projects, without private time and space. Always to live life in public view is to live a life for others; indeed, it may be to live another's life. The mystery of the self, the paradoxical intersection of darkness and light, of evil and good, necessitates private life.

Once again, however, inclusion suggests itself. One mystery of the self is that it needs others. The inclusion of others, however, depends at the same time on their exclusion, while the self explores its mysteries. Henri Nouwen says it best:

> When we do not protect with great care our own inner mystery, we will
> never be able to form community. It is this inner mystery that attracts us
> to each other and allows us to establish friendship and develop lasting
> relationships of love.[23]

Private life means both exclusion and inclusion. It is to the dimensions of
private life as inclusion that I now turn.

Inclusion and Private Life

As I suggested earlier, private life, like freedom, has two fundamental
dimensions. Exclusion is similar to negative freedom, "freedom from." It
entails limitation on interference by others in an individual's life. It draws
lines and builds walls. In the conventional understanding of things, this is
all there is. What goes on behind the walls is not a matter of public concern.
Yet, just as "negative" freedom exists to facilitate "positive" freedom, these
walls around private life exist to facilitate relationships and ways of life,
ways of life that must be inclusive if the meaning of private life is to be
fulfilled. The notion that "anything goes" behind the wall of privacy is one
of the most misleading about private life and, clearly, about its relationship
to public. Thus, the inclusive side of private life must be seen in balance with
its obvious exclusive side. Like positive freedom, inclusion is freedom "to"
enter into certain ways of life. Private life includes who and what a person
cares for.[24] The self is defined not only by what it sets itself apart from, but
also by the persons and the truths to which it is loyal.

The inclusive dimension is the purposive, dynamic side of private life. It
has two characteristic qualities: intimacy with others and integration of the
parts of personal life. These two qualities, but especially the first, lead private
life toward the public sphere.

Exclusive private life without links to the public sphere is dangerous, as
James Glass's work on the private lives of delusional patients shows.[25] Unable
to cope with threats to identity posed by the assaults of external reality and
the limitations it places on the would-be omnipotent self, the delusional
schizophrenic regresses to the private world of infancy, thereby rejecting the
public world. This is the exclusionary side of privacy with a vengeance. The
consequences are horrifying, as the persons, places, and things of the external
world become transformed in the inner world into dire physical, emotional,
and psychic threats. The only defense available is to create a new world and
a new language of power, aggression, and domination in which the patient
is alternatively totally controlling and totally controlled. Survival is pur-
chased at the cost of severing all consensual relationships.

The schizophrenic is sick precisely because there is no balance or tension
between the inner and outer world. Indeed, it is to get rid of the tension that

the inner world must absorb the outer. "In delusion the private totally absorbs the public (or at least what is public for the self). What consensual reality perceives as the distinction between public and private disappears for the schizophrenic, and the autonomy of delusion absorbs the action of the outer."[26]

The only way out of this prison, Glass argues, is to retrieve the self from inner isolation, to enable the hurt self to receive life through therapeutic empathy. Therapy begins a journey back to trust, to entry into the terms of the social contract, to consensual and limited reality in which sorrows, struggles, and limitations are accepted and shared. The consensual world, the public world, grounds human development and justice. We might say that recovery requires a bridge between the private and the public worlds, a bridge the delusional person must be willing to cross and allow others to cross.

Religion is the best indicator of the unity of the inclusive and exclusive sides of private life. Religion first of all integrates the fragments of life and world. Because religion refers to something beyond human life and control that holds together the splinters of the world, it interprets the world and its diverse, contrasting, and conflicting phenomena. It does the same for the fragments of personal identity, helping to knit them into some kind of integral whole.[27] My argument is not that religion alone performs these functions or that religion best performs them; rather, I simply assert that integration of the pieces of life and the world is a fundamental role of religion for its adherents. Religion's integration of cognition, affection, and behavior clearly places religion within the inclusive side of private life.

Under conditions of personal, social, or natural fragmentation, integrity is difficult, if not impossible. Integrity refers to the orientation toward truth, toward integration of one's ideas, interests, beliefs, and patterns of behavior. I am not arguing that religious faith guarantees integrity or that only believers have integrity. Rather, the point is that religious belief provides a framework for personal integrity. The sacred enfolds one's own norms and principles. The transcendent focus of belief becomes a ground for integrating the plurality of principles.

Similarly with trust and intimacy. If the world is fragmented and unreliable, if people are disconnected monads, then it becomes difficult to trust them or to entrust them with one's secrets. When, however, the world is somehow unified, there is a ground for including others in one's private life, for sharing self (including virtues, vices, and revealing stories) with others, particularly others with the same religious beliefs.

Integrity

One dimension of the inclusive side of private life is integrity. Withdrawal behind the boundaries of private life is required to develop, maintain, and explore integrity. Time and space away from others provides the occasion for discovery of truths and principles worthy of commitment. Moreover, they furnish the occasion for reflecting on behavior in light of truths to which the person is already committed. Modification of commitments also requires privacy. It is certainly true that truth and one's commitment to it cannot be accomplished entirely in isolation. Others help. But the presence of others, their gaze and their opinion, also distract from the individual's relationship with the truth. Their approval and disapproval, their high or low opinion of oneself, provide an essential external referent, but by that very fact they externalize the self and fragment it. Integrity refers to integration of the self as character, to pulling together one's good and bad experiences, as well as the contributions of others, into a personal quest for truth and for commitments that reflect it. As Simone Weil says, the collective is always dangerous to truth.[28]

Integration of character is vital to social and individual life, a fact particularly recognized by J. S. Mill: "A person whose desires and impulses are his own—are the expression of his own nature, as it has been developed and modified by his own culture—is said to have a character."[29] Liberty is valuable for Mill, not in and of itself, but because it is essential for integrity of character.

Conscience is another way of speaking of integrity as an inclusive dimension of private life. There is, of course, social conscience. Individual conscience, as Mill knew, is shaped by others. At same time, however, conscience is primarily individual, personal. It directs moral judgment and moral behavior and calls behavior to task when it fails to live up to personal standards. Conscience is the watchdog of integrity.[30]

It may be objected that the whole idea of inclusivity as a dimension of privacy is undermined by this discussion of integrity. The objection runs like this: the discussion of integrity, character, and conscience only shows that private life as exclusivity is needed for developing these qualities. It does not show that they are elements of private life. Private life may be a means to the higher goods of integrity and so forth, but this does not mean that they are part of it.[31] Can it really be said that inclusivity is essential to private life in the same way that exclusivity is?

The response to this objection does not argue that integrity is an essential part of private life. Integrity is what it is and not part of private life, though private life is a necessary requirement for integrity. To this extent the objection is sound. The critical contention of my argument, however, is that private life cannot be understood apart from inclusivity. That is, private life cannot be understood or its importance appreciated simply as withdrawal, for the purpose of the withdrawal is critical to comprehending it. One withdraws *from* someone or something *in order to* include or make part of oneself other persons or things. This purposeful, inclusive element bears an essential connection to private life. Only the sick withdraw solely to withdraw. Healthy persons seek privacy to pursue some good—integrity, pleasure, truth, intimacy. Exclusion lacks meaning without this reaching out to include qualities impossible in a wholly public or a wholly withdrawn way of life. Truth, integrity, conscience, and character are fundamental values sought in a healthy use of private life and qualities the pursuit of which requires some substantial degree of private life.

Trust

Integrity, I have argued, means private life reaching out to truth and principle. Private life also involves reaching out to other persons in trust and intimacy. The former is the less intense, the latter the more intense, relationship.

Trust has not received much attention in recent philosophical literature, perhaps because of the influences of contractarian and utilitarian models of social relations, which are of limited utility in understanding trust. Indeed, many variants of social contract theory could be described as descriptions of relations among fundamentally distrusting, autonomous equals. Yet trust is a basic need in society. Everyday actions require trust in friends, loved ones, acquaintances, and strangers. Husbands trust that their wives will not stab them as they sleep. Friends trust friends with confidences. Coworkers depend on mutual good will to accomplish their tasks. Shoppers trust that grocery store workers have not poisoned the food. Annette Baier says, "We inhabit a climate of trust as we inhabit an atmosphere and notice it as we notice air, only when it becomes scarce or polluted."[32] The havoc occasioned when ordinary, trustful expectations depart (for example, when Tylenol capsules are tampered with, friends betray secrets, and coworkers begin snooping on one another) reveals individual and social dependence on trust. Trust is utterly basic to integral private life, and utterly fragile.

I am not arguing that trust is always justified or appropriate. There are occasions and even professions in which distrust, or at least wariness, is prescribed. My perhaps painfully obvious point is that trust is fundamental to normally operating, tranquil social life. How is trust related to private life?

Trust can certainly be conscious, though most of the time in ordinary life trust is an implicit personal attitude. In times of reflection, as in writing or reading this book, one might consider the dozens of occasions of trust each day. Or when someone must be explicitly trusted with a rare and unusual thing, such as a psychiatrist being entrusted with deep personal experiences, one might very well consciously consider the fact of trusting. Normally, however, one does not, and this is for the best. For trust does its best work unobtrusively and unreflectingly. To think about it too much is to undermine it.

These considerations suggest that trust is less a social relation (though I shall discuss public trust in the next chapter) than a fundamental personal attitude with crucial social consequences. Trust reveals just how closely personal attitudes bear upon public life. Note how quickly a social group, whether a political party, a work group, or a neighborhood can deteriorate when a fundamentally distrusting, suspicious person comes on the scene. Yet trust of others is fundamentally private, because it is a highly personal attitude toward the world, involving trust of nature and trust of self.

We trust that trees will not fall on us during a springtime walk in the woods, that the woods do not contain ghosts, and that the sun will rise each morning. There is a certain regularity in nature that we can rely on for our psychic security. In the moral realm, most of us most of the time can trust ourselves to take on responsibilities, such as a job assignment, allocating the paycheck to family needs, marriage, and child-raising. Could we not trust ourselves in such situations, we would be powerless to act. If we cannot trust ourselves in a certain setting, we (if prudent) avoid the temptation. The fact that some cannot trust themselves and that some are terrified of nature only reinforces the point that for most people trust is so fundamental to their identities that they act (or fail to act) on it unreflectingly.

Because trust is so basic to identity, it seems to me to be a fundamental constituent of the psyche and, as such, private. Only I know the limits of my trust, the suspicions and fears that I hide from even close friends. The shape and texture and size of my trust (and my fear) go a long way to defining who I am. Trust has religious dimensions, for it is closely related to faith in God, the world, others, or myself.[33] Beliefs, emotions, and behaviors are closely tied to the level of one's trust, and to the objects in which one places it. The form of trust in transcendence and action based on that trust is close to the form of religion. The core of a person's life is touched when we begin to question who or what or how far he trusts, and on what occasions.

Yet trust is among the inclusive elements of private life, for we have seen how naturally it reaches out to include other persons and things. At the same time that it defines who I am, it attaches me to others. It makes me willing to come into contact with persons who, without my trusting them, would be perceived as deadly threats. To trust someone's good will is to become vulnerable to that person. There is truth in the Hobbesian account of the state of nature, which describes any human relationship, in or out of society, lacking trust. "Trust in some degree of veracity functions as a *foundation* of relations among human beings; when this trust shatters or wears away, institutions collapse."[34] Trust is like an iron gridwork extending from person to person, forming the underlying structure of society.

Intimacy

The inclusive side of private life contains not only unity of character (integrity) and a fundamental disposition toward the natural and social world (trust); it also includes intimacy, which refers to particular relations between persons touching the most personal areas of individual life, including erotic love, friendship, prayer, and religious ecstasy. Intimate relations are private because fundamental to self-definition; they are core experiences of personhood.[35] Because they involve others, intimate relations are inclusively private. Yet they require privacy as exclusion, because their existence depends on excluding all but the intimate others from participating in or observing intimate activities.

Robert Gerstein has demonstrated that intimate relations could not exist if we did not insist on privacy for them.[36] Intimate relations, Gerstein argues, require losing oneself in an experience, which is the opposite of observing it. To be observed in intimate experience is to make the participant aware of her actions as an observer would be aware. Hence, it destroys or transforms the intimate experience. Intimate relationships, out of which grow intimate experiences, give meaning and significance to life, Gerstein continues, but they are also fragile and open to being used for self-indulgent reasons. Observation reminds the participants of this and displays for them the possibility of using a relationship, rather than enjoying it.

Charles Fried has also explored this relation between the sense of ourselves and intimacy with others. Love and friendship, he argues, "involve the voluntary and spontaneous relinquishment of *something* between friend and friend, lover and lover. The title to information about oneself conferred by privacy provides the necessary something."[37] By conferring the right not to share (exclusivity), private life creates what Fried calls the "moral capital" spent in friendship and love (inclusivity). Privacy, Fried contends, also supports the mutual respect on which friendship and love depend, and it modulates the degrees of friendship and intimacy by control over the quantity and quality of information shared with intimate others.

Institutions of Private Life

I have discussed private life principally in terms of individual persons. This is appropriate, for the features of private life are most clear in personal life. As the discussion of inclusivity has shown, however, private life also involves special relationships between persons. It is but one step from relationships to institutions, for institutions regularize and structure relationships.

Certain institutions have a special relationship to private life, being themselves considered private. These are principally the institutions of family, marriage, and friendship, which provide rituals, stories, memories, and artifacts that create a common intimate life. Yet these institutions are not divorced from public life. Michael Walzer reminds us that kinship and love are not completely isolated from politics and the market and that, while politics and the market affect marriage and family, it is also true that marriage and family often impinge upon the spheres of politics and economics.[38]

Indeed, one purpose of such institutions is to mediate between the private life of persons and their intimate relations and the public world of government, economics, and culture. As true as this is of such traditionally private institutions as marriage and family, it is even more true of such "quasiprivate" institutions as neighborhood, work, and voluntary associations.

It is difficult to know whether to classify such institutions as quasi-private or quasi-public. Each has realms of (limited) exclusivity and each contains intimate or potentially intimate relationships. But each also plays important social roles and is traditionally subject to public law and custom. These institutions help define the border between public and private life. This function is especially true of religion.

Is it possible for religion to be wholly private? Note that my definition of religion does not exclude this possibility. The development of religion in contemporary culture, especially in America, reinforces it. Sociologists, journalists, and commentators have wondered about the persistence of religion, especially institutional religion, in America, given its clear decline in the rest of the developed world. America seems the exception to the predictions of secularization theory that religion plays a more isolated and, ultimately, a progressively smaller public role as modernization progresses.

In the late 1960s Thomas Luckmann constructed a now well-known argument that religion does not disappear or become less important in secularized society. It becomes invisible, privatized, but not less important.[39] Though religion in Luckmann's view is a social construction, it becomes internalized and individualized, and these mechanisms define "personal identity as a universal form of individual religiosity" (70). Thus all religion possesses a social and an individual side. Luckmann argues, however, that modern society has created the possibility of privatized religion (chap. 6). First, rapid social change makes it difficult to pass on the official religion to children. Second, Western religions like Christianity, Judaism, and Islam have created differentiated, specialized religious institutions. Once society becomes religiously pluralistic, and under conditions of rapid social change, the existence of specialized religious institutions defending (now often competing versions of) the "official" beliefs and practices makes tension possible within individual believers between the "official" version and their individual religiosity.

Religion then takes on characteristics of consumer society, "autonomous" individuals selecting from the available assortment of ultimate meanings, constructing not only personal identities, but also individual systems of "ultimate" meaning (97-99). As long as these systems of ultimate meaning are based upon a reality transcending the human, an individual, private religion is certainly possible within my definition. The seeming strength of institutional religion in the United States can be explained in conformity with this theory by the fact that here, for historical and cultural reasons, secularization is occurring *within* the churches. They are containers for privatized religion.

It is possible to deplore this situation and recognize its problematic effects, as Luckmann does in pointing to the "dehumanization of the social structure" (116). Doing so, however, does not deny the possibility, indeed the dominant reality in modern society, of private religion. If religion *can* be essentially private, perhaps it *should* be essentially private. Therefore, if private and public can and should be separated anywhere, religion is the place. Religion, like family, marriage, and friendship, becomes fundamentally, if not essentially, a private affair.

In short, it seems possible to agree with all that I have said about private life and even about its connections with public; yet even in agreeing, it is possible to argue that *religion*, at least in the modern world, is so deeply a part of the exclusive side of private life that it must be regarded as fundamentally private. Religion, in this view, is a matter of autonomy, a matter of individual choice. It is focused on those parts of private life (shame, the personal) that are most exclusive. Even if we grant religion a connection with integrity, this quality is the most exclusive of the inclusive features of private life.

Luckmann's own argument, however, though it explains much that is happening in American religion, also suggests a problem with this line of thinking. Curiously, in view of his claim that religious privatization is unlikely to be reversible (117), he also regards privatized, consumer religion as unstable. Absent social and institutional support for private belief, the individual must depend on the more "ephemeral" support of other "autonomous" individuals. The disappearance of such support persons, especially with family disintegration, entails the instability of these new, flexible systems of ultimate meaning (105-6). This should not be surprising, given Luckmann's argument that the origin of religious meaning for each individual is social; indeed, socialization for Luckmann is a religious phenomenon (chaps. 3 and 4). If Luckmann is correct about the social origins of religion and the instability of private religion, can religious privatization last?

This is not to say that there is no advantage to regarding religion as private in many respects. In the American context particularly, privacy has become a strong argument for state noninterference, a bulwark of the doctrine of separation of church and state. This doctrine, limited as it is, as I shall argue in the final chapter, does help to protect religious liberty and religious conscience. For example, statutes and constitutional interpretations have afforded protection to conscientious objectors to war, sabbatarians in employment, the privacy of church records, the freedom to form religious associations, to express religious belief and to proselytize, and to form alternate schools.

There is, of course, controversy on all of these issues. Do legal exemptions to protect religious liberty provide improper public support for religious institutions? Is home schooling an acceptable accommodation to private religious belief, or does it undermine socialization to public commitments? This last example returns us to my basic contention that, important as the private face of religion might be, it cannot be regarded as simply private. The public does have a responsibility to educate its citizens for public membership, a responsibility as real as the family's responsibility to educate its children in its own religious beliefs and traditions. Home schooling and religious schools can be permitted as recognition of the value of religious conscience only on the condition that their curricula recognize the public interest in education and the curricular guidelines and standards that implement that public interest.

These reflections support the following conclusion. Neither my definition of religion nor the development of religion in the United States precludes that religion can be, for many individuals, essentially private. Moreover, formal, legal recognition of a zone of privacy for religion has beneficial public consequences. Yet religion need not be wholly private, and there is nothing about religion, apart from historical contingency, to make it so. Religion does have a public side as central as the private. Moreover, privatized religion is inherently unstable and may have, as Luckmann suggests, negative social consequences. In order to examine these matters, however, it will be necessary explicitly to consider the nature of public life and the public side of religion.

3

Public Life

> The primary good that we distribute to one
> another is membership in some human com-
> munity.
> —Michael Walzer, *Spheres of Justice*

The present chapter articulates three themes. First, public life is essential to human development, for it is the sphere of mutual participation. But the public is a broader sphere than the political. Politics is one form of public life; there are others of equal significance. Second, religion is fundamentally public. Religion itself is a sphere of participation, but religion is also related to politics in crucial ways. Third, religion therefore occupies dangerous territory. It inhabits the broad expanse where public and private life meet and overlap. Religion is not the only inhabitant of this uncertain terrain, but it is one of the most prominent. The dangers are that religion will travel into the purely public and political territory, that politics will invade religion, and that the public–private overlap will be misconstrued.

The Meaning of Public Life

Charles Taylor argues that private life cannot be comprehended apart from public life, for the private world is immersed in the public.[1] Public life, however, is as mysterious as is private, though not because it mirrors the depth of private life. Rather, the breadth of public life makes it mysterious and complex. Personal, intimate relations delimit the private world. The difficulty of describing it reflects the soul's intricacies. The public world, however, incorporates the complexity of collectivities. In ordinary language we speak of "public" officials, thereby suggesting citizenship and politics. But we also speak of "public" buildings, meaning simply that they are open to all. We speak easily of public opinion, public enterprises, public information, and public service. But it is not at all clear that they refer to the same kind of relationships, nor what relation they bear to that strange collective, "the public."

The *Oxford English Dictionary* confirms this breadth. As we expect, "public" is the opposite of "private." Yet "the varieties of sense are numerous and pass into each other by many intermediate shades of meaning. The exact shade depends upon the substantive qualified, and in some expressions more than one sense is present; in others the usage is traditional, and it is difficult to determine in what sense precisely the thing in question was originally called 'public.' "[2]

The modern world has developed a loose set of referents for the adjective "public."[3] Public, for example, can refer to players on the economic market. Here the term aggregates individuals and their preferences, as in the phrase "public demand for coffee." Public also refers to the phenomena of clientage, when the public world is conceived as a set of interest groups controlling social distribution through conflict and compromise. The idea of the public interest in interest-group politics seizes this conception. Yet another use of the concept implies a medical metaphor, the public being thought of as patients benefiting from the policies of government or business. They receive the therapeutic outputs of policies—for example, defense, clean water, or jobs.

A fourth modern meaning of the term "public" suggests consumption. According to this view, "public officials" are public because they regulate and promote consumption, as in "the public consumed x million pounds of cream cheese in 1986." Individuals are linked by their additive ingestion of material goods. Finally, a fifth modern view refers specifically to government functionaries, "public officials," who have responsibility for seeing that goods and services are delivered to demanders, clients, recipients, or consumers. Here the key values are management and efficiency; the field is public administration.

Three qualities stand out. First, the diversity of "public" is striking, as hundreds of uses of "public" can be comprehended under them. This very comprehensiveness, however, hints at the modern vacuity of the term, for when so much can be comprehended, there can be little firm meaning. Second, despite the diversity, most uses conceive of the public aggregatively. The public becomes a convenient collective term for the sum of the differences of thousands of individuals and their essentially separate lives. Third, most of these senses of public are passive. The "public" itself doesn't do anything. Individuals consume or receive or are managed. Individually they pursue money, career, consumption, or interest; together they do nothing of consequence.

The relative poverty of public language and the relative richness of private is confirmed by the different weights of derivative terms. Privacy has a rich normative meaning and carries substantial influence in moral discourse. It strongly supports the right to private life. This is why, despite its not being mentioned in the Constitution, privacy has taken strong root in American constitutional law. Publicity, however, does not suggest a corresponding right to public life. Instead, private individuals and groups seek publicity for their individual projects. The idea of a right to public life falls dully on modern ears. Such a right is embodied, if at all, not in derivatives from "public," but in concepts like citizen and citizenship.

These modern senses of public life have been challenged by the recovery in political theory of a participatory sense of public life. Return to citizenship and the "civic republican" tradition in Western political thought have given vigor to this challenge. The new literatures of community and character also have contributed to an idea of public that stresses wholes rather than aggregates, joint action instead of passive reception.[4] Citizens replace consumers. Interest-group alliances give way to civic friendship.

This chapter explores the meaning of public life in the sense carried by the idea of citizenship. I focus on active participation in a public that is more than an aggregate of private individuals. However, I do not intend to review all of the debates and discussions of the last three decades on citizenship, community, civic republicanism, and participatory politics. Although I refer to this literature in the next section, it is only to set the stage for my portrait of public life. While I recognize the important differences among the different strands of this literature, I shall not attempt to untangle them. I am more interested in their similarities, for it is the fundamental difference between public and private life that they emphasize, as well as the essential personal and political goods flowing from public life.

Therefore, in the next section I work toward a definition of public life. Then I address the relationship between politics, religion, and public life. In the fourth section I consider two sides of public life. Finally, I address how public religion shares the dangers of public life, but also can counteract them.

Defining Public Life

The Common World

In its most elementary sense, public life is participation in a common world. To participate in public life is to become enmeshed in the worlds of the other members of society, both those of acquaintances and those of strangers. Mutual involvement creates a world common to all, shared by all in at least a minimal way. While I shall soon discuss a richer sense of public life, initially a minimal sense suffices. We can understand this minimal sense by attending to Benn and Gaus's criteria of public life.[5]

The first criterion is open access to space, activities, participation, information, and resources. Private life tends toward restriction of access, restriction prompted by shame, secrecy, mystery, and imperfection. Ultimately, private life can degenerate into a world of delusion in which no common terms connect persons. Openness guarantees, even forces, common life as different individuals bump into each other while taking advantage of open access.

Accountability, Benn and Gaus's second criterion, even more actively creates common life. In private life agents act on their individual accounts, justifying their actions according to personal standards, and are responsible only to themselves or to selected others. In public life, on the other hand, persons are accountable because they are officers of the community, and it is the community that has the right to hold them responsible to common standards. Codes of professional ethics are the formal recognition of the accountability professionals owe each other for the quality of their common world.

Finally, the criterion of interest refers to those who will be better or worse off for action taken. As the effect narrows to a few or a single individual, the matter becomes private. As it broadens toward the entire society, it becomes public. An interest affecting an entire society is common to its members, connecting them in at least that minimal way.

Yet the notion of public defined by these criteria is minimal, because it reflects merely the simple, but vital, fact that only a social context makes individual behavior intelligible. The unintelligibility of delusional behavior to any but the delusional person demonstrates this truth. Humans do not confront reality immediately, but only through symbols, particularly language, and symbols necessarily are jointly created. "Everyday life is, above all, life with and by means of the language I share with my fellow men."[6] Language, distinctively human and distinctively social, is the elemental life of the common world. Its very existence reflects shared experience and shared symbols. Language is fundamentally public, though private life makes use of it. In its most minimal sense, the public world is open and common to all, and symbols are the fundamental building-blocks of public life.

Public life, however, is more than simply common. Public life is a distinctive part of the common world, possessing an irreducible political dimension. If public life were only what I have so far described, there would be no need for giving it a particular designation as "public." "Social life" would do just as well. "Public life," however, adds to social life a reference to power, especially shared power. For public life signifies active participation beyond mere access to the elemental common world. One may share in the common world with only the most minimal exertion. Though language and symbol must be personally absorbed and shaped, no particular effort is required. One may share in the common world in a more or less passive way. Public life, however, demands active participation, special and even strenuous effort. Public life entails power.

Politics: The World of Shared Power

Hannah Arendt's most distinctive contribution to political theory was to revive the idea of public life as active participation in shaping the common world. The common world for her is not a world to be absorbed by individuals, but a world to be created by their striving with and against one another. Therefore, the public world is principally the world of politics and power, for the fragility of the public realm demands constant recourse to power.[7]

Politics, according to Arendt, is not the pursuit of self-interest, nor is it the defense of individual goods. For Arendt the public world is a brightly lit stage for appearance. Politics supports this stage. The public world does not consist in the personal qualities of individuals that link them together, but in the public, political space itself. It is, like a table, a space that both binds and separates.[8] In the public realm people are united by the space between them, though their joint inhabitance of this space also fulfills them personally.

The space that separates and joins is a function of irreducible human plurality, and plurality necessarily means politics, with its conflict, competition, and self-creation/revelation. But it means as well democracy, equality, and freedom. Politics characterized by equality, freedom, and participation in debate and action defines the shape of the public world precisely because different human beings seeing the world from different perspectives must live together in the same space. So they must be free to define both that space and themselves, and the only way they can do so as persons (not as passive objects of imposed rule) is to confront one another on equal ground and contend for their own public visions. To be human, we must engage in action, that is, in politics.

The political world, therefore, is the realm of individuality and of distinctly human excellence. It defines the space where human beings can appear to one another, thereby assuring them that their experience is real. For even intense private experience seems less real than public, for no one save the self, which may be deceived, confirms it. The public is the world itself, common to all, fashioned by human artifacts and affairs, the reality that both binds and separates. This world needs permanent things; it needs traditions and memories to create the possibility of generations in whose memory the individual person may become immortal. Hence, the public world relies on the innumerable perspectives and locations of a plurality of persons marking the same object. Public life, then, is the life of seeing and hearing each other from different perspectives. It incorporates both individuality and plurality.[9] Rather than the disappearance of self in community, public life means the appearance of self as unique.

For Arendt the public world of politics creates the possibility of beginnings, hence of freedom, for it interrupts the cycle of bodily necessities to create something new. The greatness and glory of politics allow the self to disclose itself (though not to show off). Yet public life is frail and uncertain. Actions have no end; they are unpredictable and irreversible. Therefore, for Arendt, politics is not about means and ends, but about the confirmation of self and the possibility of freedom to overcome the natural ruin of the world. Law-making and power are not politics, but only the boundaries that create the space between persons necessary for the deeds and words that are politics.[10]

If the public world, according to Arendt, is anything other than free, open, equal, and competitive participation, it disappears into the privacy of individual interest pursuit. As human plurality requires a public, political world with these qualities, to abandon the public world is to flee or reject the human condition. Humans are, as Aristotle said, political animals. This vision is not utopian, for Arendt recognized that public life in her sense is rare and fragile.[11] Active citizens participating in the shape of their common world are few in most periods and absent in many, whether from individual lethargy or tyrannical rule. Nevertheless, periods of revolution seem spontaneously to generate public spaces and active citizens for at least brief periods, and these periods stand as shining examples of the possibilities of human life. Arendt's vision of public life challenges all politics that settles for less than it could be.

Yet public life in Arendt's account is also less than it could be, for her sharp division of public life from private leaves it strangely empty.[12] It is never very clear in Arendt just what it is that active citizens talk about and over what they compete. Hanna Fenichel Pitkin has made this critique of Arendt most effectively, while at the same time strengthening her fundamental insight in such a way as to reinforce the political character of public life.[13] Pitkin argues that if the material concerns of private life (some of our imperfections that need completion) are excluded from public life, so are those persons so exploited that only material concerns hold significance for them. What, then, is the benefit of politics? What keeps citizens together and what do they talk about, if not their private interests?

Admitting private concerns into public life, however, need not reduce politics to competition over self-interest. Public life can differ from private and still be active and participatory. Pitkin amends, and I believe, strengthens Arendt's account of public life by returning to Aristotle, to whose account of politics Arendt herself is indebted. Aristotle pictures public and private in a way similar to Arendt, but for him politics concerns justice, a concept oddly absent from Arendt's theory, and justice involves economics—therefore individual, private interests. But justice does not privatize the world. Rather, political speech, the language of justice, transforms private interests into public interests.

Justice, the public thing *par excellence*, keeps the advantages Arendt discovered in public life, while endowing it with content. A public life concerned with defining and realizing justice builds on plurality and requires collective action, for every citizen is capable of the language of justice, and each has a perspective on justice. Though justice is not simply a form of equality, the politics of justice requires political equality and active citizens. And the politics of justice calls upon the collective responsibility that is a hallmark of public life. Public life is not the aggregation of private interests, but the transformation of private interests into public goods through public debate. Properly amended, then, Arendt's theory of active political participation sharply reveals the essence of public life.

The most significant exegesis of participation in public life to emerge from the experience of the 1960s and 1970s was Carole Pateman's *Participation and Democratic Politics*.[14] This slim work masterfully reviewed the criticisms of the "elitist" theories of democracy, summarized the participatory theories of the late eighteenth to the early nineteenth centuries, and examined the empirical evidence for the value of participation, in both politics and the workplace. Inclusion of workplace participation is important, for, despite Arendt's argument, public life is not limited to politics. Though politics is the paradigmatic form of public life, not everything public is political, nor should it be. Citizenship in other forms of public and quasi-public life balances political activity.

Pateman emphasizes three results of participation. Participation helps to develop individual self-worth, freedom, and competence. Participation facilitates acceptance of decisions. Participation integrates individuals into the community. These three results mark the significance of public life.

The first result focuses on the benefits of participation for the individual. One who takes part in decisions affecting her life learns the value of her intelligence, judgment, and experience. She is worth something, because she discovers and exercises particular talents among her peers. Her freedom is enhanced, because she can exercise her ability to make choices and to have those choices count. Finally, a sense of competence derived from taking part in common action contributes to self-esteem and dignity. Competence radiates from a sense of mastery (not domination) in which an individual is able to have and to know that she has an impact on future events. To make a difference demands taking responsibility for the difference one makes. Participation is thus a training ground in which individuals learn to become responsible persons. Because becoming a moral person requires responsibility, participation in public life is a duty.

Acceptance of decisions promotes social stability and legitimacy. Stability and legitimacy can be coerced or contrived, but genuine, active participation in public life makes such forced order less likely. Persons taking part in decisions feel more committed to them and to the institutions through which they are made. They also know that these decisions, in part at least, reflect their judgments. In participation, as we have seen in Arendt and Pitkin, we encounter persons with views different from ours. We can, however, more readily accept their role in the decisions made if participation has revealed to us their point of view.

Finally, participation in a group stimulates commitment to that group.

Participation generates a "sunk cost" that binds one to the group into which the resources are plowed. In other words, I become a member of a group more readily by working with its members than by observing its activities. Participation enhances membership in the public, thereby creating and shaping the public at the same time.

I might add to Pateman's arguments the point that a public defined by active participation by responsible citizens is more likely to resist abuses of power than one without active public life. Citizens are more likely than subjects to keep politics within proper bounds and to object when it exceeds them.

More recent expressions of the idea of a participatory public life and its value can be found in the works of Michael Walzer and Benjamin Barber. Let me briefly summarize significant contributions they make to the notion of public life as active participation.

Walzer's theory of justice as complex equality based on different spheres of life is by now familiar. What is particularly important to recognize in the context of this discussion is that the idea of membership is crucial to the definition of the spheres on which the theory depends. And membership is meaningless for Walzer without participation. Thus, the idea of participatory citizenship is a leitmotif throughout *Spheres of Justice*. Citizenship is the critical element of community, for shared meanings constitute communities. Therefore, politics, especially democratic politics, is fundamentally related to community, for meanings cannot be shared without members' participation in a common life. Citizens share meanings; subjects have meanings imposed upon them. The same is true for the distribution of goods entailed by justice. Thus, for Walzer, citizenship and democratic participation are crucial even in the most "private" areas of life.[15]

Membership in a particular community and in its common life implies inclusion of some and exclusion of others, and this exclusion may be viewed as problematical for a democratic, equalitarian politics. However, exclusivity has a flip side. Justice requires that all admitted to membership be given or be placed on the road toward the rights of full members of the community. No second-class status is allowed.[16] Distribution, especially of security and welfare, should be arranged to enhance and maintain membership and communal participation. Thus Walzer's account of justice ties it to participation just as firmly, but for different reasons, as Pitkin's amendment of Arendt's theory of public life. Public life, they agree, is essentially connected to participation and to justice.

In *Strong Democracy* Benjamin Barber claims that we suffer not from too much, but from too little democracy.[17] Though arguing that an excess of liberalism has undone democratic institutions, Barber does not intend to attack liberalism itself. For there is little wrong with liberal institutions that cannot be cured by strong doses of political participation and reactivated citizenship. The crisis of democracy is that political apathy has grown as a greater and greater number of public things have been relegated to the private sphere. Barber contrasts strong democracy with pure or direct democracy and with liberal or representative democracy. His fundamental contention is that the common life of community, built by public and participatory institutions, must cease being a servant to private interests. For the common life in fact establishes the conditions for freedom, justice, equality, and autonomy.[18]

Nevertheless, in opposition to the nostalgic literature of community, Barber does not make community prior to individuality. Rather, community is created through participation by free individuals. Community, public goods, and citizenship are three interdependent parts of a single democratic circle, a true public. Participatory institutions and common action, the principal features of strong democracy, have as their fundamental purpose community-building or the creation of public interests, common good, and active citizens.[19] Moreover, participation educates personal judgment about facts, ideas, people, and institutions.[20] Making judgments is a fundamental constituent of maturity and responsibility. For Barber the civic role is sovereign over other roles. Citizenship, Barber argues, is not necessarily the highest or best identity, but it is the moral identity *par excellence*.[21]

Barber—like Arendt, Pateman, and Walzer—stresses the intense value of citizenship and political participation. But with his theory we begin to reach the limits of the idea of the public as politics. For there are other forms of public life than politics, and public life itself is subject to significant limitations. Nevertheless, the general argument of the theorists of participation is valid. The principal defining characteristic of public life is active, free, and regular participation by equal citizens in their common life. Politics, therefore, is the paradigmatic form of public life.

The Political, the Public, and Religion

The temptation for advocates of public life is to identify public life with politics, which is certainly a problem in Arendt's theory. For her the public is political; forms of life that look public but lack the distinctive features of politics are, for her, "social." The social world is ambiguous, "public" in some sense, but neither politics nor household management. What the social truly is, she contends, is politics as housekeeping, "that curiously hybrid realm where private interests assume public significance that we call 'society.' "[22] The same tendency toward the dominance of the political world appears in Barber, for whom the civic role is sovereign.

I am particularly concerned in this book with politics as a public institution and with its relation to religion. Politics and power are distinctive and vital forms of public life; yet politics is not the only form of public life. It is one constitutive element. Other forms of life, other institutions, have features of public life and make many of the same contributions to personal and political development as politics. Arendt worried that the exaltation of private life would squeeze out politics and, therefore, public life. The mirror danger is that exaltation of politics constricts other forms of public life, relegating them to the private realm. Such is the fate of religion in the developed world. Once this happens, politics becomes identified with the state or with governmental institutions, and a genuine public world of participation disappears into a sea of power, manipulation, and administrative detail. Other public institutions have independent grounds of existence and are not part of the state. The strengths of public life also spring from them. Moreover, they themselves have political responsibilities, rights, and duties.

In making this argument I understand politics as participation in the comprehensive ordering of the life of a group or institution. Politics is collective debate and decision making about the common good of a whole. In this sense, politics is a necessary and legitimate part of the life of all groups and institutions. I distinguish this from politics in the strict sense. Politics in this latter sense is participation in the ordering of an entire society. As such, it always involves the disposition of instruments of power and force. Politics in this sense is public. But so is politics in groups and institutions smaller than the society as a whole. What is objectionable is the tendency of politics in the strict sense to swallow up other politics.

I have specifically in mind here such public and quasi-public institutions as neighborhoods, academic institutions, parishes and churches, voluntary associations, unions, and civic boards and commissions. This is not an exhaustive list. Such institutions may properly be called public or quasi-public, because their dynamics can be plotted along the continua formed by the criteria of public life: openness of access to resources, space, and information; accountability to constituents and to the larger society; and broadness of interests affected. These institutions define common worlds, where integral parts of life are shaped and shared. Of course, the public features of these institutions may in fact be minimal in some societies or in all societies at some time. These institutions may exhibit features that are little more than collectivities of private interests. That is, the question of whether in any particular setting they are public or private, quasi-public or quasi-private, is in large measure empirical.

The point, however, is this. Normally such institutions occupy the space between the purely private and the purely public, helping to maintain a rich and diverse fabric of individual and social life, a mosaic of private and public life. The more they are absorbed at either end of the spectrum, the more Arendt's descriptions of liberal, interest-group society and of totalitarianism ring true. I have already discussed those institutions closest to private life: family, friendship, and intimate association. Here I want to distinguish from politics proper other institutions close to the public side of life, and to iterate their distinct value.

Such institutions will be public if they demonstrate the features of open-ness, accountability, and broadness of interests. Their publicness also necessi-tates, in an Arendtian sense, promotion of crucial political values such as identity, equality, and freedom. It would be tedious to try to make an exhaustive list of such institutions and to examine their characteristics against the criteria just specified. Moreover, it would be pointless, for I have admitted that any such institutions might in particular societies not exhibit such features at all. We could spend all day disputing whether a specific institution 'tis or 'tisn't.

Fortunately for my purposes it is only necessary to demonstrate that institutions other than politics can be public and can fulfill some of the needs for public life performed by politics and political participation. This demonstration, when added to the perhaps painfully obvious fact that if politics alone fulfills the needs for public life, both political and personal freedom and equality are in jeopardy, should reinforce the contention of this section that there is a wider sense of public life beyond politics and that not everything public is or should be political in the strict sense.

The Public Worlds of Religion

Fortunately, politics is not the only form of public life. The public side of religion demonstrates this clearly. From the perspective of those who stress its public aspect, privatization is, far from being the essence of religion, a tremendous danger. Michael Harrington, himself an atheist, places consider-able importance on its public role and on the evils of private religion. "Political theology," he says, "rightly understands that privatization is the great enemy of religion in the modern world—not, as some sociologists think, its salvation. All those theologies which accept that premise . . . are . . . uncritically affirming the bourgeois norm of the private man."[23] The idea of religion as wholly or essentially private is modern, reflecting particular historical ideas and conditions.

Yet even such modern thinkers as Hobbes, Locke, and Mill gave religion a significant public role, according to Eldon Eisenach.[24] Although the logic of liberal political philosophy is most often expressed in self-interest, natural liberty, reason, individualism, and the desire for self-preservation, Eisenach argues that these liberal thinkers believed that human beings inhabit a world of history and tradition alongside the world of freely reasoning, contracting individuals. They argued that tradition and a duty of obedience to God are needed to deal with the historicity of society, punishment of criminals, life and death questions, the motivation for self-sacrifice, and the presence of religious belief.

Eisenach's argument is not that liberalism needs religion in some absolute sense or that religion is an essential part of public life, only that key figures in liberalism saw it in this way. Yet this fact suggests the deep paradox of attempting to relegate religion to the private sphere. Eisenach's argument is reminiscent of John H. Hallowell's argument that early liberalism was "integral." Public and private reason, public and private religion were part of the same fabric in the early development of liberalism. Recent liberalism, however, splits these sides asunder, divorcing the religious dimension of morality from individual interest calculation. With such a split, integral liberalism can only decay.[25] Thus split apart, reason becomes public, because it must be rooted in arguments and proofs accessible to all. Yet political life becomes rooted in private desire, for it is the individual and his wants that drive politics. Hence, the paradox: politics, the quintessential public realm rooted in private desire, divorced from public reason.

Religion reflects the particularities of historical contingency, and this is the key to its public side. When political theory considers religion at all, it tends to derive it from some universal need for meaning. Such a view, however, is part and parcel of religion's privatization. Any need for meaning is individual and can be satisfied by individual nonreligious belief systems as well as by religion. I am not arguing against a "need for meaning" that religion can satisfy. I only argue that it is not the essence of religion to satisfy such needs. Instead, I contend that religion appears in human life as historically contingent, particularistic, and community-bound. That is, religion appears publicly. Religion's public contribution lies in its embeddedness, its traditions and rituals, and its emphasis on human dependence and limitation.[26]

Although this approach to religion seems to weaken claims to truth and universality of meaning made by particular religions, I argue in chapter 7 with respect to the general significance of tradition, history, and narrative, that contingency does not rule out truth claims. Indeed, it enhances them. So I shall not repeat that argument here. Beliefs about the sacred find confirmation in the history of a group or in events experienced or witnessed by many individuals, who can be questioned publicly or who testify publicly to the beliefs' validity. Religions are communities of memory, repositories of collective, public traditions, stories, and experiences stretching through time. Even those claims most rooted in the mystical (and therefore seemingly private) experiences of charismatic leaders seek validation in the common experiences of followers. The experience is communicated to followers who receive it in public ways such as dancing, singing, shouting, healings, scourgings, and so on. The claims are validated (partially, at least) by the public experience following them. Even religions that focus on the physical and spiritual purification and perfection of individual holy persons feature communities of disciples.

My claim is not that religion is true, but that it is public. I do not contend that religion is not private, but that private religion is the historical exception. The public side of Catholicism, Judaism, and Islam is especially clear. That we might think otherwise is perhaps a result of evangelical Protestantism combined in America with the privatizing dynamics of liberal culture. Even a Protestant theologian like H. Richard Niebuhr, who reflects profoundly on personal responsibility and the radical existentialism of Christian decision making, knows that these are deeply linked to the traditions and the communities of the faith.[27] The point is not to denigrate the private side of religion, which is so deeply ingrained in American culture, but to see the public way religion can confront the easy individualism of modern life. A harder, more mature individualism would come to grips with the location of self in family, in other institutions, and in a particular, historically contingent culture. Such an individualism would situate the self within the demands of various authorities and communities and the harsh realities of the social world.

Religion, perhaps uniquely among human institutions, brings to the person who is faced with these demands the experiences of tradition, authority, and community, as well as those of dependence, failure, and temptation, that serve as resources for personal judgment. Religion has the special responsibility to teach and nourish a tough, embedded individualism. Religions possess significant resources for this job. They contain authorities and rules; stories, memories, and traditions; and teachings on social ethics. Religions include images of God as judge, ways of understanding justice as well as mercy, and explanations of sin and tragedy. They include also forms of community, discipline, roles, hierarchies, and moral demands. This is why religious motivations are so often behind movements of civil disobedience and passive resistance such as Gandhi's campaigns, the civil rights sit-ins, and Operation Rescue. Religion so intimately connects to public life that it constitutes a public space and a forum for participation as fundamentally important as politics.

Religion as Space for Participation

Religion, in its institutional manifestations, particularly in America, is a vehicle for the kind of participation essential to the definition of public life. Even those who favor religion's public importance often miss this aspect. For there are two ways to look at religion's public role. The first acknowledges religion's significance in shaping character and virtue and recognizes this as a vital public contribution. The second discerns religion's participatory side. Tocqueville's great contribution was to see and recognize the significance of both.

The first is the most commonly recognized, as demonstrated by the popularity of that famous passage already quoted in chapter 1 in which Tocqueville observes that religious leaders exercise their most important public role by influencing the morals of the citizens, but that they do so only because they refrain from direct political involvement.[28] Religion inculcates habits of stability, moral decency, domestic tranquility, and public good. Self-interest alone cannot construct the authority necessary to freedom. Some notion of the public good, responsibility to others, and a higher good must motivate self-interested individuals to undertake the sacrifices necessary for daily peace and civility and a common good transcending their individual goods. Religion, by supplying a positive notion of duty and goodness, provides a necessary foundation in individual character and virtue to support a democratic polity.

Those founders steeped in the republican tradition recognized the significance of religion as an indispensable prop to republican virtue. Religion and education go together, for religion sustains the lesson of education that moral virtue underpins civic virtue, and religion fosters moral virtue.[29] Religious commitment toward a consciously chosen set of ends liberates political action. Democratic politics requires vision and discipline of character.

True as it is, this idea of religion's moral and visionary role has two key limitations. The first is that this function of religion is compatible with the public-private split. Religion here operates through private character, and its beneficial effects come when it remains within the circle of individual and family. Indeed, according to Tocqueville (and here he comes to friendly terms with contemporary liberalism), religion can only have beneficial effects if it is disestablished, if church and state are separate. The second limitation of this role of religion is its focus on utility. On this view religion has public utility when it supplies the virtues not directly part of public life. Though considerable truth adheres to this perspective, and though I do not deny religion public utility, this perspective tends to reduce religion to those of its private aspects having public usefulness. Moreover, this notion identifies religion with its functions. Therefore, should anything else satisfy these functions, religion becomes dispensable.

I conclude that though religion's role in promoting the virtue requisite for democratic politics is increasingly noted, this role is compatible with traditional understandings of the split between public and private, politics and religion, state and church. Another aspect of religion, this more directly public, is less often noted, but it lodges in Tocqueville's analysis as a kind of counterpoint to his major theme. One of Tocqueville's prominent themes is the danger of the isolated individualism made possible by democratic equality and freedom. He finds in America a number of institutions that dampen individualism's effects by pulling people out of themselves, drawing them to interact with others and to see points of view different from their isolated, self-interested ones. The most important of these institutions are the jury system, township self-government, the natural aristocracy of lawyers and judges, a vigorous free press, and voluntary associations, especially religion.[30] Note that the first two of these are close to death as vehicles of participation.

The general point I wish to make is that religion can be public and participatory. Religion involves not only an individual's direct relationship with the sacred, but also interaction with other believers. There are spaces and occasions for participation in shaping the common, public life of a group of believers. Religions, particularly those relatively well-institutionalized, display a wide variety of such occasions. American religion, as Tocqueville recognized, has specialized in these institutional forms. Believers participate in church governance (especially in those religions with congregational polities, but even in the Catholic Church more recently), in staging liturgies and assemblies, in parish bazaars and festivals, and in church-sponsored community service or civic projects. All are opportunities for participation with others in taking responsibility, making collective decisions, compromising, expressing one's views, and acknowledging the contrasting views of others.

In short, religion is a form of public life. There is no contradiction between its private and its public aspects. Indeed, they reinforce one another and correct each other's extreme tendencies. Religion's public role is especially important in a context where the dominant public institution, the state, takes the form of a large, impersonal, distant provider of goods and services. Richard Bernstein argues that "if there is to be a renewal of public life, a communal basis for individuals coming together, it is to be found outside those great impersonal abstractions of society and state."[31] Religion is one basis for a renewed public life, an opportunity for public participation and responsibility. Public life is not limited to the realm of the state or politics. Religion is more than a reflection of other publics or a useful complement to the larger public. Religion is and can be a space for many kinds of public participation.

Religion and Politics

Religion's relation to politics grows out of its participatory features. That is, because participation in religion brings citizens together in a relation different from their other relations, religion bears on the power around which politics organizes. Because the later chapters take up their relationship in detail, I shall only speak generally here about religion and politics.

Religion is public not only because it is itself a space for participation, but also because, as an association of believers, it appears in public. It makes demands on the political order for space for its own activities, for freedom of conscience and freedom of worship for its believers. It may also demand building permits, exemptions from public duty for its clergy, special consideration in the drawing of municipal ordinances, and so forth. Religious organizations may also claim priority over the political in the moral and legal rules for social order. They may claim greater legitimacy in the exercise of public authority, and they may challenge the political realm for the loyalty of citizens. In these and similar ways, religion not only enters the public realm, it becomes itself public. And it becomes political.

The interaction and clash of power (or claims to power) make the intersection of religion and politics dangerous. For the great temptations are to combine religious and political power in such a way as to make one the servant of the other. Yet the response to the danger must not be denial of the public side of religion. For then a potential challenger to the dominance of political power outside its own proper sphere may be lost. That is, religion in its public role may serve as one of the voices to which political power should be responsive in formulating public policy. Pluralism and political freedom depend on the availability of channels of influence and of different perspective. Religion can serve as one of these channels. Moreover, in more extreme cases, public religion may also directly challenge a move toward tyranny by political power. Alternate sources of authority are necessary when political forces exceed their authority.

The Duality of Public Life

The sections above have argued the advantages of public life. But public life has its peculiar tyrannies. In this section I shall first pull together some themes of the previous sections to outline the salutary facets of public life: loyalty, trust, narrative, and identity. Then I shall consider the deleterious features of public life in preparation for the next chapter, which treats the strengths and limitations of private and public life.

The Virtues of Public Life

Public life balances the limitations of private and moderates its negative tendencies. Remember that private life is subject to the vacuity of consumption, to lying, shame, and deception. Left to myself, I am strongly inclined to stay to myself. I wish to hide my weaknesses and imperfections, and therefore also my talents, from outsiders. Ashamed of my mistakes, I decline to act lest I commit further mistakes and have my limitations discovered. As Arendt's analysis of private and public life suggests, we are too often tempted to have our life together administered by experts, so that we can gorge ourselves in the private life of consumption or hide ourselves within the right to privacy.

Hence the value and necessity of public life. In public life, the consumption of private goods must be balanced by concern for the common good. The demands of justice transform the pursuit of private interest into public. Truth, too, possesses a public dimension. That private life is essential for the discovery of truth is only half the story. Falsehood and truth are distinguished through public tests. Ideas and insights into the relationship between ideas must be demonstrated and defended before others. A community of inquirers who support, criticize, and appraise one another's ideas is crucial to the advancement of knowledge, whether in science, politics, or religion. The openness that characterizes public life therefore is essentially related to the discovery and validation of truth. The liberal idea of the marketplace of ideas reflects this aspect of public life. There is ultimately no such thing as a private truth, though private life is necessary for the discovery of truth. This way that public life balances and confirms private is its first and most obvious benefit. Its light reveals and brightens the darkness of private life.

Loyalty

Why should the demands of public justice matter to an individual wrapped up in private consumption and in guarding secrets? These demands in fact may not matter. Public justice is too often only a phrase, an illusion, or a cynical slogan itself concealing private greed. There is nothing automatic to the private-public balance.

There is, however, in human beings an impulse to loyalty to ideas, ideals, persons, or institutions beyond the self. The institutions of public life, especially but not exclusively the political, are a normal locus for this loyalty. The human quest for meaning inspires this impulse, for it does not take limited human beings long to discover, under normal social and mental conditions, that their private selves are poor containers for meaning. While public and quasi-public groups and institutions may also be weak vessels, they are not so obviously insufficient as the individual heart and mind.

The simplest way in which public life in its various manifestations provides meaning for individuals is by providing roles for them.[32] Roles pull people out of themselves, suggest standards and goals for action, and connect them to others in stable ways. Roles such as mother, supervisor, assistant professor, representative, and priest help to define the duties and responsibilities of persons and to structure relations with other persons, such as child, employee, dean, voter, and congregant. Acceptance of a role means acceptance of the duties associated with the role, and duty moves a person away from self-interest toward concern for other interests, even toward justice. These duties and the norms associated with them provide content for the speech about justice and injustice that Aristotle finds distinctive about human beings and that forms the foundation for public life. Although the dynamic of justice suggests that stable social roles and duties may not be sufficient and that probing beyond their limits will be necessary, these roles constitute a starting point for public debate.

To recognize the importance of roles and their consequences is to realize that some ways of life are truer to their implications than others. This recognition leads to the next one—namely, that commitment to a way of life is necessary if it is successfully to be followed. In short, the idea of social roles leads naturally to the idea of a way of life and, from thence, to commitment and loyalty. Even theorists preoccupied with private interests have not been able to deny the significance of these ideas, for they constitute a perhaps suppressed, but always present theme in liberalism, especially in its religious perspectives. As Eldon J. Eisenach says,

> In this view, political man cannot be comprehended as a bundle of legal rights and duties or as a physical container for the endless play of desire and aversion. In a historical and religious perspective, the political capacity of man is his ability to act on his conscious commitment to a way of life.[33]

The significance of loyalty for public life should be clear enough. The give and take, the conflict and compromise, the burdens of freedom, could not survive the struggles of power without loyalty to the wider public, whether the political realm or another public realm. Loyalty to a source of meaning anchors freedom and participation to specific contexts in which freedom and participation find meaning.

Loyalty to such a center of meaning becomes a source of dignity, a dignity impossible to find in sordid preoccupation with personal pleasure and self-aggrandizement. Public service, either through political/elective activity or civic responsibility, supplies a form of dignity unavailable in private life, despite its satisfactions. The dignity derives precisely from the acceptance and execution of responsibility in public— that is, in full sight of all participants, who thereby become acutely aware of successes and failures. Such responsibility demands a certain bearing compatible with the particulars of the assignment. Thus the unease surrounding the often demeaning rituals of political campaigning in America. The bearing of the campaigner seems at odds with the demeanor, the dignity, demanded by the responsibilities of law-making or of executive office.

In like manner, active involvement in debate and collaboration with others in the affairs of one's church, neighborhood, labor union, or vocation/workplace, provides a similar source of dignity and a reinforcement of loyalty. They draw one out of self-occupation and allow recognition and appreciation by others of one's talents and achievements.

At the same time, they expose weakness and failure. These can be profitable motivations for improvement, but they can at the same time become excuses for fleeing the public realm, leaving it for expert administration.

Fleeing, however, simply makes the public impersonal, thereby destroying its special character. An impersonal public realm inspires meager loyalty, so it resorts to rules and to coercion, thereby transforming its distinctively public character into a form of private tyranny, ironically administered for the "good" of its subjects. Thus, without public participation, the realms of government and business, even of church and union, become daily assaults on human dignity and destroyers of loyalty. Indeed, they end by transforming loyalty into one form or another of fanaticism. What I have just said about loyalty has an analogy in trust. Trust is certainly personal and private, but trust is also a public phenomenon. The public realm helps to establish social and personal dispositions toward trust.

Trust is naturally interpersonal, for it involves an attitude toward others. In the public realm participation directly affects trust. Participation with others in political or other public activity may certainly lead to distrust, if the others prove untrustworthy after direct experience with them. I do not mean to suggest that every person and every institution in the public or quasi-public sphere is automatically worthy of trust. However, only direct, active participatory experience can test the trustworthiness of such persons or institutions. Large institutions of a nonpublic sort, bureaucracies for example, may be reliable, but not trustworthy.

Narrative and Identity

Walzer contends that "men and women take on concrete identities because of the way they conceive and create, and then possess and employ social goods."[34] The public realm is, as Arendt saw, vital to acquiring identity. Social goods, shared in common, debated in public, provide reference points for understanding the self unavailable to the private self and its limited introspection. To have something of my own, even something private and secret, is indeed necessary to shape an identity, but I can only discover and explore what is my own through encounters with others. These encounters primarily occur in the public world, where, willy-nilly, I have to interact with others, defend my ideas against theirs, assess my interests in light of theirs, and discover ways of competition without mutual destruction and of cooperation without self-abnegation.

The self alone cannot fathom itself. It can begin to understand itself through signs and symbols devised with others and used as means of conflict and cooperation.[35] Witness what Aristotle said about the distinctive qualities of human beings. They are not simply gregarious; they do not simply make sounds indicating their respective pleasures and pains. Human beings create a public world through language that "serves to declare what is advantageous and what is the reverse, and therefore serves to declare what is just and what is unjust."[36] The "therefore" is not meant, as the context makes clear, to equate the advantageous and the just, though that seems to be the function of language in Hobbes; rather, it indicates the topic of justice (public) language. The public realm is speech about justice, and this speech draws on, as Pitkin argued, individual perceptions and articulations of interest in order to discover and create a common life out of separate lives.

The connection with narrative is this. Public accounts of both justice and interest evoke old stories and create new ones, stories in which individuals find a place and an identity and in which a common life is portrayed. When we give accounts of our needs and wants, we tell stories of our experiences, stories whose political and religious origins are particularly prominent. When we appeal to justice to justify these needs and wants and to help our story turn out better, we appeal to the ideals of our society developed in its past experience, its history embodied in the stories of its founders and heroes and ordinary people, who carved out a life together. The public language of justice is not abstract; it is, as Plato demonstrated, a language appealing to specific ways of life and to the stories of people who follow these ways of life.

As we tell, create, and reshape our myths and stories, we situate ourselves with respect to our fellow inhabitants of the public realm, and we create and reshape collective stories at the same time. Our situation is always vis-a-vis someone else's, and there is no way to avoid learning this if we take the risk of joining the speech and action of public life, whether in politics strictly speaking or in other public realms. Therefore, public life makes an essential contribution to shaping individual and collective identity, and this contribution is inseparable from the narratives that give concrete shape to the public realm.

The Vices of Public Life

But these positive contributions of the public realm are not its only features. As crucial as it is to flourishing individual and communal identity, public life has its own diseases: communal pride, lust for power, manipulation, and jingoism, to name a few.

Public Versus Private

Public life is prone to interfere with private life. It demands conformity, success, and fame, all of which place severe tests on integrity. Fear of public exposure reinforces the deception and the fleeing of public life that so often follow shame and guilt. Public life magnifies real or perceived imperfection, tempting the person to hide in private. Or, paradoxically, public tastes mask imperfection and inflate the pride of persons who would otherwise know that their works and their souls are flawed.

In addition, the public world tends to demand that all trust, all intimacy, all autonomy, all personal relations, and all political speculation—the special contributions of private life—serve public purposes. In short, public life is greedy. It strives to transform the goods appropriate to private life and the necessary times and spaces of private life into means for public goods or into public goods themselves.

Community and the Public

One of the most insidious forms of public imperialism is the metamorphosis of public life into some form of community. This phenomenon takes the forms of nationalism, jingoism, racism, or totalitarianism. The source of the error is transference of intimacy from the private to the public. Community, a form of private or quasi-private intimacy, becomes conformity to race or land or ideology. The speech, language, ritual, and tradition that are essential elements of community do have their analogues in public life. There are legitimate public traditions; there is a common language and speech of public life; and the public world has its rituals. But these have a different quality from their genuine communal form, which is more appropriate in the intimacies of private life. Public speech is different from family conversation.[37] Public, especially political, life has gone drastically wrong when it attempts to be family. Public life, however, frequently welcomes this invasion of the public by the private.

The invasion is welcome because the power, the conflict, and the stresses and strains of genuine participation make public life fragile. Therefore, public life seeks stability by violating its proper limits. The solidarity of community looks appealing from this perspective. Nationalism is one manifestation of this tempting vision. In the public realm, however, these qualities of community manifest themselves as conformity. Loyalty must be earned, freely given. In assigning loyalty, the person does not relinquish freedom or the right, indeed the duty, to criticize. Loyalty requires criticism. Community, genuine intimacy, dictates a deep sharing of selves, of experience, of principles, stories, and struggles. This kind of intimate sharing is not possible in public life, unless it is manipulated through emotional appeals, fears of external threats, and evocations of shame, guilt, and imperfection.[38]

Public life is exclusive, as is private life: the members of particular publics must be identified and marked off from those who are not members. But it should be relatively easy to join a public group, and this sets public exclusivity apart from private. The exclusivity of private life is intense, for what is shared is deep and personal. When the exclusivity of public life approaches this degree of intensity, and it too often does, then it has exceeded its bounds. The Platonic tendency to regard the public bonds as bonds of *philia* marks the limits of public life, suggesting the primacy of the personal, for friendship is principally exclusive and private.[39]

I have argued that direct participation characterizes public life. This means that public life, as opposed to bureaucratic life, is personal. Yet compared with private life, public life is relatively impersonal. Public participants share episodes of their stories, and they discover and develop parts of themselves that cannot be discovered and developed in private life. Nevertheless, the public face is always a mask, which is not and cannot be dropped in public.

This fact explains the titillation associated with questions about Gary Hart's sexual behavior and the state of his marriage during the 1988 presidential primary season. The real state of his marriage and the real Gary Hart cannot be known publicly, no matter how much is revealed, for something will always be held back, known and experienced only by himself, his wife, and intimate friends. Thus in the campaign, we are both eager to learn all about his secret behavior, for there is a thrill in the public revelation of private things, and also uncomfortable with public discussion of adultery.

Here we approach the boundary that both separates and links public and private life. Private character has public consequences. Or, better, a single character acts in both private and public life. The point here, however, is that this character is more personally known in private than in public. Thus impersonality haunts public life, becoming an excuse for avoiding legitimate questions of character. The impersonality becomes as well a temptation to transform the genuine personal and participatory life of the public into impersonal expertise and bureaucratic administration.

Public As Sovereign

The combination of the impersonality of public life and its simultaneous temptation toward conformity is particularly dangerous when the idea of the sovereignty of public life is broached. Though I believe there is a sense in which public life directed toward the common good has a certain priority over private goods, there is also a vital sense in which personal life, the central mystery of private life, takes priority over public life. Sovereignty does have a legitimate place in our conceptual vocabulary. Some conceptions of public life, however, come dangerously close to unitary conceptions of life in which the private is submerged into and indistinguishable from a part of the public. For example, Benjamin Barber says that

> civic activity, though omnicompetent only in unitary democracy, stands in lexical priority to all social activities in strong democracy. Because it is public it orders and guides all forms of private activity. These private forms may be more valuable and more precious than civic activity, but they are

nonetheless only possible in a framework of public seeing and within a workable public order.[40]

Barber's language, while it distinguishes the omnicompetence of public activity in unitary democracy from its sovereignty in strong democracy, comes very close to identifying the two. This danger is always present. Because it is more comprehensive than the private, the public is likely to think of itself as more important in all respects. Because religion has its public side, it is subject to the corruptions of public life. But religion also has qualities essential to counteracting them.

The Vices of Public Religion

So far, I have emphasized religion's salutary public functions. Its destructive side, however, is not far to seek. Indeed, neither passionate fear of nor commitment to religion is ever far below the surface of even calm seminars on religion and politics. Usually there is an edge to questions and comments revealing an emotional commitment beneath the surface of dispassionate discussion. Nor should this be surprising.

Religion's public side manifests two qualities particularly dangerous in public, its passion and its universal claims. These two qualities in turn produce two major dangers: religious domination of public life, and the combination of religion with political ideology.

The first danger occurs when religious passion and religious claims to totality find little resistance from other public institutions. Religious passion and totality are always present as part of religion's claim to transcendence. Because this claim tends toward an account of all reality, it inclines toward a total account of life, organizing, explaining, and justifying all action. Therefore, religions often generate elaborate systems of belief, institution, and ritual applicable to all areas of life and claiming total jurisdiction over the individual believer and the community of believers. In its extreme form it claims the right to govern the total life of an entire society.

I must qualify this strong statement of the dangers of the universal claims of religion. Some religions are more susceptible than others.[41] Those that permit or require structural differentiation between the things of God and of Caesar are less vulnerable than others. For example, the Lutheran idea of the kingdom of God and the kingdom of the world allows an autonomy to the latter that protects it against religious usurpation. Shiite Islam, on the other hand, makes no such separation.

Religion also touches directly on the heart's deepest passions. Indeed, one of religion's major intentions is to explain, moderate, and control those passions. Yet it often releases human passion. And this too is one of its purposes. Indeed, one way to govern passion is to release it under controlled conditions, which is one of the purposes of ritual. But playing with passion is a tricky business; it may go out of control. Alternatively, religious leaders may employ control and release precisely as a means of social power. State officials may seek to dominate religion in order to wield this power themselves.

This danger of religious passion and totality generating mechanisms of social command is particularly strong in Western religions, such as Judaism, Christianity, and Islam, because they have religious leaders and structures readily identifiable and readily tempted to claim jurisdiction not only in their specific religious realms, but also throughout all social and political jurisdictions.[42] As they claim total jurisdiction they run into other groups claiming similar jurisdiction or into secular and religious groups favoring pluralism. Religious violence, civil war, assassination, terrorism, and international conflict are all-too-common results of this impulse, as the recent histories of Iran, Lebanon, Northern Ireland, and other parts of the world racked by religious violence demonstrate. Western religion, however, is not the only form in which the universal impulse is present. Witness also Sikh and Hindu violence in India with its combination of religious and nationalist fervor.

The second danger of public religion is less dramatic and, initially at least, less destructive, though it is more subtly subversive of religion itself. This danger is the absorption of the religious impulse into political ideologies. I am not referring here to the religious dimensions of political ideologies themselves, a subject I put aside (for purposes of this book) in my definition of religion. Rather, I mean the danger of religious belief becoming assimilated to an existing political ideology. The best illustration of the danger of religious totalism is the Iranian regime of Ayatollah Khomeini. The new religious right furnishes the best illustration of ideological absorption, where religious leaders have baptized laissez-faire economics and nationalist foreign policy.

In assimilating religious passion and totalism the political ideology captures the religious beliefs in such a way that a particular set of political beliefs becomes identified with the expression of religious beliefs. As George Marsden puts it, "The fact is that religion and power is a very volatile mix. . . . Religious convictions can all too easily become a sort of wild card that one puts together with whatever political bias one happens to hold."[43] In the first danger, religious passion absorbs the political. In the second, political ideology absorbs religion. For example, some religious leaders of the nineteenth and twentieth Centuries have identified Christianity with capitalism (the new religious right) and some with socialism (liberation theology). Such identifications join economic theory with religious belief in unholy wedlock.

Although the first danger more likely produces violence, each is dangerous to both religion and to politics, for each obscures the proper border between public and private life and between religion and politics. The dangers are different, but each threatens pluralism, freedom, and democracy.

Religion and the Vices of Public Life

Religion need not succumb to its particular dangers. When it does not, it provides a check on the dangers of public life. I have indicated above how public life becomes impersonal, jealous of the private, imperialistic, and conflictual. Many of these qualities spring from the fiercely agonal, egoistic public forces discovered by Arendt. Because of these forces, the public cannot be a community of like-minded, harmonious, sharing friends. The public, and especially politics, cannot take the place of family and friendship or other forms of community. Competition, self-interest, and ambition always interact with concern for the public good. One contribution of religion is to moderate, mediate, and serve as an alternative to these competitive forces.

There are two principal ways in which religion accomplishes the task of moderating the dangers of public life: first, by serving as a refuge or retreat from the public realm; second, by challenging that realm.

The family has been called a "haven in a heartless world," and there is some truth to the label. Religion too forms a haven. The solidarity of a community of friends and fellow believers, the solace and forgiveness offered by religious rites, and participation in common efforts on a small scale can counteract the heartless, individualized, impersonal, utilitarian, competitive public world. Especially in a liberal society, with its emphasis on cool and skeptical rationalism, pragmatism, tolerance, moral relativism, and individual freedom, religion furnishes a source of warmth, emotion, and shared principles. "Clearly for many Christians and other religionists in America the church more or less approximates the community they seek but too rarely find in liberal society."[44] The local church may afford a community of worship, satisfy aesthetic needs with its art and ritual, counteract the pragmatism and skepticism of public life, and suggest in its affirmation of transcendence a meaning for public and private life otherwise not available.

Religion also supports, along with family and school, a system of behavior control. Religion reinforces right and wrong ways of acting and beliefs about moral and immoral behavior, and so can control some of the wilder passions of the heart. In doing this, religion indirectly serves as a refuge from politics, for if the institutions of religion, family, and school fail in this task of control (as they seem to in modern times), then the more impersonal and physically coercive mechanisms of the state will take over the task.[45] Even worse, religion will seek to coopt the state (or vice versa) to enforce moral principles that have lost their ability to gain the assent of the majority of citizens or to regulate the actions even of believers. This is the path taken by the new religious right.[46]

Religion, however, can serve as a refuge and retreat from the worst side of public life only if it does not fall into the trap of privatization. The danger today, in America at least, is that religion has been deeply infected with the general individualism and privatism of American culture.

The second way that religion counterbalances the dark side of public life is by challenging it. Though the requirements of the public language of justice, freedom, and common good are designed to draw self-interest toward the public good through the meeting of differences in participation, the agonal, ambitious side of public life often triumphs over justice and the common good. Sovereignty, force, and imperialism overwhelm the fragile participatory space and the mutual recognition of interests and needs. Because religion possesses a system of principles and beliefs independent of the political realm, and because it tends to advocate idealism and perfectionism in realization of moral principles, it can contest the imperialism and cynicism of political life.

The challenge may be direct or indirect. The church, simply by being itself, may by its very adherence to principles challenge a public realm that has lost connection with principle.[47] Or the church might directly enter politics to challenge immoral laws or policies, as many religious abolitionists did in the decades before the Civil War.[48] Either way, religion confronts politics when its principles and way of life contradict those of the political realm. Of course, institutionalized, relatively public religions can challenge politics more effectively in these ways, which is another limitation of privatized religion. Note also that it is very difficult for civil religion and for faiths closely allied to political life effectively to dispute the political realm.

Thus religion walks a thin line, serving as a challenge to and as a refuge from politics. It performs either of these tasks best when it displays a balance between the private and public sides of religion. Religion must be in contact with, but not absorbed in or too closely allied to politics. This balancing act once again suggests metaphors of tension and of borderlands. These metaphors must now be unpacked.

4
The Border of Public and Private Life

If I am for myself only, what am I?
If I am not for myself, who will be for me?
—Hillel

In this chapter I wish to draw together a number of threads of the argument so far concerning the place of private and public life in politics and personal life. I am particularly concerned to state clearly the contributions that private and public life make to personal and political development. But I want to show clearly as well the limitations of each form of life. The limitations of each alone suggest the need to pay close attention to their area of overlap. This area, and especially religion's place in it, forms the core of the rest of the book.

The Contributions of Private Life

Private life makes irreplaceable contributions to both personal and political development. Most contributions are implicit in private life's features of inclusivity and exclusivity and need only be drawn out. I shall classify these contributions under three headings: autonomy, intimacy, and freedom.[1] Although I discuss these contributions in terms of individual private life, the same points are valid, *mutatis mutandis*, for the institutions of private life. Families, friends, and churches also promote autonomy, relationships, and freedom.

Autonomy

The value of personal autonomy and the contribution that private life makes to it are familiar in liberal culture and political theory. J. S. Mill's defense of individual liberty against political and social authority is rooted in autonomy. An area of private life is necessary, and its protection from public interference required, in order that individuals have relief from oppressive social conventions and pressures for conformity. Freed from these forces, persons have the opportunity to develop their particular talents, to become unique individuals, and to legislate for themselves principles, standards of conduct, and ways of life. The individual in control of his own life, because he can control access to information about himself and exclude others from unwanted access, possesses the resources for dignity and self-respect. Dignity depends on concealing various facts and activities; self-respect on living according to one's own standards, even in the face of pressures to abandon them. Self-respect depends on integrity. Private life is the place for reflecting on standards and resisting pressures, as well as for concealing guilt and imperfection.

Another and related aspect of personal autonomy is creative originality, a trait particularly valued by Mill. Creativity requires finding one's own voice, artistic, intellectual, moral, and political. Constant bombardment by other voices makes it difficult, perhaps impossible, to hear and cultivate one's own. Thus, private life, time and space away, at times, from all others or, at other times, in the presence of selected intimate others, nourishes creativity. Indeed, creativity proves impossible without private life. The mystery of creative originality and the mystery of the self are fundamentally the same. Research and writing, painting and sculpture, moral and scientific thinking all require solitude. This is not to say that privacy and solitude are the only things needed. All of these activities profit from interaction with others and with the public.

Finally, private life enhances and makes possible another use of personal autonomy, the opportunity for particular experiences that are good in themselves. Some experiences are inherently good or pleasurable, but are only or best enjoyed in solitude or with a few intimate friends. I have in mind such things as mystical religious experience, a tranquil walk, and a good book. Separation from others and the ability to decide when and where to pursue such experiences are critical to their enjoyment. At the same time, these experiences also depend on the qualities of integrity and trust linked to the inclusive side of private life. This is so because they are nonconsuming. Their experience depends on receiving gifts from others or from nature without reaching out to grasp and appropriate what is received. That is, one must trust that the experience is not a possession to control. One must have a large enough sense of one's own completeness not to need to determine how the experience will turn out.

Intimacy

Relief from social conventions and the opportunity for experiences good in themselves are also highly relevant for personal relations. Private time and space away from social conventions and pressures are necessary for intimate relations and their special qualities to flourish. Exceptional experiences are heightened when they are shared, not indiscriminately, but with a few intimate, trusted others. So a deep tie exists between the contribution of private life to personal autonomy and to personal relations. Indeed, cultivating intimate relationships constitutes one of the highest uses of autonomy.

There is no possibility of beginning or sustaining intimacy without private life. Intimate relations dissolve under the glare of nonintimate observers. Indeed, even the observation of one circle of intimate relations by members of another circle can be destructive. Close friends are not invited to observe marital intimacies, and spouses need time apart with friends.

Intimate relations are so vital to human flourishing that even if private life made no other contribution, facilitating intimacy would be all the justification needed to grant it large scope. Intimate relations both remind us of and help us to overcome our limitations as embodied creatures. When we think that we are invincible, friends and family remind us otherwise, by their own obviously limited existence if not by explicit warnings. The private world, even more than the public, is a world of context and contingency, of biologic and psychic boundaries to pride and ambition. We can get away with things in the public realm that our friends and family would laugh or cry at. That is why people from small towns like to spend Saturday nights in the big city. It's easier to pretend there.

Yet just as private life reminds us of our limitations, intimate relations help us to bear and even overcome them by giving us others to share our burdens. Having secrets means that we have secrets to share—that is, we have surprises, guilt, and forgiveness to convey in order to forge intimacy. Friends help us to discover our imperfections and to realize that these faults are not fatal to intimacy. Private life teaches us our limits and provides us with intimate others to share them.[2]

The centrality of religion, therefore, in reminding believers of their limitations and in helping them bear them should not be surprising. To the extent that religion is deeply part of private life, it is involved in frailty and healing. Before the transcendent, of course, frailty is most obvious. Therefore, religious belief, feeling, and action is oriented to explaining and justifying handicaps in face of the divine. Yet religion also provides rituals, justifications, and beliefs that allow debilities to be borne with grace and dignity.

Freedom

Public life is certainly the principal ground of political freedom, but private life also advances it. Private life provides relief from social conformity displayed as political uniformity. If all of life were lived in public, resistance to conformity would require superhuman strength. Private life, however, provides a refuge from such pressures. Such is its "negative" contribution to political freedom.

On the positive side, private life supplies the occasion for perfecting political understanding and devising plans for social change. To be involved in politics is to learn a great deal about human beings and their behavior. Yet unless a person can withdraw periodically from the political struggles to reflect and to compare political to other insights, political learning is truncated. Politics becomes unlimited when detached from other experience. Politics does not carry its own meaning; it has significance as part of total human experience. Politics is also imperialistic. Left to itself, it absorbs all energies and translates other forms of life into its own terms. Private life frustrates this distortion.

Similarly, political activity is typically shortsighted, wedded to the social and economic status quo. Plans for long-range social, economic, and political change have little possibility of formulation without withdrawal and reflection in privacy. Private life grants the freedom to consider possible plans of social change, even of radical change, plans unlikely to emerge in the same fashion in the heat of political struggle. Private life contributes as well intimate friends to support one's political efforts, the integrity to act in the face of contrary pressures, and the trust needed to act at all.

The Limitations of Private Life

Despite these essential values, private life cannot stand on its own. Public life is its necessary complement and antagonist. Private life's insufficiency is double. Individuals cannot standon their own, the obvious conclusion of virtually all political thought. But, less obviously, individuals cannot stand together if their only bonds are the interests of private life. This point has been the burden of much contemporary criticism of liberal politics and political theory, so I shall not belabor it.[3] Rather, I wish here only to suggest the limitations of private life as they are rooted in the temptation to dwell within the exclusive side of private life and in the exaltation of personal autonomy over intimate relations and political freedom.

The Limitations of Private Consciousness

One of the features of the exclusive side of private life is imperfection. We do not wish the less than perfect to appear in public. Indeed, we may legitimately postpone public appearance until imperfections have been remedied. Yet imperfection is the natural lot of all human projects. Therefore, human beings are greatly tempted toward illegitimate concealing, dissembling, and lying to make the imperfect appear perfect. This temptation gathers more strength when shame and guilt enter. Thus, without the constraints of public life, lying tends to become endemic, endeavoring to keep imperfection, errors, faults, crimes, and injustices hidden behind a facade of perfection. Of course, the ultimate victim is the individual liar, who inevitably has to believe the lies in order to make them convincing, which might explain President Reagan's account of the budget deficits during his administration. We lie to ourselves in order to lie to others. To maintain personal autonomy we cut ourselves off from creativity, close relations, and political freedom, all of which are undercut by falsehood.

Thus Sissela Bok, who sensitively assesses the place of justifiable and unjustifiable lies in personal and public life, finds that private life cannot stand alone. Because of the power of the lie, lying can only be justified when it can be defended by (at least potential) public reasons. The public overcomes the limitations of private conscience. The requirement to test justification in the public court balances the too often easy court of one's own conscience. The person who can justify a deception publicly, which is a greater burden to bear than hiding the deception, is more mature than one who cannot or does not care to. Public justification requires a constant effort of imagination, particularly to imagine oneself in another's position, and strong institutional incentives. Bok argues:

> Moral justification . . . cannot be exclusive or hidden; it has to be capable of being made public. In going beyond the purely private, it attempts to transcend also what is merely subjective.[4]

Private life supports truth and integrity, but that is only half the story. Truth and integrity decay without public justification.

The political manifestation of private deception is interest politics, the descent of the common good into the pursuit of public support for private advantage. Private interests possess a legitimate place, but public interest requires justification and, ultimately, transformation of private interests in public terms. The problem of the 1960s and 1970s was not that the personal became political with the entry of private matters like sex, feelings, family, children, and personal hang-ups into the political arena. The problem was that the political ultimately became personal. Increasing privacy in the modern world, without the means of linking private life to public institutions, yields increased alienation.[5]

Private life in and of itself is blind to justice, for it tends to place the self in a different category from others. Private life easily becomes an irresponsible refuge from the moral duty to act responsibly and to pursue public justice. Such culpability is exceptionally frequent in modern consumer society. It is all too easy to forget the public while wrapped up in private consumption, as Tocqueville warned. Public life is not simply attractive, though it does have its allurements. Public life is also a duty for moral persons concerned with justifying their action. To close one's eyes to injustice is to participate in it.

These considerations point to the limitations of the prerogatives of private life. In addition, in the singularly modern emptiness of the soul these limitations are clearly illustrated.

The Narrative Character of the Self

No one has commented so forcefully on vacuity of soul in the modern world as Walker Percy.[6] Through a series of "quizzes," thought experiments, and imaginative exercises, Percy shows how a "self" (a revealingly modern word) cut off from all social and culture moorings is literally lost in the universe, completely mysterious to itself, though it "knows" more about the universe than ever before. This emptiness of the self explains twentieth century consumer society: "The self in the twentieth century is a voracious nought which expands like the feeding vacuole of an amoeba seeking to nourish and inform its own nothingness by ingesting new objects in the world but, like a vacuole, only succeeds in emptying them out."[7]

Though such vacuity is nothing new, the modern idea of the private self necessarily produces and even exalts such emptiness. For this idea of the self depends on private life as exclusion, therefore on separation of self from others. This separation then tends to generate a world constructed by the private self, a world without the untidy dangling threads of life connecting self to others in unplanned and undeniable ways. The public then disappears and the self is thrown back on its own meager resources alone. When, according to Marvin Zetterbaum, this idea of the self arises, "the self begins to speak of itself grandiloquently as subject, as individual mind, self, or ego, the center or agent of consciousness, and, in so doing, not only radically alters the vocabulary of political theory but also fundamentally changes our perception of political things." This self, in its quest for self-expression and self-fulfillment, threatens to "dissociate the private and the public altogether."[8] Opposed to this idea of the self, characterized by the inflation of the exclusive side of private life, is the idea of the self as narrative. Political theory is beginning to recover this idea, as it realizes the weakness of "thin" theories of the self and begins to explore narrative and historical theories of selfhood.[9] These theories have argued that we cannot abstract people from their cultures, with their very particular histories, traditions, and stories, without stripping them of their humanity. But histories, traditions, and stories are public, shared. They connect the private lives of particular persons to the private lives of particular other persons. Such connections begin to create a public world, a common history and common stories linking private life to private life and, ultimately, private to public life. Selves embedded in narratives, traditions, and histories are not empty, or at least resist emptiness, because the stories provide a solidity, a resource on which they draw for strength and constancy in the midst of demands for submission to fashion.

Religion is one of the most embedded institutions of private life. Religions typically contain rituals, stories, and traditions whose origins may be so deep as to be shrouded by the mists of memory. Grounding in such obscure, but powerful, forces is much of what it means to be a Methodist, a Jew, a Moslem, or a Catholic. The very embeddedness of religion helps to overcome the emptiness of the self and to link it to a line of fellow believers stretching from the distant past into the dimly perceived future. Thus religion, considered only in its private aspects, helps to surmount the limitations of private life itself. Of course, it is just such traditions and rituals on the part of religion that demonstrate that religion itself is more than private and that religion is a vital institution linking private with public life.

I must leave this point at this temporarily undeveloped stage, for narrative is one of the primary connections between public and private life and the primary focus of chapter 7. The point, however, is that the narrative idea of self reminds us of the essential limitations of private life and points toward public life.

The Limitations of Public Life

Public life by itself is as limited as private. Without both its links to private life and, at the same time, boundaries between public and private life, public life's impersonality, tendency to conformity, and imperialism are dangerous to freedom and dignity. Public life sundered from and made superior to private life produces a split personality. How I appear in public comes to be divorced from and ultimately to violate my private identity.

Public life is subject to a double limitation, a limitation particularly striking in politics. First, public life is not private—a simple enough truth, but one with profound consequences. As public life is not private, it does not possess the strengths or make the contributions of private life. The relationship of public life to such contributions of private as trust, integrity, autonomy, and political freedom is problematical. There is a public form of trust, but it cannot replace private trust, for such trust is one of the very constituents of private life. Public life tests integrity severely, for it encourages deception to conceal the imperfections of private life. The imperialistic aspects of public life also threaten to submerge personal autonomy and the aspects of political freedom particularly nurtured in private.

Second, public life is not community. Therefore, its relation to intimacy, shared values, tradition, and common stories is problematical. The particular and vital contributions these make to human flourishing cannot be made by politics or other forms of public life, no matter how hard they try. Though it possesses its own important goods, particularly loyalty and participation, and though it remedies the more threatening aspects of private life, public life is prone to distort its particular goods by magnifying them beyond their proper limits. Instead of balancing the limitations of private life, it wishes to absorb private life. Instead of facilitating community, it desires to become community. Instead of facilitating the ordering of goods, it wishes to become the sovereign good.

Distortions of the good can be detected and challenged by personal judgment. Someone must have the vision and the courage to see and to say, not that the emperor is naked, but that he is wearing the wrong clothes, that the public person has stolen the wardrobe of private persons. Firm grounding in the moral and social goods of private life can empower a person to see and to say what is wrong in public life. Certainly it helps if the person's vision is aided by public experience, but public experience may leave one too close to the distortions to detect their true outline and colors. Private life furnishes the distance vision requires. Churchill's warnings about Germany in the 1930s furnish a dramatic example.

The ultimate limitation of public life is that private life is in some sense prior to it. This principle may be illustrated by the fact that a person may legitimately opt out of public life, particularly out of political life. Even in a democratic society, a person may have morally good reasons for not participating in public life or in certain parts of public life. It is indeed morally puzzling to make voting, let alone more extensive forms of participation, mandatory. But it would be very odd to say that a person could legitimately opt out of private life. That would mean fleeing himself. It would preclude all intimate relationships, particularly love and friendship. There would be something morally and psychically obtuse about a person, no matter the motives, who declined to have any private life.

That a person may decline public, but not private, life suggests a certain limitation to public life and a certain primacy to private life. What, however, are the "certain" limit and the "certain" primacy? To argue in this way is not to argue that private life can do without public or that private life is prior in all ways to public. It only suggests that at the boundaries there is a particular relationship between public and private that gives preference to the private. But this may be true only at the boundaries. And, as I have been suggesting throughout, a boundary not only separates two things, it also defines and structures a relationship between them. It links them in certain ways.

The Idea of the Border

Private life and public life are different. Theories that collapse one into the other are mistaken. Private life is defined by such "exclusionary" phenomena as the personal, shame and guilt, imperfection, and mystery and by the "inclusionary" phenomena of integrity, trust, and intimacy. As distinctive experiences of human life, these form a tapestry of interwoven patterns defining a particular form of life. Public life has other distinct qualities. These include active participation in a common world, loyalty, trust, and narrative. The public world is closely associated with power and therefore with politics. Though the political and the public are not coextensive, they fit closely.

Natural differences thus distinguish public and private life. Qualities differentiating them provide criteria for assigning particular experiences or forms of activity to one or the other. Yet, though public and private are different, they are not unrelated. The preceding pages have brought us to the point of seeing public and private as distinct yet overlapping. Difference and distinction do not mean separation. Both are parts of the life of individuals or groups, and this life has a unity, or at least aspires to one, that transcends the distinction between public and private. Earlier pages have principally focused on the distinctions. The following chapters examine closely some areas of commonality.

In the next two chapters, I discuss virtue, character, and language, especially political and religious language. Chapter 7 considers narratives and institutions, other human properties tying public to private life. Narratives and institutions depend on common traditions, histories, and rituals, and I say something about these as well. Character and virtue lie on the border of public and private life, but they are most firmly rooted in private. Language, however, is most clearly public. Finally, narratives and institutions, especially religion, are squarely planted in both realms. The description of these concepts takes some time to unfold, for it is important to specify as carefully as possible what these concepts accomplish, as well as what they do not accomplish.

Because religion embodies character, narratives, and institutions, it occupies the borderland between private and public. More precisely, perhaps, religion suffuses private life, yet is itself a public thing. Other institutions also inhabit this territory, and religion's relation to public and private is not singular. Yet religion makes distinctive contributions to public and private life and, therefore, to politics. At the same time, politics has something to teach religion.

I have used the metaphor of the border between religion and politics and between public and private life. This metaphor requires a more complete explanation, though certainly metaphors are useless if too precisely defined.

Religion brings a dynamism to both private and public life, because it is one of the principal inhabitants of the border territory between public and private life. Borders are places of tension, and such tension is responsible for a good deal of the creativity, and sometimes bloody confrontation, that occurs on any tense border. The metaphor gets complicated, as two borders, involved with four phenomena, intersect. The border between religion and politics is itself important, as is the border between public and private. These are not the same borders, but they do intersect.

Perhaps it would be best to try to diagram the intersections, but that would require greater artistry than I possess and would make the metaphor too literal in any event. Let me simply indicate that what I am trying to express is that religion partakes of both public and private life. Therefore, it is neither wholly one nor wholly the other. It possesses its own special characteristics and its singular dynamic because it resides partially in each realm. Therefore, religion is instructive as one of the clearest examples of the connection between public and private life. Moreover, religion is a good example of how the tensions between public and private play themselves out.

The border metaphor becomes stretched thin here, for it suggests either a definite line separating nations or a no-man's-land between hostile territories. Though these suggestions themselves may be useful in certain ways to point to the distinct features of public and private and to the tension between them, religion (and other institutions on the border) clearly demonstrates that public and private are simply different emphases in human life, not separate metaphysical entities. Religion, like the family, includes both public and private characteristics. It is private from certain perspectives, public from others. We may speak of it as occupying the border or as existing in the area of overlapping spheres of life, as long as these metaphors are not taken too literally.

At the same time that religion resides on the public-private border, there are a variety of spheres within public life itself. As I argued above, politics is not the whole of public life. There are other forms of public life as well, though politics in the narrow sense is a most important component of public life, one that plays a special role relating to the order of public life as a whole. However, if there are different publics within the public realm as a whole and if religion is one of the publics, then it must touch politics as another of the public realms. Therefore, there will be a religion and politics border within the public realm, just as there is a border or area of overlap between public and private (with religion as a prominent resident of that territory).

Sometimes, then, I shall speak of one border and sometimes the other, and I hope not to confuse them. But if some confusion results, it shall be merely a reflection of the complex interactions as four different areas of life intersect. That matters are thus complicated is not an artifact of our conceptual poverty, but rather an artifact of the way the world really is, an untidy but richly rewarding arena of tension and cooperation, of aspiration and failure. The following chapters concentrate on some of the stories located in this tangled domain.

Although I cannot review the history of political philosophy as it bears on private and public, a long tradition of speculation contemplates just this issue, and many theorists have concluded that the inner and outer worlds, the private and public worlds, are linked.[10] In the *Apology* (28A), Plato has Socrates say, "A man who really fights for the right, if he is to preserve his life for even a little while, must be a private citizen, not a public man." Yet this same Plato makes the analogy between soul and *polis* the ruling metaphor of the *Republic*. It is safe to say that Plato wrestled with the nexus but did not abandon it, whereas Aristotle assumed the attachment. Etienne Gilson characterizes a strong religious tradition that outer peace and virtue depend on inner tranquility when he says, "Not until the social order becomes the spontaneous expression of an interior peace in men's hearts shall we have tranquillity."[11]

There is, I believe, a truth to this notion. I have already suggested various ways in which private compensates for the weakness of public, and vice versa. And some of the things I shall say in the following chapters reflect this compensation. Nonetheless, this notion easily misleads. For the interaction of public and private (and, I shall argue, religion and politics) exhibits tension. Public and private support each other up by pushing against, challenging one another. A wall may be anchored to a foundation, or it may stand by pushing against a beam connecting it to another wall, which is pushing in the opposite way against the same beam. The connection between private and public is similar to the latter. If it were like the former, either public would have to be the foundation for private life or vice versa. I have argued already that one does not grow out of the other.

The following reflection illustrates the idea of balance in opposition. Because private life may be the occasion for contact with transcendence through truth, trust, or mystery, it needs the support of others. Transcendence is frightening, and supportive others (a public) help the person to bear it. Yet private life may also be the occasion for delusion, so it needs the correction of others. Support implies harmony, but correction suggests tension. Yet private life needs both. Even more, the same supporting public must also challenge, so the relation between private and public always will be touched with tension. Similarly, there are public episodes of transcendence and delusion. The former are incomplete without private appropriation, and the latter can be challenged by individual witness (the emperor's new clothes). From the public side, too, tension fulfills the need for support and challenge.

The contention that public justice means transforming private interests into common goods intimates the tension between private and public life. Their relationship must be political and dynamic, if private interest is to be transformed and if public goods are to be prevented from slipping into private hands. Change and transformation require pushing, pulling, and tugging. The private pulls against other private interests and against the public, while public pulls against private. It is inaccurate to say that public and private are opposed, for each transforms the other. Each needs the other; their struggle entwines them.

Finally, as W. L. Weinstein says, "there are tensions between the ideal value set on something seen as essentially private and free and what is understood to be its actual value in social reality."[12] For example, club memberships, as they involve intimacy, should be private. Yet in the social world they often function to exclude women or racial minorities from political, economic, or social benefits, thus violating public justice. If so, as the Supreme Court has recently recognized, they are effectively public, even though so treating them strains their otherwise properly private character.

My account of the strengths and limitations of private and public has highlighted the connections between them. But I have not described the connections or the ways in which they complement one another. Only after that description will the specific form of the primacy of the private be clear. And only after accomplishing that will it be possible to explore the most distinctive ways in which religion bears upon public and private life.

5

Argument on the Border: Political and Religious Language

> The mind—the culture—has two little tools,
> grammar and lexicon: a decorated sand bucket
> and a matching shovel. With these we bluster
> about the continents and do all the world's
> work. With these we try to save our very lives.
> —Annie Dillard, *Teaching a Stone to Talk*

In this marvelous image Annie Dillard captures the centrality of language. She does not exaggerate. Language, clumsy as it is, makes us human; through language we do all our work, private and public. At the most elemental level private and public interlock through language. Yet if we restrict ourselves to one vocabulary, we hinder our ability to do the world's work. That is the danger to which Bellah and his colleagues point in *Habits of the Heart*. We have different languages available for different tasks and appropriate in different arenas of life. That plurality is enriching; so we must resist translating everything into one conceptual language. Further, it would be a mistake to forbid the participants in different language arenas to speak with those in other arenas. I shall first consider the meeting of public and private in the general features of language. Second, I shall show how specifically political and religious language entwine them even more closely. Finally, I shall discuss the limits of religious language in political debate.

Language and Public-Private Life

The Character of Language

Language is a fundamental constituent of human sociality. Humans never confront reality directly; contact is always mediated by symbols. That is why the first years of life are spent learning the names of things. Toddlers do not bruise their foreheads by bumping into undifferentiated reality; they stumble against chairs, tables, radiators, doorjambs, and refrigerators. At least they do so in Western society. In other societies and other symbol systems, they bump into other objects with other names. The power of names in primitive cultures is well known, but advanced culture has not left this magic completely behind. A person who knows the names of things, even ordinary objects, possesses far greater control over them and over his life than a person ignorant of their proper names. For confirmation, visit a hardware store and try to describe that odd-looking thing fitting into the strange-shaped part of the furnace.

Names inhabit the symbol systems that mediate reality, and they are social creations. Admittedly, intimates give special names to highly significant objects; hence, family nicknames and private jokes. The most intriguing example may be the "private" languages of identical twins. Nevertheless, the scope of these "private" languages is minimal; successful maneuvering in the world requires internalizing the social, public language.

Language is certainly the most significant symbol system. The human form of sociality takes its shape from language-using. We create categories of thought, which in turn transform the world, for particular cultural purposes. Public and private are, first of all, categories of thought created through language. Therefore, they are entwined in language and the functions they serve within that system of symbols. In the American lexicon, public and private are, partially, defined by their opposite functions. This definition, however, does not separate them; rather, it joins them in specific ways. Like other opposites, love and hate, for example, they do not exclude one another.

So far my argument is not particularly profound. That we are language-using creatures and that, therefore, public and private are interwoven through their roles in language is an important truism, but a truism nonetheless. Elementally, public and private are associated words in a common symbol system. There are, however, more profound linguistic unions of these concepts.

In James Glass's work on delusion, the connection between private and public language is not simply a convention, a simple social creation.[1] Rather, their union is literally a matter of life and death, a struggle by patient and therapist with no predetermined outcome. Language bridges self and world. Every person creates a private language—that is, particular words, particular ways of speaking having meanings special to that person. We might say that they have personal connotations. Proper names are obvious examples. "George," "Betty," "Alice," "Anderson," "Simpkin," "Vasquez" are always associated with the Georges, Bettys, Alices, Andersons, Simpkins, and Vasquezes we have known. Equally obvious are emotionally laden words, such as father, mother, wife, husband, friend, comrade. But even ordinarily non-laden terms, such as table, cattle, airplane, and computer, bear specific connotations for particular individuals.

Each person has special words, phrases, or styles of speaking that carry personal significance. Ordinarily these are formations, or sometimes deformations, of the shared language. Private and public meanings connect in fairly clear ways. Sometimes public and private connotations frustrate one another; for example, the public benevolent connotations of "mother" and the private connotations created by an abusive mother. Yet the gaps and tensions between private and public language do not separate them. Both the harmonies and the tensions between public and private meanings help define a person's identity and establish the relationship between that identity and other persons. If there were no gap between public and private language, private life would be impossible. The private would be wholly absorbed in the public, producing tyranny. Conversely, if the gap were too great, both tension and harmony would disappear, and the person would become delusional, living wholly in a private world.

Properly functioning language attaches public life to private through both congruencies and disharmonies. Proper functioning has to be maintained by efforts from the inside and the outside; that is, the efforts of the individual to communicate, thus to shape the language, must be met by the efforts of others to communicate with her. This mutual struggle to use and to create language defines both public and private language, thereby connecting public and private life.

Let me try another demonstration of this linguistic confluence of public and private life. One of life's most important tasks is to discard the illusion that the universe revolves around the self.[2] The job is important not simply for social reasons, but because the self cannot be conscious of itself as a person unless it differentiates itself from the rest of the world, recognizing that the self does not rule the world.

This shedding of illusion happens through language. Identity grows not only through shared symbols, but also through the struggle to understand which symbols can and cannot be shared. In other words, the self, realizing the world is shared with others, learns that it is not omniscient. But it also learns, again in language, the particular shape of the world from the individual's unique vantage point.

Note that the features of language discussed in this section point to the argument from narrative in chapter 7. Stories, traditions, and rituals interweave public and private, and these social products must be individually appropriated and socially communicated through language. According to Alasdair MacIntyre, conversations, which are enacted narratives, connect both sociality and the unity of a particular life. "What I have called a history is an enacted dramatic narrative in which the characters are also authors."[3] We are part of our own (private) dramas and of the (public) dramas of others. Indeed, even this way of putting it too strongly implies separation of public and private life. Our drama is indeed ours, but it is a play within the dramas of others.

Political Language

That language associates public and private life reflects the social character of humanity. Does its political character also make a distinctive contribution to the association? The language of politics accents such concepts as justice, freedom, equality, power, election, and rule. If one cannot speak this language, is one humanly diminished? Or only limited in the same way as one unable to speak, say, Swedish? Politics is a useful language, like Swedish; is it, like the language of love and friendship, more than just useful?

If we follow Arendt's lead, political language, public language *par excellence*, is essential. Those who cannot speak the language of love are fundamentally crippled. Similarly, full human development, indeed the possibility of the appearance of all dimensions of the human condition, depends on politics. Public activity, the speech and action of the realm of power, create and confirm identity. To be without a space for appearance is just as inhuman as to be without love or friendship. That is the deepest tragedy of the democratic movement crushed in China in June 1989. The public space of Tiananmin Square became simply empty space.

Public life strictly speaking is the world of politics. The public values of participation, of balancing the weaknesses of private life, of loyalty, of public trust, and of narrative are clearest in politics, and these values make vital contributions to human well-being. Ability to speak a second language is optional, but sharing responsibility for a collective future, where such opportunities are available, is not.

I part company from this Arendtian celebration of politics, however, in two respects. First, private life has a certain primacy over public life, particularly over politics. One may, reasonably, choose not to engage in political activity. Second, and closely associated, politics is not the whole of public life. Public life—that is, some collective responsibility, where such responsibility is available (tragically, it is not in all societies)—is essential to human flourishing. To share responsibility, to participate and to place loyalty in some public realm, such as neighborhood, workplace, club or other voluntary association, church, or university, adds a dimension to human life unavailable in the private realm. But it is not essential that politics, strictly speaking, constitute this public realm. Religious language in its own way, for example, links public and private, and it may substitute for political language where the latter is not spoken.

Nonetheless, I believe that politics, and its particular language, makes a vital contribution on the public-private border. Dialects of this language grace other public realms, but the pure language and its unique contributions are spoken only in politics. In arguing the virtues of political language, I am not implying that politics is easy, that it exists commonly, or that its provenance inevitably spreads. Indeed, one of the tragedies of human history is that this pure language has been spoken so fitfully. Genuine participation and sharing of power is rare and, therefore, a gift to be cherished and extended.

Political language, as I understand it, concerns justice, freedom, participation, and persuasion. The languages of administration, control, command, force, and the like, often associated with politics but really idioms of hierarchy, are important human languages. But they are not political, and they do not link the public and private worlds.[4] They swallow the space between persons necessary for political language, and they establish ranks in place of the rough equality among persons on which persuasion depends. What specific contributions does political language make to connecting private and public life?

Some connections are implicit in previous chapters and need only a mention here. Justice most obviously links public and private, and I have already indicated how, drawing especially on Pitkin's discussion of Arendt. Just as on the stage, if the characters risk nothing, there is no serious drama, so in political life. What is at stake in politics is the connection between private lives made possible through political action. Public goods can jeopardize private goods. Justice warrants the risk of attaching private to public good.

Our private interests concern us not only absolutely but also relatively. We contemplate our political power and ability not only in themselves; we also compare them to the power of other members. Indeed, political power and ability are meaningless except in comparative terms. Our power is either less than, equal to, or greater than that of others. Equality thus automatically becomes a political concern, part of political language. Indeed, the *political* struggle for power is always a struggle at the margins, within a context of rough equality. Justice, involving as it does justification of equalities and inequalities, transforms individual, private concern for relative amounts of power into regard for the total distribution of power. One's particular share cannot be justified except in terms of a fair total distribution. Therefore, an initially private concern for power becomes part of a public debate over the justice of the whole distribution. Actual participation in the discussion—that is, actual use with others of the language of politics and its lexicon of equality and justice—reinforces the connections. Participation means that we have to speak with others who have more or less the same power as ourselves and to justify to them our defense of change or of the status quo. They must do the same. This debate, conducted in political vocabulary, therefore interweaves public and private concerns, interlacing private lives and their particular shapes, needs, and wants with public life and its requisites, strengths, and limitations.

The previous paragraph used the example of relative power, but other initially private concerns work the same way. Questions about how I as an individual am treated by the courts must be phrased in political debate as regard for everyone's right to equal justice before the law. Interest in my rights to speak, debate, publish, or avoid cruel and unfair treatment by law enforcement agencies must appear in public as interest in similar fair treatment for every person. The availability of work for myself becomes advocacy for work for others and for collective ways of assuring it. Just distribution of the burdens of taxation, military service, and land use do not abstractly pertain to the whole society; they touch particular individuals, deeply affecting their private lives.

I am not arguing that every individual comes to be altruistically concerned with the needs of every other person. Nor do public justice and equality always triumph over private interest. I do not contend that individuals inevitably appreciate the priority of public justice. Indeed, the risk of politics is that the politics of interest will devour justice. Rather, I argue that irrespective of actual motives or moral insight, the fact that political debate must *use* certain language and vocabulary forces an association of private interests with public interests, links private life with the exigencies of public life. This requirement does not determine the shape of the links or the form of the association, but it does make such links and associations necessary. When the encounter of one private interest with another can bypass the language of justice and public good, then the end of politics, and the beginning of tyranny or of administration, is close.

Religious language bears important similarities to the aspect of political language just discussed. The question of an individual's relationship with the transcendent inevitably raises the same questions about others. What is the connection between the salvation of one person and the salvation of others? Religious language in and of itself does not supply a determined answer to this question. Different religions answer it in different ways. But religious language is inevitably led to confront the question. The issue of belief implies a relationship to a community of believers.

The political vocabulary of citizenship and freedom suggests similar connections between public and private. The structure of Michael Walzer's discussion of the spheres of justice indicates this truth very well.[5] Walzer's argument depends on a delicate tension. He separates as much as possible spheres of life such as family, work, religion, leisure, and politics, so that their distributive principles do not invade each other. Their languages, in the terms I am using, are distinct. Yet Walzer also constantly shows that public and private life are not radically separate and that their interaction varies, and should vary, historically and culturally. The spheres cannot be entirely separate, though interaction should happen at the margins.

Walzer resolves the tension between separation and interaction through politics and the language of citizenship. He argues that democratic politics has a major role in defining the principles of distributive justice *within* each sphere and in establishing and maintaining the boundaries among the spheres. In other words, each sphere is its own public, one that needs citizens who deliberate actively about the distributions within that sphere. Politics itself is a particular sphere with its own distributive principles to be worked out by citizens, but it is also that sphere in which citizens with the freedom to debate, discuss, and disagree (the nature of citizenship itself) work out the proper boundaries among the spheres of life. The language of citizens, unlike the language of subjects, means the freedom to participate actively in shaping the future, not of one's own life, but of the common civic world.

The language of freedom implies a difference between private and public life. Absent this boundary, the demands of private life would crowd out free debate in the public world, or the demands of public life would abolish private freedom. But differences are not impenetrable barriers. The boundary between public and private life is important, but only because the self-awareness and freedom that make us persons depend on the ability to move back and forth from one territory to the other.[6] Life is not restricted to one or the other sphere; citizens cross the boundary. This ability is the essence of the distinction between citizen and subject. Subjects are merely private persons with no political rights. Only citizens legitimately possess rights in both private and political life.

The language of freedom boasts the same implications as the language of citizenship. To be free is to cross boundaries. The freedom of subjects within their particular spheres is a mean sort of freedom compared with the political freedom of citizens. Political freedom means freedom within the political realm, of course; but it cannot exist without private freedom as well. The converse is not true; therefore, the language of citizenship and political freedom demonstrates the interlacing of public and private life.

Finally, political language invokes both public and private life because it entails conflicting principles. Citizenship, justice, equality, freedom, election, voting, and the like are meaningless without different interpretations. The language of justice and equality show this clearly. The language of justice embraces debate about differing interpretations of equality and inequality. Freedom and citizenship influence the boundaries between public and private life. And perceptions always vary across borders. Elections and voting are meaningless without choices—that is, without differing perspectives on the best persons or parties to take the lead in defining justice and public good.

Political language, in other words, always embodies contrasting ideals. The paragraphs above have emphasized the way in which political language links public and private by transforming private concerns into public. They have implied a "realistic" perspective in which private interests come first and are only later transformed into public goods. Reality, however, is more complicated than this. In some cases, individuals or groups adhere to principles that they wish to realize in both public and private life. Individuals holding high ideals often have little understanding of the interests at stake or of individual and social limitations. They do not grasp the ways in which private interests and different conceptions of the good have to be mingled and compromised. Politics teaches this lesson. As Roberto Unger puts it:

> To anticipate the ideal, the individual must be able to see and to build in his own life a connection between the personal and the historical resolution of the problem of the self. The link is established by the action, political in the most ample sense, through which he strives to make the ideal actual and thus to move beyond the logic of the everyday and the extraordinary.[7]

Politics and political language teach idealists, as they teach realists, the margins of their vision. Religious idealists expressly need instruction. Religion often brings, and should bring, vital principles to the attention of politics. But religion often forgets the realities of public life and the difficulty of realizing ideals. Politics, therefore, has something to teach religion.

Politics and Religious Language

Language links public and private life; therefore, it seems plausible to speculate that language would play a critical role in connecting religion and politics. The contemporary debate over religious language in political discussion reinforces this suggestion. Fears about the imposition of religious belief are sparked as much by religious arguments used to support policy positions as by the positions themselves. It is disturbing to have Scripture quoted in a political argument as conclusive proof for the superiority of free enterprise or for the necessity of abolishing nuclear weapons. What can those who disagree respond to such arguments? Rather than linking religion and politics, language seems to tear them asunder.

A New Kind of Civil Discourse

Though I advocate toleration and pluralism, what is important in this context is that these also are part of *our* story; they form the backbone of *our* political traditions. If religious language is to enter political debate, it must do so within American traditions of political discourse. Therefore, to discuss religious language and political life requires leaving the general discussion of languages and examining the languages of a particular culture. In other traditions, religious language may possibly enter on other terms. Our heritage is one of liberal democracy, of civil and religious pluralism, and of tolerance of divergent religious and political views. Any kind of civil discourse open to religion must incorporate these features. There is no alternative to pluralism apart from radically overturning our moral, religious, and political traditions. A new kind of civil discourse incorporating religion is possible, I believe, far short of revolution.

The difficulty of describing such a discourse comes from both politics and religion. The descriptive difficulty parallels the problems of sustaining such discourse. This discourse requires locating language that can be understood by all or, less optimistically, most participants in the dialogue. Yet conflict over religious terminology makes common linguistic ground elusive. Each faith needs to remain true to its own linguistic and narrative traditions. To enter political discourse seems to require surrendering the distinctive expressions that so deeply form the identity of each religious community.

Take now the dilemma of political actors. They are most responsible for maintaining, strengthening, and extending the heritage of civil talk. To do so, they must find ways to incorporate new religious, ethnic, political, and occupational groups into the dialogue. Each of these groups brings its own terminology, and all must learn to understand one another. Political actors (here I include elected and appointed officials, party activists, and active citizens) must discover or invent ways of translating unique idioms into the common idiom so that the groups may talk to each other and so that policies responsive to as many groups as possible may be articulated. Any group insisting on its own distinctive concepts makes it extremely difficult for political actors to accomplish their vital linguistic work.

Vibrant political language includes concepts originally peculiar to certain groups, religious groups included. Such concepts, however, lose their distinctive flavor as they enter the common vocabulary. Originally one group's private possession, they become part of the common heritage. The concept of covenant, for example, became transformed in the last three hundred years from its distinctly biblical roots into the concepts of compact, contract, and, ultimately, constitution.

Now the dilemma for religious groups intensifies. To enter the political dialogue, to take part in public policy, they appear to have to surrender their distinctive identity. To enter politics, they must learn a new language and translate their unique ideas into that language. Yet something is always lost in translation. Attempting to find common language, one is tempted to set aside or deny what is essential to one's identity. Sensitive to the enormity of the problem, Stanley Hauerwas emphatically asserts that the Church's first social task in any society is to be itself. "The Church must serve the world on her own terms."[8] Doesn't this preclude entering a political discourse in which other actors set the terms?

Religious groups deeply involved in secular activities rightly fear this loss of identity. Catholic social welfare agencies, receiving government and nonprofit funds for counseling, food distribution, and parenting classes rightly wonder how they are different from any other public or nonprofit social welfare agency. A Methodist hospital, accepting Medicare and Medicaid funds and abiding by their regulations, a hospital operated by medical personnel with their own distinctive ethical and professional norms, rightly wonders how its identity is any different from a Jewish hospital, a public hospital, or a proprietary hospital. To speak the world's language, you have to learn it so well that you may forget your own or, worse, confuse it with the world's.

The alternatives create major difficulties. If the civil discourse of a pluralist society must accept religious groups on their own terms, speaking their own language, then civil discourse is in danger of breaking down. If every group claims the right to speak its own language, it becomes impossible to stake out common linguistic ground. Moreover, to take this alternative is to accept religion into the territory of politics, rather than keeping contacts limited to the border. Better to accept separation of church and state, severing all contact, than to allow this option.

Yet the other alternative is to force religion to speak only in secular terms if it wishes to enter political discourse. The only acceptable arguments are those equally accessible to all. No distinctive religious values, concepts, or positions may be articulated in public, political discourse. This alternative demands that religious groups risk their identity to enter politics.

To speak only in terms accessible to public reason is to make the border area irrelevant. In this case there would be no religion-politics interaction, only *political* argument. Yet, ultimately, every political or ideological group advances positions rooted in principles and premises central to its beliefs and not others. Concerned not simply with winning particular issue battles, it hopes to convince others of the rightness of its principles. Should religion have to be different in this respect? Must it alone abandon all attempts at conversion when it enters politics? The special dangers of politicized religion and religicized politics are all too real. Religion *is* different and, therefore, has to play by different rules. But this conclusion does not mean that it must abandon all distinctive language in order to enter the civil conversation.

Kent Greenawalt and Civil Discourse

Kent Greenawalt has made the best recent contribution to the debate about how religious conviction can appropriately be recognized in political decision making.[9] Greenawalt properly works from within the perspective of liberal democracy in the United States. That is, he works within the tradition of a particular society to ask how religion can appear in public in that society. His model of liberal democracy includes public nonsupport for religious truth, substantial separation of church and state, and public laws based on secular objectives.[10]

Greenawalt focuses principally on the complex question of whether religious language and imagery is ever permissible for citizens and public officials in debate and decision making with respect to particular public policies. Greenawalt discusses this question with great subtlety and with notable respect for both religious convictions and rational, secular argument in a liberal democratic polity. My discussion of Greenawalt's position will summarize his conclusions and their grounds, conclusions that nicely complement the tensional model of religion and politics I have developed. At the same time, however, I want to go beyond Greenawalt's position to reinforce my primary contentions that religion is itself an important field of public-private interaction, that the appearance of different arguments, including religious, in civil discourse is a vital occasion for citizenship and participation, and that public discourse is the ground on which the mutual challenge of religion and politics takes place.

Greenawalt evaluates the claim, implicit in some theorists such as John Rawls and explicit in others such as Bruce Ackerman, that religious convictions are out of bounds in the civil discourse of liberal societies. Policy discussion in these societies may recognize only publicly accessible reasons. Such reasons are those accessible to all citizens. Religious arguments, by their nature, are not publicly accessible, being persuasive only for believers. The general problem is how far liberal democracy must rely on rationalism. "The centrality of this problem is evident once one understands that the argument against reliance on religious convictions often comes down to an argument *for* reliance on premises that are deemed rational in some way that excludes religious convictions."[11] Though Greenawalt very effectively criticizes this position, he neglects the equally important problem that the exclusion of religious conviction from civil discourse in a liberal democracy relies on a theory of reason that is rooted in the public-private distinction. Despite this omission, Greenawalt effectively addresses exclusive reliance on publicly accessible reasons in political discourse.

May good citizens of a liberal democracy properly rely on their own religious convictions when adopting policy positions? Greenawalt concludes that on many of the most important policy issues of today, the answer is "Yes." Barring reliance on religious conviction would preclude sources of insight with considerable practical significance for vast numbers of religious persons. For many important ethical, moral, and political positions it is impossible to disentangle religious reasons and nonreligious, publicly accessible reasons:

> Legislation must be justified in terms of secular objectives, but when people reasonably think that shared premises of justice and criteria for determining truth cannot resolve critical questions of fact, fundamental questions of value, or the weighing of competing benefits and harms, they do appropriately rely on religious convictions that help them answer these questions.[12]

Although, Greenawalt argues, religious and moral convictions are inappropriate grounds for restricting conduct absent a claim about harms,[13] most issues do admit of religious input.

Publicly accessible reasons are incapable of making conclusive judgments about what Greenawalt refers to as the "borderlines of status." Status judgments, such as those involving the nature of the fetus or of animals or of the environment and the extent of protection they deserve vis-a-vis human persons, are judgments where "reliance on religious convictions remains appropriate, since protection of the physical integrity of entities deserving moral consideration is a kind of protection that is called for in terms of secular objectives, and the religious convictions are used to reach judgment about which entities deserve protection."[14] Religious convictions may also appropriately be relied upon in making complex judgments about the facts in policy areas such as welfare assistance, proper forms of punishment for crime, and military policy. Moreover, Greenawalt contends, religious judgments are proper where clashing values are at stake, for example in issues such as school prayer and conscientious objection to war.[15]

So far Greenawalt's conclusions bear on the grounds on which ordinary citizens may arrive at judgments about complex policy issues. His conclusion is quite strong that, concerning issues such as those mentioned above, citizens may aptly rely on their religious convictions, just as they might on moral or philosophical convictions. As he says, "If all people must draw from their personal experience and commitments of value to some degree, people whose experience leads them to religious convictions should not have to disregard what they consider the central insights about value that their convictions provide." Moreover, "The implicit demand that people try to compartmentalize beliefs that constitute some kind of unity in their approach to life is positively objectionable."[16]

There are a good many nuances and qualifications in Greenawalt's position and its supporting argumentation that I cannot attend to here. But the perspective of the border between religion and politics and public and private life and of their mutual interaction should provide considerable reinforcement for his conclusion that ordinary citizens cannot and should not be expected to divide their religious from their political convictions or their private from their public life. One nevertheless may still ask about the form of appropriate discourse in a liberal democracy. Even if citizens may rely on their religious convictions in making personal decisions about voting and policy issues, may they employ such convictions in political debate and may public officials call upon such convictions in their discussion of the issues? In addition, may religious officials properly enter political life articulating their religious convictions as grounds for political decisions?

Greenawalt approaches these questions prudentially, articulating guidelines rather than unyielding principles. These guidelines are rooted in certain assumptions about American politics: that a consensus obtains on organizational principles; that political discussion will be primarily in secular terms; that respect for religious belief prevails; and that one may be both religious and a participant in liberal democracy. If these assumptions are false, or in countries without such conditions, his prudential guidelines would require modification. Based on these assumptions and building on his earlier conclusions about the place of religious convictions in the decision making of ordinary citizens, Greenawalt arrives at the following conclusion concerning the appropriateness of religious convictions in political discourse:

> The government of a liberal society knows no religious truth and a crucial premise about a liberal society is that citizens of extremely diverse religious views can build principles of political order and social justice that do not depend on particular religious beliefs. The common currency of political discourse is nonreligious argument about human welfare. Public discourse about political issues with those who do not share religious premises should be cast in other than religious terms.[17]

Policy discourse, in other words, should be principally secular in order that the danger of divisiveness in a religiously and politically pluralistic polity not be exacerbated. Prudentially and ordinarily, according to Greenawalt, it is unwise for religious groups to endorse candidates, and organizing interest groups on religious lines is also inapt. Moreover, for similar reasons of avoiding divisiveness and keeping political debate primarily secular, it is very troubling for religious leaders to hold public, especially executive, office. Extreme or unusual cases provide exceptions to these guidelines, but these are the normally appropriate rules in American liberal democracy.[18]

Greenawalt's argument here has the virtue of maintaining the border between religious and political discourse, while not insisting on a rigid separation. Political language is distinctive and has special functions; therefore, it is wise that it remain primarily political—which is to say, in a liberal society, primarily secular. Moreover, such guidelines have the further advantage of keeping politics out of religious life. They ensure that civil society cannot enter too deeply into religious territory. The general shape of interpretation of the free exercise and establishment clauses in American constitutional law has the intention of maintaining these advantages. The free-exercise clause keeps government out of religious life, and the establishment clause places boundaries on religious institutions to keep them within their appropriate sphere. All well and good so far, but the specifics of constitutional interpretation are another matter, as we shall see.

One problem is that Greenawalt's guidelines, standing alone, create a nearly unbridgeable chasm between religious and political life and come very close to reintroducing a public-private split that his discussion of religious conviction and publicly accessible reasons implicitly recognizes as false. Fortunately, Greenawalt qualifies his general conclusions in such a way as to avoid these problems. His qualifications and exceptions to the general rules move in the direction of recognizing how religious participation may reinforce civic participation and how religious perspectives can challenge political ones without usurping their place.

The first qualification is that the primacy of secular political discourse does not apply to political discourse with coreligionists. Fellow-believers may fittingly discuss policy issues in religious language, for here each knows and accepts the language. It is their vernacular, and it is, therefore, apt that they employ it. Thus Catholics may (and probably should) discuss nuclear deterrence among themselves in terms of the Catholic just-war tradition and recent teachings of Catholic bishops. But Catholics discussing deterrence with non-Catholics should seek a common political language. It seems to me that Greenawalt's argument here neatly links religion and politics, but at arms' length, as in my tensional model. As that model requires, religion and politics meet, religious beliefs apply to political topics, and political perspectives enter religious thought, but believers entering the specific political realm do so seeking common ground with all participants.

Yet I would allow even wider scope to religious language in a pluralist political community.[19] Members of a language and belief community cannot leave their deepest beliefs behind when entering the political debate, even if that debate is the civil discourse of a liberal society. This point holds for proponents of secular belief-systems as well. Liberals cannot desert liberal assumptions, and Marxists cannot desert their foundational principles in discussing public policy. It would be unfair and intolerant to demand such abandonment, especially in a pluralist polity. Similarly, a Moslem or a Christian cannot be required to speak non-Moslem or non-Christian language when entering politics. Moreover, there is no universally accessible secular political language transcending all basic beliefs.

Members of religious communities, like proponents of ideological or philosophical positions, need to use lucid political and policy arguments and empirical evidence where available to show how they move from deepest principles to specific policy positions and proposals. No fundamental principles are self-applying. The policy and political debates into which religious believers enter will be a mixture of different languages. The task of participants in a genuinely civil and tolerant public discourse is to bear the burden of trying to understand and appreciate, not necessarily to agree with, the deepest principles and the policy arguments of those with whom they disagree. To learn Swedish is not to become a Swedish citizen, but rather to appreciate Swedish language and culture. Just so, to learn to understand Jewish principles and political language is not to become Jewish, but to acquire a wider appreciation of the diverse civic world. Conversely, religious believers need to learn and appreciate secular, political language for the same reasons. Public, civil discourse is genuine to the extent that participants learn to speak with one another in their differences as well as in their shared language.

Greenawalt suggests four other, less controversial, exceptions to his general principles, exceptions that also provide appropriate, border-type links between religion and politics.[20] First, religious language and imagery are fitting when religious persons are writing or speaking one step removed from ordinary political advocacy. Greenawalt uses the example of an article written *about* Jewish perspectives on welfare reform for an audience principally of non-Jews. Here the attempt is not to try to convert the audience to Jewish ways of thinking about policy, but to explain such thinking. This point would reinforce my extension (in the preceding two paragraphs) of Greenawalt's first exception.

Next, Greenawalt allows religious *leaders* to address policy in religious terms. Why? Simply because religion is their special area of expertise. Thus, Catholic bishops properly address Catholic perspectives on the economy when they testify before Congress. Because religious convictions do bear upon policy questions—as Greenawalt has already argued—it is not out of line for religious leaders to make those connections. He does caution, however, that they should cast their arguments in as generalized a form as possible without losing the distinctive religious edge. For example, he might suggest, citations of scripture to *prove* a point are not proper, nor is calling down the judgment of God on those with other policy positions, but citations of scripture to *illustrate* the reasons why the religious leaders take the positions they do might well be permissible.

Additionally, religious language is appropriate in general media when one is attempting specifically to reach cobelievers through these media. For example, a Methodist official might address Methodists through a *Times* op-ed piece on the death penalty.

Finally, policy discussions may figure in proselytizing that draws attention to the political and moral implications of religious belief. For example, a politically active person considering conversion to a particular faith would legitimately be interested in the political implications of the prospective beliefs. Religion and politics would legitimately be mixed in a discussion between this person and a member of the prospective faith.

Greenawalt also allows for the possibility in public discussion of an appeal to very general and widely shared religious premises, such as some elements of civil religion and religious imagery. Specifically, he allows employing religion, not to support *particular* policy positions, but rather to enjoin divine assistance, emphasize human fallibility, call people to act on their consciences, and remind citizens of subjection to higher judgment. He finds these acceptable for traditional reasons—that is, they are part of the common public and private heritage of this particular liberal democracy. They are best exemplified in the rhetoric of Abraham Lincoln.[21]

These exceptions, together with my modification of Greenawalt's general argument about religious language in political discussion, serve to inform all citizens in a pluralist society of the implications of perspectives different from their own. They also serve to enrich the views of the audience and to suggest alternatives that otherwise would not occur to them. Religious discussion, in short, can play a necessary and salutary, though circumscribed, role in public discourse in a liberal democratic society. For religious adherents have a parallel obligation to attempt to understand the perspectives of nonbelievers and of believers in other religious traditions.

Proponents of religion might object that, despite Greenawalt's exceptions to his general principles, religion is allowed to play a role only where shared secular premises do not settle an issue. Secular argument takes pride of place. This objection, however, must fail. Political language does have its own dimensions, value, and validity. Therefore, it must possess a very wide scope, and this scope is properly politics and public policy. Therefore, it is fitting, especially in liberal democracy, that secular, political discourse have pride of place in the public realm. Political argument must always play the major role in settling political issues. This priority keeps religion muted in political debate, taming its dangerous political tendencies. Religion must always seek political links between general principles and particular policies.

Although Greenawalt does not emphasize the challenge that religion can make to political argument, he does suggest that many of the most important policy issues are not resolvable through secular, publicly accessible reasons. Therefore, despite the fact that political argument must be primary, given the proper place of religious conviction in political decision making and the wide scope of the exceptions allowed to the general principles, the border area between religion and politics will be the scene of very lively discussion and debate. But that discussion and debate will be conducted at the border, not at the political center. Precisely because of its distance from the center, religious belief will have the opportunity of challenging conventional, secular perspectives and of presenting alternatives not otherwise available.

Some theologians and students of religion suggest a similar perspective. George M. Marsden, for example, argues that secularism is not the primary threat to religious conviction. We should, he believes, resist the exclusive dominance in the public realm of a sectarian *world view*, but believers should push for a pluralism of world views. Religion should have a certain distance from the public square, but should be welcomed into public debate. Robin Lovin points out that the search for criteria of public, political truth is different from the search for criteria of truth within specific religious traditions. Therefore, religious convictions entering the public realm need corroboration from other communities of meaning. Until such corroboration is forthcoming, religious groups should hold back from making strong truth claims in the political sphere.[22] Corroboration requires dialogue with other religious and nonreligious traditions, a dialogue entailing a language not exclusively rooted in particular religious traditions. It entails, moreover, tolerance of the tensions generated by plural traditions seeking both common ways of speaking and faithfulness to their roots. The tensional model of religion and politics provides a way that liberal democracy can achieve tolerance. As the different participants seek common ground, they begin to discover the Arendtian virtues of the public realm in a new way.

All will not be sweetness and light. Not all religious persons will adhere to civil discourse. Not all political actors adhere to civility. Yet the value of the preceding argument is to show not only that religious and political language can properly interact, but also that there are some kinds of issues on which religious language gives a perspective unavailable to purely public reason. Moreover, there is a way in which religion, as part of our cultural heritage, may become a repository of principles and traditions from that heritage that otherwise might be neglected. Sometimes those principles are needed to call politics to account when it might ride roughshod over important principles. There is, in short, an entirely proper role for religious language to be the language of challenge to dominant political forces. When that happens, the religious language looks like an invader from across the public-private border. But it invades speaking a language neglected, but not forgotten, in the political realm. And it must be willing to learn from politics political ways of speaking, even as it challenges dominant political forces.

A few illustrations of these principles might show their import for contemporary issues and controversies. I cannot hope to provide full arguments for the positions I take, but only to suggest the line of argument growing from the principles. The controversy over prayer in public schools demonstrates the limits of religious language in public. Although the public schools are not political realms strictly speaking, they are created and governed by political entities. Therefore, significant care must be exercised over any entry by religion into their domain. Organized prayer, devotional services, or scripture readings, even if voluntary, introduce deeply religious language into that domain. Prayer is paradigmatically religious and should be reserved for religious settings. Though "moment of silence" practices might pass muster if prayer is not at all suggested, prayer and religious devotion as such should not be part of the public school curriculum.

There are, however, some corollaries of this position. Because prayer for many persons is an integral part of education, private, religious schools have a vital place in American pluralist culture. Such schools respect the diversity of languages and sublanguages and provide ways within the outlines of this culture's definition of public and private life for many forms of religion (and not just religion) to exist together and to develop their own traditions and voices. Tuition tax credits and/or school vouchers would be a way to maintain the independence of public schools from religious influence and to support the pluralism at the heart of our traditions.

Another corollary concerns other forms of religion in public places. Though the Supreme Court has found prayers by legislative chaplains before law-making sessions to be constitutional, such a direct invasion of distinctly political space by religious language is good for neither politics nor religion. On the other hand, the furor over religious symbols on public property, such as creches, crosses, and menorahs, during holiday seasons is hardly necessary. Though there are certainly reasonable limits, such displays should not provoke dismay. They are most appropriately seen as simple acknowledgment, at rather limited times of the year, of one facet of American culture—that is, the significant role played by religion in the formation of our traditions, values, and principles. They should be no more offensive than reenactment of Pilgrim thanksgivings or pictures of George Washington and Abraham Lincoln in February. They could, indeed, help to develop appreciation and tolerance of different languages and beliefs in a plural society.

With respect to other issues, ones less directly focused on religious expression itself, such as crime and punishment, protection of the environment, and welfare reform, religious language should have no privileged place. Religious traditions may indeed have concepts that have significant bearing on such issues—for example, stewardship (environment), sin and repentance (crime and punishment), and compassion and justice (welfare reform). Yet these concepts cannot be directly translated into policy proposals. They need other, political arguments. Therefore, scriptural/theological principles should not be directly cited as conclusive evidence for proposals. Such principles inform thinking, but they should be forced also to encounter the hard reality of scientific and political data.

Finally, there is abortion, possibly the most contentious issue on the public-private and the religious-political borders. Precisely because abortion does involve difficult questions of the status of the fetus, and because abortion involves life and death, religion has a very important place. First, it is appropriate for religion to form the conscience of politicians and voters on the question of fetal status. Second, because life is at stake, it is appropriate for religion to challenge easy assumptions and convenient practices. But, third, because the first two conclusions run the danger of allowing religious language into the heart of political life, politicians and particularly religious leaders and leaders of the "pro-life" and "pro-choice" movements must be most careful not to state their positions simply in religious terms or to provide religious reasons as their primary arguments. They must, instead, search diligently for ways to translate positions into public terms. Fourth, it is important to make a distinction between the legitimate role of religion in attempting to persuade people of the rightness or wrongness of abortion and religion's role in abortion legislation. Abortion is a matter for moral as well as for strictly political debate. Religious arguments might indeed have broader scope in the former than in the latter. Appealing to religious sentiments to convince persons of the moral status of abortion can be permitted wider scope than in strictly policy debate. Finally, legitimate discussions in religious terms within religious communities should guard against inappropriate spillover into the political realm, which was the real danger in the 1984 furor over the attack by some Catholic bishops on the abortion positions of Catholic politicians such as Geraldine Ferraro and Mario Cuomo. Just because religion cannot and should not be excised from public debate on fundamental issues like abortion, we should monitor very carefully the ways in which it appears in the public, political realm.

6

Character, Virtue, and Religion

> ... I don't actually take much stock in
> the collapsing culture bit: I'm beginning
> to see it instead as the conduct of life
> without input from your soul.
> —Saul Bellow, *A Theft*

In some ways the most obvious place to look for connections between private
and public life is in the persons who do the living in each. Just as private
persons shape their lives according to their characters, the character of
public actors determines the direction of public life. The virtues constituting
character channel the confluence of public and private life. Indeed, even
more profoundly, character undergirds and unifies the distinctive territories
of public and private. They are overlapping spheres because both ultimately
trace back to the human person.

This argument is not easy to make, nor is it easily accepted. As Alasdair
MacIntyre insists, the idea of virtue is fundamentally at odds with modern
politics.[1] Liberal politics is uncomfortable with and suspicious of any suggestion that politics promotes virtue or builds character, or that it depends on
either. Character and virtue are private qualities. The union of public and
private character that brought down the 1988 Hart presidential campaign
made most liberals distinctively uncomfortable, because a union of politics
and virtue challenges the liberal separation of public and private life. Yet
certain cultural developments signal greater openness to the public significance of character.

The most prominent signal is the increasing acceptance of the idea that
public schools should be concerned with character education. "Value-free"
individualistic education is under attack from left, right, and center. That
the schools should inculcate honesty, diligence, respect for others, sexual
restraint, citizenship, and other virtues, while by no means universally accepted, no longer represents a shocking position in educational policy. Curricular reform toward a more "classical" core of general education at the
collegiate level also manifests this general position.[2] It is perhaps inevitable
that liberalism confronts character education in an era of cultural politics.

Culture affects character formation, and the state depends on the character of citizens and public officials to restrain self-interest and passion and to prevent toleration and skepticism from degenerating into cultural anarchy. The steeper the slippage toward cultural disorder the more evident the connection between culture, character, and politics.

A second signal of a new openness to virtue language is the growing advocacy in political theory of virtue and character as foundations to reform or replace liberalism. The theoretical dichotomy between politics and private character is now just as questionable as the dichotomy between public and private life. To advocate character and virtue as qualities most profoundly linking public and private is not as heretical as it once was.

Character and Virtue

Character conjoins the specific moral qualities, the distinctive marks that make persons who and what they are.[3] Character also joins internal qualities with social roles. Virtues, about which I intend to speak more extensively, are qualities of character. They constitute specific attributes of identity. Character is a whole; virtues are parts. Listing a person's virtues tells much about her, but the list is not the person; nor is it her character. Character unifies the virtues and relates them to one another and to the demands of specific roles.

Virtue enjoys a revival in contemporary philosophy and political theory.[4] I shall concentrate on virtue as a quality of character, a firm and stable disposition to act in certain ways. I want to show how this idea of virtue links private and public life. In doing so, I realize that I am leaving aside a whole range of important questions. These include metaethical questions, such as "Why be virtuous?" I also take for granted the identification of qualities of character that are virtues. Though I realize that these are difficult issues in ethical philosophy, I want to avoid them in order to concentrate on other questions more directly related to the aim of this book. These questions involve whether there are purely private and purely public virtues and what role the virtues play in linking public and private life.

In the sections below, I shall discuss a number of virtues, not only heroic virtues such as courage, but also ordinary virtues such as frugality and hard work. The fundamental question is whether private and public virtues differ fundamentally. If so, then perhaps the idea that virtue unites private and public life is erroneous. Separate virtues might be appropriate to each form of life. Individuals could display virtue in private life, for example, without thereby being virtuous in public life. A military officer might manifest private, family-oriented virtues—kindness, diligence, frugality, and so forth—and yet be vicious in his public, military duties, compulsive, angry, and disregarding of life.[5] Many theorists of virtue, however, argue that the public-private distinction is antithetical to an ethics of virtue.[6] The first section below considers those virtues most clearly related to private life; the second, those associated with public life. The burden of my argument is that the "private" virtues have public connections and the "public" virtues private implications. The concluding section argues the falsity of the dichotomy by discussing key virtues of both public and private life.

"Private" Virtue

Liberal society thinks easily of virtue and character in private terms. They are commonly assimilated to that most revealing of words, "lifestyle." One makes one's own individual choice to be honest, truthful, patient, and so forth, a choice unchallengeable and unassailable in the privacy of one's own life. Many of the traditional virtues are naturally associated with and naturally supportive of private life. Whether one thinks of "heroic" virtues such as the courage of a mountaineer, the integrity of a person who turns down a lucrative financial offer in order to pursue a religious vocation, or the "ordinary virtues" of persons who with frugality and hard work support their families, the virtues represent and reinforce particular ways of life chosen by particular individuals.

Though it would serve no useful purpose to attempt an exhaustive list of the virtues most closely associated with private life, some indication of their range is necessary to support and illustrate the argument of this section. James Wallace and J. Budziszewski supply helpful classifications and illustrations. Wallace describes the virtues of "conscientiousness" and the virtues opposite to self-indulgence. Such dispositions as honesty, faithfulness, and truthfulness represent the former; temperance, self-control, and restraint represent the latter.[7] Budziszewski distinguishes four dimensions of excellence (or virtue): intimate, integral, practical, and political. The first two are the most clearly private, intimacy and integrity being fundamental qualities of the inclusive side of private life. The intimate virtues include courtesy, devotion, loyalty, complaisance (not complacency), and a quality between frankness and reserve (perhaps honesty, rightly understood). The integral virtues include resiliency, constancy and strength of will, courage on one's own behalf, self-respect, and patience.[8]

The importance of such virtues in private life is evident. Integrity, intimacy, and trust themselves are principal qualities of private life. Truthfulness, hard work, restraint, and faithfulness are vital in the discovery of identity. Resiliency, courage, self-respect, truthfulness, and restraint are critical in coping with secrecy, shame and guilt, imperfection, and mystery, qualities representing the exclusive side of private life, that part resting on the desire and need to conceal parts of one's life.

Many of these virtues testify to a sense of duty and to an intrinsic motivation for life that help the individual to perform in generally beneficial ways, to build character and identity, to anticipate the future and coordinate plans. They are, as Yves R. Simon shows, won at high cost, in effort too frequently today devoted to external, material goods. Such goods of private life, goods of the soul, are lasting: "In contrast with the modern approaches, all of which appear to want to assure human dependability with the least cost in effort to individuals, in the Aristotelian tradition becoming good and true is primarily a personal achievement."[9]

So the connection of these virtues to private life is clear. Yet the same virtues that advance private life also promote public. First, notice that some of these "private" virtues have public counterparts: courage and loyalty, for example. Second, some private virtues have obvious beneficial public effects. Public officials personally honest, hardworking, frugal, truthful, self-respecting, and devoted, for example, can be expected, *mutatis mutandis*, to bring these qualities to their public duties. Third, ordinary citizens with these same virtues will produce effects in the public realm that transcend their private effects. Hard work, frugality, and loyalty have aggregate economic effects, for example.

Beyond such connections between private virtue and public life, however, are more profound ties. Wallace argues that the (private) virtues of conscientiousness can motivate individuals to act in socially beneficial ways in what he calls "Hobbes situations"; that is, situations in which general conformity to a certain mode of behavior is collectively advantageous, but in which individual nonconformity (as long as most individuals still conform) is individually more advantageous—in short, the free-rider problem. Competitions, joint undertakings, and disarmament treaties are common examples. The public realm itself has many characteristics of a large Hobbes situation. As Wallace says, "A function of virtues that are forms of conscientiousness is to resolve this opposition in individuals [between individual and community goals] in a way that is beneficial to individuals and communities."[10] Private virtues make joint participation possible. When calculations of individual self-interest counsel refraining from social cooperation, virtuous dispositions conduce toward publicly beneficial behavior. Benevolence or altruism cannot be counted on to motivate individuals toward social good. A sense of duty, a habit of honesty, and self-respect might.

Character, the meeting point of the virtues in a person's life, suggests a way of life (not a "lifestyle"), and a way of life carries certain necessary moral parameters. Private virtue is not simply a matter of choice and will, but also of discovering the implications of a way of life. It is difficult to imagine, however, that the implications of a way of life will be entirely private.[11] Public officials ought to discover that their private commitments to honesty make demands of their public speech. This is not to say that public and private honesty are precisely the same, but only that they entwine in fundamental ways. In short, the "private" virtues intersect with the public. It is difficult to expect public virtue from elected or appointed officials in a social context that undermines private virtue. When, for example, the urge to get rich quick overtakes the virtues of thrift, delayed gratification, and discipline, it is difficult for government to resist the similar urge—hence government finance by lottery and deficit spending. Therefore, it avoids the heart of the problem to focus on ethical questions in public life (for example, Gary Hart, John Tower, and Jim Wright) apart from ethical issues in private life (pulpit scandals, stock manipulation, and faked scientific data). When private virtue runs amok, can public virtue be far behind? Neither religious moralizing nor public handwringing can solve the ethical problems, especially not if they are addressed to the private or public dimensions alone.

"Public" Virtue

Yet public and private honesty are not the same. Public figures owe honest answers to questions that private persons have no obligation to answer. Deceptions justified by the public interest would be dishonest in private life. So the connections between public and private virtue do not require their identity. Stuart Hampshire, for example, distinguishes public from private morality on the grounds that the former, which involves moral reasoning on public matters, has greater requirements for explicitness, but also fewer scruples, than private moral reasoning.[12]

Political life does have characteristic virtues. Justice is the political virtue *par excellence.* Justice supports freedom, equality, stability, and peace. Injustice deprives some persons or classes of persons of what is their due and creates, even justifies, revolution. Injustice means that freedom is denied or diminished for some persons or classes, thus violating the premises of liberal democracy.

Though these effects of justice and injustice are widely acknowledged, it is tempting to limit public virtue to justice. In this view, justice is not the public virtue *par excellence*; it is the only public virtue. Such is the tendency of liberalism. Moreover, liberal theory tends to conceive of justice in a procedural way, firmly divorcing it from a substantive, characterological base. Yet, were this notion of justice able to sustain liberal politics and political theory, discussing justice in terms of virtue would be superfluous. If justice is a principle, a demand, a standard, a value, why call it a virtue?

The liberal conception of justice has been attacked most notably by Michael Sandel, who argues that liberal justice cannot remain procedural, but implies substantive commitments, and that character is a necessary foundation for justice. William A. Galston argues that justice is not enough to ground liberal society; even on liberal terms other virtues are needed, virtues such as tolerance, civility, self-restraint, courage, humanity, industry, and truthfulness.[13] Justice, important as it is, cannot do all the public work. Wallace and Budziszewski catalogue other public virtues.[14] Under the heading of practical virtues, the excellences that sustain social practices and institutions, Budziszewski lists such possible dispositions as diligence and reliability. Under the heading of political virtues, he considers justice and "the civic disposition." Wallace lists courage as a practical virtue, for it preserves practical reason. It sustains practices and institutions in the face of challenge. The virtues of benevolence such as kindness, compassion, and generosity are public as well, for they manifest direct concern for others' well-being.

How do these virtues complement and support justice? How do they facilitate public trust, loyalty, and participation? Citizenship is most clearly public, but it might best be considered a compendium of virtues rather than itself a virtue. Citizenship requires and calls forth tolerance and civility. Citizens participate, and their participation frequently revolves around contending interests and conceptions of justice. Therefore, public life is irreducibly plural and inherently conflictual and competitive. It would fly apart without tolerance and civility. Civility deflects unproductive antagonism so that public debate might focus on genuine issues. Its work issues in compromise. Personality clashes, real and imagined insults, and partisan rigidities diminish when individuals exercise civility toward one another and when social practices and customs channel interpersonal exchanges in civil directions. Personal pride and partisan passion block justice.

Tolerance allows public persons to bear the burden of respecting other public persons, working with them, and disagreeing with them, especially when they believe them to be profoundly wrong. The temptation, when we profoundly disagree with someone, is either to convert the person, to make him a permanent enemy, or to become indifferent to his views and his fate, dismissing him from sight and mind. Public life, however, cannot function properly with these strategies. Participatory institutions require citizens to communicate with others, respect them as much as possible, and acknowledge their perspectives. This is not easy; it is in fact an impossible ordeal without the virtue of tolerance.[15]

Courage, diligence, and reliability are virtues crucial to the success of all public institutions, political and otherwise. Bad luck, internal and external challenges, apathy, hostility, disease, and inertia work against their survival. In the face of these, loyalty can travel by itself only so far. One may be loyal to a political regime, a business enterprise, or a neighborhood. But destructive forces erode and finally shatter loyalty. Participation may be fun for a while, but it becomes difficult and discouraging when apathy or fear, for example, infect the body politic. Virtues like courage, diligence, and reliability allow individuals and institutions to meet these challenges and to survive them, even to grow and develop through them. Moreover, from instances of bravery in the face of external challenges, from times of hard work and diligence in the face of deadlines, apathy, bad luck, and disease, institutions build up the stock of narratives and traditions so vital to public life. Accounts of the valor of individuals and groups become the stories that define public identity.

Public institutions meet challenges, but they also facilitate positive exchanges, and they need such exchanges. If public life were only conflict, competition, and hard work in the face of hostility, it would be a mean life indeed. Public institutions, politics included, need the benevolent virtues at least some of the time. Public kindness, compassion, and generosity cement loyalty, make participation an occasional joy, and add to the stock of traditions constituting institutional tissue.

But these virtues are not simply public. Take the benevolent virtues. Benevolence (normally) is supererogatory. But institutions cannot do without it. Kindness, generosity, and compassion powerfully unite individuals, forging bonds of trust and intimacy. These virtues can also overcome shame and imperfection to forge such bonds. Because benevolent action is voluntary, it benefits giver and receiver, building self-esteem and self-respect in both. Thus benevolence fosters mutual good-will, forestalls antagonism, and fosters a cooperative atmosphere.[16] The virtues of benevolence, then, touch both public and private life, bringing public commitment out of private benefit.

Similarly, the public virtues of courage, diligence, and reliability have counterparts in private life. The challenges to public institutions described above also challenge the intimate institutions of family and friendship. Love and affection go only so far in marriage; then constancy, hard work, and courage—not to mention generosity, kindness, and respect—must take over. The most private things too, contemplation and self-knowledge, have their fears and terrors; to face them requires courage, courage that can be learned in public life. Tolerance and civility also strengthen private, intimate life. The members of a family are often strangers to one another; often fundamental disagreements damage the relationship. Good manners are not just for company and strangers. They also preserve the family table.

So the public virtues also assist private life. Public character reflects and affects private character. Politicians must have a sense of the moral weight of their action. Character consists in learning which moral costs are worth paying. As Bernard Williams, perhaps paradoxically, puts it, "We need to hold on to the idea, and to find some politicians who will hold on to the idea, that there are actions which remain morally disagreeable even when politically justified. . . . [O]nly those who are reluctant or morally disinclined to do the morally disagreeable when it is really necessary have much chance of not doing it when it is not necessary."[17] Prices paid in private create the character expected in public. Conversely, those who discern moral weights in public life can apply those lessons in private.

Mentioning responsibility insinuates the most significant virtue linking public and private life. It is impossible to know whether responsibility is more public or more private. It characterizes a whole life, public and private. Responsibility constitutes the most profound confluence of public and private.

Virtue: Private and Public

Responsibility suggests the unity of life. Responsibility disposes one to act dependably in all circumstances. The responsible person lives one, unified life and displays one, unified character. Such a person does not possess separate private and public characters such that the virtues of one side of life may ignore those of the other. The lessons of responsibility absorbed in private life carry over to political participation, and vice versa.

The idea of the unity of life is today neither common nor popular. The ubiquity of "lifestyle" demonstrates just how foreign is the notion of the interdependence of virtues and of character as a unified field of action. "Lifestyle" suggests that individuals pick and choose among a wide variety of personal characteristics, values, and behaviors, assembling unique combinations of personal orientations. The unity of such an assemblage consists in purely personal taste. Because this assemblage represents a style, it, like other fashions, may change substantially over time. Given this notion, the idea of the unity of life makes no sense. It is not surprising that terms such as virtue and character are "out of style."

Even by the time of America's emergence as a republic the languages of public and private virtue were diverging. The republican idea of public virtue had acknowledged its dependence on private virtue, but the development of a commercial republic suggested privatization of virtue, and indeed virtue came to be more and more restricted to private life. The idea that private, economic virtue sufficed to support a republic became over time more acceptable than the notion that a republic demands high levels of public citizenship.[18]

To the extent that virtue appears at all in modern, success-oriented, economic society, its connections with life's satisfactions appears upside-down. Remarking on the cynical put-down, "If you're so smart, why ain't you rich?" Annie Dillard comments, "The notion still obtains . . . wherever people seek power: that the race is to the swift, that everybody is *in* the race, with varying and merited degrees of success or failure, and that reward is its own virtue."[19] In this atmosphere words uniting public and private life, like sacrifice, duty, honor, responsibility, and obligation, struggle to escape mocking cynicism.

Nevertheless, the languages of virtue and character naturally entail the unity of life, both public and private. Though all recent theorists of virtue stress the interdependence of the virtues and the unity of character, I shall focus here on the most familiar of these accounts, that of MacIntyre.[20] MacIntyre observes that someone who possesses a virtue can be expected to manifest it in different situations. It would be odd to speak of someone having the virtue of self-control, if he exercised it only on Friday afternoons at the corner tap. No, he possesses the virtue if he is disposed to control himself in a variety of temptations to indulgence, temptations that might all apply to private life, but also could involve public life. The virtue, in short, is defined not by the external situation alone, but by the unified, consistent way in which the same self responds to different situations. Therefore, virtues manifest the unity of the self or (MacIntyre does not emphasize the word, but it is the best available) character.

For MacIntyre the unity of life is a narrative unity. The stories of the self link life together from beginning to end. What an agent intended to do is always relevant to judging what she actually did. Intentions, however, are teleological; they refer to what the person is trying to accomplish, and these goals are part of the narrative of that person's life, her history. Actions become intelligible only when we can fit them into the continuing development of a person's life, with its particular past and its future purposes. If a person's actions make no reference to where the person has been or is going, they are incomprehensible.

Stories are paradoxically both unpredictable and teleological. We have goals, but we cannot tell how nature, the actions of others, or our own reactions in particular situations will affect the path from our beginning to our end. The continuity in the identity of persons lies in their character and its stories. Persons become responsible in terms of their histories. Here the unity of a life is found, for to give a satisfactory account of one's action is to refer to its place in the story of one's life.

The virtues, therefore, are central to a unified, responsible life. A person can live his story, pursue his quest, only through habitual dispositions that make it possible for him to hold firmly to the course that he must follow on that quest. This notion of character, virtue, and self would be open to the charge of individualism, except that each person's life is embedded in communities and their living traditions. As MacIntyre states, "The story of my life is always embedded in the story of those communities from which I derive my identity."[21] The virtues are both part of and sustain traditions.

Thus the virtues are both public and private because they form part of a unified character in which public and private life are part of one story and because they form part of the story of a community, of intertwining individual stories that delineate the public and private lives of members. The idea of virtue then connects with narrative and tradition and their function in individual and communal life.

The argument from narrative is not the only way to support unity of character linking public and private virtue. Simon, for example, specifies three ways in which the virtues are interdependent.[22] First, prudence connects all the virtues. Applying the virtues to particular situations is not a logical derivation from general rules, but a creative judgment finding the right answer for *this* situation. Second, each virtue needs the others for its own perfection. In order, for example, to be temperate, a person needs courage. By the late nineteenth century Chesterton could remark that the modern world had gone mad because it was full of the old Christian virtues wandering in isolation. Some cared only for truth; others for pity; still others for humility. Because they could no longer balance one another in a unified life, they went immediately to their extreme forms.[23] As Chesterton saw, any virtue cut off from the others will quickly run to a destructive extreme. The passion for justice divorced from prudence and temperance creates havoc. Third, if a virtue is totally lacking, this creates insuperable obstacles for other virtues. An honest person who lacks the virtue of courage, for example, will not long remain honest. This does not mean that in order to have one virtue one must have all to the same degree; it means only that one must have them all to some degree.

It might be argued that demonstrating the unity of a life is not the same as demonstrating the unity of public and private life. That is true. The idea of the unity of character does not entail that public and private life, or even public and private virtue, are the same thing. But my argument does not depend on their identity. I am not trying to show that all virtue is one or that public and private life are really the same. I do not deny the plurality of virtue in the sense of their being many virtues or the different degrees of different virtues that constitute differences of character. Rather, I am arguing that these virtues are not independent. The unity of the virtues and of character means that private virtue grounds public participation and that such participation helps to shape private virtue.

Stanley Hauerwas puts the matter quite well:

> In the past it was assumed that a person of virtue, even if not directly involved in politics, served a political function. The person of integrity is a political resource; his character makes possible a society that would otherwise be impossible. When we can't count on the other person to be virtuous, we must then rely on institutions, most often the state, to rectify our inability to trust someone. . . . The more we rely on the state to sustain the relations necessary for social life, the less it seems we need people of virtue—and that's how the whole vicious cycle begins.[24]

Religion, to the extent that it inculcates virtue and to the extent that it insists on the unity of life and of virtue, plays both a public and a private role. Although there is variation among religions in this respect, it is common of religion to attempt to unify different strands of life and to be concerned with the dispositions of character of adherents. Tocqueville identified this inculcation of virtue as religion's principal public role.

Character is crucial here, for it is character, not subjectivity or intimate reflection, that appears in public. Character is not just public roles and not just private reflection, but their more or less smooth meshing. Thus it is quite possible for the private and the public to be out of joint, because the social context in which character unfolds will not accept every role. Hence Don Quixote's problem. My argument does not imply that a person's public and private lives will always fit comfortably together and produce personal or social harmony. Quite the opposite may happen. The point is not that public and private will harmoniously mesh. This depends on the particular character and the particular public setting in which it must act. Rather, the point is that there is a deep connection between character's public and private virtues and, therefore, between how a person lives in public and in private.

The temptation is to want the public-private border to be harmonious and tidy, to have clear definitions of the edges of each form of life and definite specifications of the limits of each. Clear rules, we think, mean peace and harmony. Yet Elshtain reminds us, "A harmony of purposes, ends, virtues, and identities is achievable *only* if we so thoroughly erode the bases of human existence that we willingly engage in radical and destructive social surgery."[25]

Life on the border can be harmonious or tense or, more likely, each by turns. Tensions in all areas of life wax and wane. Tensions, without intervention, always resolve themselves in some way. A stretched rubber band will eventually break unless relaxed. Even a steel bridge designed to last for decades, because it balances a series of tensions, eventually will collapse unless its components are regularly replaced. Similarly, tensions between persons or groups can be resolved (or transformed) by negotiation, violence, law, forgetfulness, or forgiveness. But they must be resolved. So with private and public life: their tensions must be resolved. Resolutions can be good or bad, creative or destructive. To say that public and private life involve one another in fundamental ways is not to say that they are always harmonious. They challenge each other, and the virtues of one side of life confront the temptations of the other. Virtue and character are fields of tension delineating public and private life.

The issue of gun control in America exemplifies the connection between public and private life and their tension. Here the public consequences of private character are quite clear. "Guns don't kill, people kill" runs the slogan of gun-control opponents. The common comparison is to the heavily armed Swiss, who have a very low murder rate. Therefore, the contention runs, it is not the availability of guns that is the problem. They are right, of course, and therein lies the shallowness of their argument.

The American rate of murder, suicide, and accidental injury by guns forces the conclusion that Americans as a people are simply too immature or too violent or too careless, in short, too character-defective, to be allowed ready access to guns. When guns are numerous and readily available, the public consequences of private character defects are enormous, thereby justifying stringent gun regulation. The legitimate use and enjoyment of guns are in tension with the public need for peace and protection of life precisely because the two are intimately linked. The linkage justifies the public remedy for private failings.

Further Reflections on Virtue

Three sets of virtues or qualities of character demonstrate well the fundamental link between public and private life. Each of these virtues is central to the proper functioning of both private and public life.

Trust and Responsibility

As I have mentioned these virtues at various places in this and earlier chapters, I shall briefly summarize their importance in public and private life. Public trust is connected to private. Though trust is not usually classified as a virtue, it is nevertheless a basic character trait, a habit of relying on the good intentions of others.

Thus trust is necessary for the existence of public life. Public life, of course, is not simply a field of cooperation and mutual support, but also of conflict and competition that warrant some skepticism, some healthy distrust of the motives of public, particularly political, coparticipants. Yet without rules of the political game and trust that most of these rules will be followed most of the time, the fragility of political life could hardly withstand the otherwise unrestrained forces of conflict and competition. Remember that politics is neither force nor rule. These need only predictability; politics needs trust. The importance of honor in public life, especially politics and the military, illustrates trust's centrality. Honor signifies commitment to follow the rules of the game, to prove trustworthy, even at great personal sacrifice.

Yet trust is also a fundamental quality of private life. The daily, ordinary intimate lives of individuals and groups would be impossibly chaotic and frightening without the disposition to trust one another. There are certain rules of the game in private life as well as public, and we expect most people (as well as ourselves) to follow them most of the time. Similarly, persons concerned with their honor and reputation in public life tend to be similarly concerned in private life, and for the same reasons. Thus trust carries across public and private boundaries and interlaces the two forms of life. It does not make public and private the same, but it does create a continuity between them.

So does responsibility. It is perhaps the most important virtue linking public and private, because it is the most fundamental. Like trust, responsibility is so basic to character that it may be difficult to think of it as a virtue. Responsibility holds character together. It integrates character's various parts and knits them into a whole by holding them to common standards. Persons do or should live their lives according to certain fundamental principles and commitments. These apply to all aspects of one's private life, work, family, friendships, and leisure. But behavior seldom fully lives up to the standards set by one's commitments. Responsibility is the quality that calls one's self to task when it falls short and encourages the self to do better. It reflects as well on the meaning of commitments and principles and on the situations in which they must be followed. So it pulls together and attempts to harmonize action with principle. Responsibility forces me to be accountable to myself.

In acquiring different virtues, I set standards for myself in different facets of life. These virtues, particularly because they are dispositions often set on "automatic" to react to situations demanding response rather than thought, need the compensating discipline of reflection. The responsible person subjects her dispositions to this discipline in private life.

But responsibility is essential to public life in much the same way. Indeed, responsibility is the most public element of character. In undertaking public life, I assume certain roles, make promises, and accept duties in such a way that I must be accountable to others for my actions. That is, I must be publicly responsible. As Glenn Tinder says, "Autonomy is going one's own way, while responsibility is being prepared to explain—to respond for—the way one is going."[26] Persons in public life can be held accountable, as the Watergate and Iran-Contra Congressional hearings vividly, if imperfectly, demonstrate. Public responsibility is the willingness to be held accountable to public principles and commitments and to discipline one's dispositions to conform to these standards. While the standards may be different, the responsibility learned in private life conduces to the habit of public responsibility. Public and private irresponsibility function in a similar way; note again the lesson of budget deficits and state-run lotteries.

Judgment and Prudence

The recent focus in political theory on virtues perforce directs attention to judgment and prudence, to practical reason. Virtue does not lie in rule-following, moral absolutism, or perfectionism. Virtue consists in practical application of principles to contingent circumstances. There is no automatic way to do this; rather, prudence joins insight into the meaning of principles with insight into the requirements of complex, changing, and unique situations.[27] Prudence is therefore connected with responsibility, and it has the same kind of function in linking public and private life. Acting morally in concrete terms requires making judgments and defending these judgments to oneself and others. In both public and private life we are called on to explain and to justify our actions. Justifications require recourse to judgments about principles and circumstances, and they attempt to persuade intimate others or public actors, and sometimes ourselves, that appropriate judgments were made.

Political leaders and citizens must learn to make judgments about policy matters, and their participation educates their judgment. It is impossible to make prudential judgments about matters with which one is unfamiliar. This is as true in public as in private life. Therefore, active participation in the affairs of both public and private life is essential for shaping practical reason. Again, the principles and the circumstances of private and of public life will be different. But prudential judgment is essential in each, particularly from the perspective of a theory of character and virtue. The dispositions of prudence carry over from private to public life, and vice versa.

Civility and Tolerance

The habit of prudence supports a civil and tolerant disposition. Persons who operate on the basis of absolute rules or who live according to spontaneous feelings or intuitions have no need of prudence. Their decisions are easy. Moreover, they have no inclination to tolerance. Legalists do not demonstrate it, because others (whether in public or in private) have no right to be different. The rules are the rules; their meaning is clear and fixed; and they apply equally to everyone. Those who see the rules or the situation differently are simply mistaken and need correction. Christian fundamentalists have a great deal to learn in this respect. They are too ready to see different points of view (evolutionary biology, the literature of different cultures, complexity in moral decision making) as *attacks* on their faith, rather than a reflection of the differences requiring the burden of tolerance.

Those at the other extreme, the radical moral individualists, have no need of tolerance, for there is no need to care how others think or act. They have their "lifestyles"; others have different ones. Such persons are not intolerant, but indifferent, except when it comes to their own sacred causes.

The prudent person, on the other hand, is disposed to the burden of tolerance and civil behavior toward those of different judgments, because he knows the difficulty of particular judgments. He knows as well that contingent circumstances make absolute pronouncements impossible. There is room for differing opinions, for different judgments. At the same time, he is not indifferent to the judgments of others, particularly toward those who arrive at very different assessments of the situation or who operate according to different principles or different versions of the same principles. The prudent person is convinced that there are better and worse judgments; all judgments are not equal. There are better and worse principles, and there are standards that apply to all human beings. Thus it is a burden to find others with very different, probably radically mistaken, ways of life or particular judgments.

Yet because he understands how difficult these matters are and how precious the need to arrive at one's own conclusions, the prudent person is inclined to treat those with whom he disagrees with the civility worthy of another fallible human being and to tolerate that person's different views.

It might seem that an emphasis on virtue is incompatible with the pluralism inherent in public life. A politics of virtue conjures visions of witch-hunts and book-burning. The description of virtue developed here should banish such visions.[28] Prudence and moral fanaticism do not travel well together. Prudence not only conduces to tolerance, as I have just argued, but the fact of plurality suggests a politics of prudence. Plurality and the particular contingencies it creates make careful judgment necessary and dispel illusions of easy moral decisions.

Tolerance and civility are virtues of public and private life. Civility treats others with the respect due to human persons and with the decency due to members of the same society as oneself. Tolerance bears the burden of human plurality. It is perhaps obvious that these qualities are needed in public life, where the existence of plurality is evident. But what about private life, where bonds of intimacy indeed may make persons very much alike? Yet even the intimate other is a stranger. Even (perhaps especially) the intimate other taxes patience. Though children become like their parents, they remain mysteries to mother and father. Their futures are unpredictable; their decisions unanticipated; their differences of principle and judgment hardest to bear. Though we are tempted to think that we need not exhibit our best manners at home, we need to treat family with the same respect and decency, indeed with greater civility, than political allies and opponents. It is not that civility and tolerance are out of place in private life, but that love transcends civility. Love makes the burdens of tolerance both heavier and more bearable.

Qualifications

I have considered primarily the virtues and the better qualities of public and private life. My arguments have perhaps suggested ways in which private and public life, private and public judgments, work harmoniously together. I hope that what I have said about prudence, tolerance, civility, and responsibility dispels fears about the tyranny of a politics of virtue. Another kind of objection, however, is appropriate at this point. Have I not neglected the deception and concealment of evil facilitated by private life and the impersonality, conflict, and imperialism implicit in public life?

This question is reasonable. The virtues are never perfected in a polity or in an individual life. Moreover, the evil, imperfection, chance, and perversity of the world frequently prevent the virtues from progressing smoothly or meshing comfortably in an individual life, let alone in public life. Budziszewski draws attention to what he calls the "desperate" virtues and the "proto-virtues."[29] The former are virtues, like courage and resolution, that sustain life when things are going wrong or character is under attack. Other virtues, like prudence, have desperate occasions, when the point of practical wisdom is to find acceptable compromises, principles being impossible to achieve in any kind of a full sense. The proto-virtues, on the other hand, are way stations on the road to becoming virtuous or realizing the virtues. Bravery, for example, is the proto-virtue of courage.

Recognizing that public and private life have their dark moments does not diminish the role of virtue or character in linking public and private life. The virtues—full, desperate, or proto—come into play in situations of conflict as fully as in favorable circumstances. In private life, virtue and character counteract the tendency to lies, deception, and selfishness. The virtue of honesty, for example, hinders the temptation to lie. The virtue of generosity counteracts selfishness. We must not forget that the virtues have their corresponding vices; it is, therefore, no part of a theory of virtue to deny evil and sin. Rather, it shows how evil and sin may be resisted.

Similarly, public life exhibits particular public vices such as manipulation, imperialism, jingoism, bureaucratization, and interest politics. The public virtues exist to counteract them. Tolerance resists imperialism and jingoism; responsibility attacks bureaucratization; the benevolent virtues rebut interest politics; and so forth. But more than this, private character is a resource for challenging public evil. Not infrequently individuals must put their principles, their resources, and even their lives on the line to resist public evil. Without firmness of character and virtues such as courage, such resistance fails. The civil rights marchers in the early 1960s are excellent illustrations. Sometimes the only honorable connection between public and private life is martyrdom. Challenge, resistance, martyrdom, and rebellion recognize the tyrannical forces that brood beneath the surface of public life. These qualities of resistance to evil, rooted firmly within the characters and the private lives of individuals, are junctions of private and public life.

These connections of tension and resistance do not all run one way. One basic function of public life is to contain the effects of private vice. Criminal law is such an obvious example that it might be overlooked. But the same is true of child abuse laws, legislation as to wages and hours, banking regulations, and pollution control laws. The public good, and the virtues that sustain it, often challenge the evils endemic to private life. So the tension between public and private life is often the tension between public virtue and private vice. Thus tension and conflict are as evident as harmony in the interaction of virtue, private life, and public life.

Tragedy and Virtue

This last truth stimulates awareness of the tragic dimension of human life, both public and private. Good and evil struggle, and the good does not always win. Illness and natural disaster strike, and health does not always follow. Rule-bound theories of morality and procedural theories of justice handle tragedy less effectively than theories of virtue and character. The classic tragic flaw is a defect of character, the counterpart of heroic virtue. We look to character to explain why individuals rise to or fall before challenges, why natural or human evils overcome some persons, and why some, through suffering, become more fully human. Similarly, the notion of national character, much subject to misinterpretation, makes some sense here. Lincoln, for example, grasped the challenge of the Civil War to American character and mission. Indeed, exemplary virtue, individual and collective, is often called forth by terrible evil. The Second World War provides the example of the French village, Le Chambon, that for years hid Jewish children from the Nazis.[30]

It is not only good and evil that clash. The most tragic conflicts occur when valid ethical directives interfere with one another. Doctors are faced with the principle of preserving life whenever possible, a valid principle, and with the duty to relieve, for example, the suffering and anxiety of hopeless, terminal patients and their families. Indeed, it is possible for public and private goods to conflict. In the mid-1980s the daughter of the president of El Salvador was taken hostage by rebel forces. His responsibilities as president and as father clashed. My argument is not that such clashes cannot occur or that the action to be taken is simple. I contend, rather, that such conflict illustrates in a particularly tragic way the interlacing of public and private life and that, in such conflicts, virtues rather than moral rules are the appropriate guides.

Some moral philosophies try to remove all conflicts, but ignore the real moral, emotional, and psychological conflicts well depicted by tragedians such as Aeschylus.[31] Virtue provides guidance in the midst of tragedy, but it also helps private individuals and public institutions to bear the effects of tragedy.

Yet virtue alone is not sufficient to explain tragedy. Only when the virtues, and character, are set within the context of the narrative unity of life can the meaning of tragic situations become discernable. Therefore, only within a narrative context do virtue and character make sense. Finally, therefore, the account of how narrative and tradition mediate public and private life must complete the account of the junction of public and private. The following chapter takes up this project.

Religion, Virtue, and Prudence

Because different religious traditions describe the virtues diversely, with somewhat disparate lists of virtues and different emphases on the same virtues, I cannot provide a universal account of religion and virtue. But I can illustrate at some length the dynamic interaction and tension of religion, virtue, and public life in one religious tradition. To do so I shall address at some length one Christian interpretation of prudence as a virtue and some of its implications.

Let me say at the outset that I am not arguing that religion is essential to virtue. I leave this question open. Certainly, theories of virtue (such as Aristotle's) can get along without religion. Rather, my point is to show how at least one religious tradition can provide a rather sophisticated account of the key virtue of prudence. Such an account, then, is available for adherents to appropriate into their characters. Lodged there, it becomes a resource for both public and private action.

The tension inherent in dialogue at the border of religion and politics calls for qualities of character properly associated with virtue. Civil discourse calls more for civic virtue than for shared theoretical perspectives, for political involvement by virtuous persons than for applied theory. Attention to the unique voices of other participants is more valuable than abstract reasoning in politics or knowledge of dogma in religion.

Robert Fullinwider has drawn attention to the importance of "anti-theory" in philosophy.[32] He notes that sophists and casuists have too often gotten a bad press in philosophical discussion, being roundly maligned as hucksters for easy morality and dominant political powers. Such indeed is the danger of casuistry and sophistry. Yet they also had the virtues of attention to detail, the art of persuasion rather than coercion, awareness of the reality of society and culture (but enough distance from it to be critical), and suspicion of grand moral theory or ideology.

Religious persons or groups entering policy discourse must be casuists rather than dogmatists. Civil discourse by religious groups is not the logical application of religious dogmas to particular circumstances, but rather the clarification of policy in terms of basic religious principles, such as forgiveness, justice, mercy, and love. This discourse requires, not abstract theory, but the judgment that comes from character immersed in the way of life of the community, including its political concerns.[33] J. Budziszewski argues that the proper movement from character to policy begins with knowledge of what is naturally good for human beings, moving to a general understanding of the excellences of character that are rooted in that natural good. These excellences must, however, then be interpreted, and the circumstances of culture are a necessary part of that interpretation. Finally, the interpreted excellences must be applied to institutions and policies, recognizing again the role of circumstances. Finally, institutions and policies loop back to educate character toward or away from excellence.[34]

The traditional virtue through which moral or religious principles are applied to practical situations is prudence, and I want here to illustrate how this virtue can accommodate radical religious principles to contingent politics in a liberal society. I do not attempt here a total theory of prudence, but only show how prudence can bear the tension between the radical demands of a particular religious tradition and the practical necessities of life in an imperfect political world.

The Radical Gospel and Prudence

In the last twenty-five years Jesus has been rediscovered as a political figure. The radical implications of the Gospel he preached have been translated into support for revolution against oppressive regimes, for a drastic restructuring of economic systems, and for active opposition to nuclear armaments.[35] The claims of prudence are not easily reconciled with Jesus' message.

The Radical Gospel

Jesus' proclamation of the kingdom is radical in two ways. First, to hear and receive the gospel demands a fundamental change of heart. Loyalty belongs to God alone; all other loyalties and commitments become provisional, subject to judgment in terms of trust in and loyalty to the Father. Because their other loyalties are provisional, followers of Jesus are pilgrims, sojourners on the earth, citizens of another city. Such citizenship breaks down the racial, sexual, cultural, and class differences on which humans conventionally rely for a sense of security and self-esteem (Gal. 3:28). Moreover, the change of heart, the new loyalty, and the universality of the gospel must be manifest in action (James 1:22-25; Matt. 7:21-24). The conflict between new and old loyalties is social as well as psychic.

This first radicalism of the gospel is familiar enough to need little elaboration; yet it is so familiar and so immoderate that its demands for love, forgiveness, generosity, patience, and compassion are too readily assimilated to the conventional ways in which these virtues are institutionalized. Generosity means giving to the United Way; patience means not yelling at the children; forgiveness means not hitting back; and so on. Such easy reductions of the demands of faith may be why the gospel includes a second kind of radicalism: very specific and very fundamental behavioral demands. "You cannot serve God and Mammon" (Matt. 6:24). "Judge not, that you be not judged" (Matt. 7:1). "But love your enemies, and do good, and lend, expecting nothing in return" (Luke 6:35). Astonishingly, "When you give a feast, invite the poor, the maimed, the lame, the blind, and you will be blessed, because they cannot repay you" (Luke 14:12-14).[36] Prudence, common sense, and decorum rebel at taking such directives literally, or even seriously, and few do. Yet these particular demands are only specifications of the radical demand of faith.

Politically, the gospel is radical in the same two ways. First, the prophetic theme that God has a special care for the poor is continued in the New Testament. Jesus identifies himself with the poor, the outcast, and the oppressed (Matt. 5:3; Luke 4:16-21). Second, the gospel is politically radical because Jesus seems totally unconcerned about how his message affects political stability or how the politically powerful react to him. Neither Herod ("that fox") nor Pilate nor the powerful priests and scribes determines his course. On the contrary, he condemns the way rulers act (Luke 22:24-27) and recognizes that he and his followers will be perceived and persecuted as a challenge to political order (Luke 21:12-15). "I have not come to bring peace, but a sword" (Matt. 10:34).

This perspective is familiar enough. The problem is: how are the radical sayings and the radical identification of Jesus with the poor and outcast to be taken? What does his subversive indifference to political stability imply? Christian thought and practice have displayed an astonishing variety of responses, most of them designed in one way or another to evade the most radical demands.[37] They are often taken as outlining an ethic of intention— that is, they make radical demands on the inner dispositions, but not necessarily on behavior. Thus the demands are "spiritualized," and the harsh sayings taken as Semitic hyperbole. Clearly, this interpretation holds for some sayings ("If your right eye causes you to sin, pluck it out and throw it away"), but not for others ("Love your enemies").

A second response softens the hard sayings by placing them in the context of Jesus' and the early Church's expectation of an immanent eschaton. Thus Jesus' demands constitute an ethic only for the brief interim before the end; they are not meant to found an enduring order. Another interpretation moves to the opposite extreme and regards the sayings as a rule of life only for the coming heavenly kingdom. Others have regarded the radical demands as serious and possible, but only in a simple, rural socioeconomic climate.

Perhaps the most widespread avoidance mechanism, however, is to regard the radical gospel as a counsel of perfection intended only for an elite few in its full measure. Perfection cannot be expected of those who must scratch out a living and raise a family day by day. The radical gospel is for monks and hermits and, perhaps, Church leaders, but it does not demand fundamental social, economic, or political transformation.

Many Christians have, of course, taken the radical gospel to heart, St. Anthony and St. Francis, for example. Most sectarian movements also take inspiration from the radical gospel. The "peace churches" are formed by Jesus' clear condemnation of violence, even in self-defense. Other groups of Christians, such as the Catholic Worker Movement, are oriented to communal living and sacrificial care of the poorest of the poor. Christian revolutionaries in Latin America take as their model the Christ who condemned oppression in the harshest language. Throughout Christian history, to use H. Richard Niebuhr's typology, both "Christ Against Culture" sectarian movements and the "Christ Transforming Culture" tradition have been inspired by the radical gospel.[38]

Whatever contributions these two traditions have made, their limitations are clear. The same Father who sent Jesus to show a new way also created the world and human beings with a need for order, culture, and stability. Those who would transform the world forget that Jesus recommended no specific plan of political change, no form of a regime, and no socioeconomic theory. The radical gospel sits side by side with the prudent advice of Romans 13, Jesus' evasive answer to the tribute question (Matt. 22:15-22), and the compromise over the application of the Law to gentile Christians (Acts 15:1-29).

The political danger of the radical gospel is ideology, for ideology supplies the specific political programs which the gospel lacks. Since a life of radical calling laden with uncertainty over how to live the call is a life in tension, Christians are strongly tempted to relieve the tension by a system of rules (legalism) or by finding an ideological solution. Even with the best of intentions radical political theology tends to degenerate into a political ideology in which human devices provide the heart of a program claiming divine sanction. The controlling ideology may be found either on the left or the right, depending more on ideological fashion than theological insight. Such naive translation of religious demands into political programs is what opponents of religious language in political life rightly fear.

This is not to say that all proponents of the radical gospel are unaware of its dangers. The problem, however, is to create a political theology inspired by the radical gospel but not captured by ideology. Prudence here makes its declaration of intent to tame religious radicalism, making it fit for political life.

Prudence

Prudence and the qualities associated with it, such as discretion, shrewdness, craftiness, and wisdom, are far more prominent in the Hebrew Scriptures than the New Testament.[39] Where prudence, wisdom, or shrewdness do appear in the New Testament, they are often treated ironically. (For example, Luke 16:8-9 and 1 Cor. 1:19.) Yet the difference is not simply between the new and old covenants, for prudence is not prominent either in the prophetic literature. Where the thirst for justice is intense, cautious efforts at reform will not slake it.

Yet the Bible at times does recommend prudence's watchful appreciation of circumstances. "Behold, I send you out as sheep in the midst of wolves; so be wise as serpents and innocent as doves" (Matt. 10:16). The parable of the wise and foolish virgins recommends foresight (Matt. 25:1-13). The follower of Christ must understand the signs of the times and discern in them the will of God. Thus prudence is more than mere cleverness or shrewdness. Knowledge and love of God and neighbor manifest in forgiveness, generosity, justice, and trust in the Father's love are the heart of the gospel. But the gospel also requires insight into the particular circumstances in which the faithful must act, as well as appreciation of the probable consequences of different courses of action. The evils of this world must not be condemned and attacked improvidently, lest the attack create worse evils and miss real but limited opportunities for good.

Prudent consideration of politics dictates that power and coercion are irremovable features of human life, which must promote the good where possible and restrain greater evil where necessary. Both Niebuhr's "Christ Above Culture" and "Christ and Culture in Paradox" traditions implicitly recognize the value of prudence.[40] The Catholic tradition enshrines it as one of the four cardinal virtues. St. Thomas transforms Aristotelian prudence into the central virtue of Christian moral and political life. Self-giving love is the supreme Christian virtue, but prudence regulates the specific means toward the end of love and makes it effective in action.[41]

Politically, prudence recognizes in stability and order the return of grace upon fallen nature. Politics is necessarily infected with sin, but materials for restraining the worst effects of sin are present in the human propensities for association, fear of injustice, and love of order.

It follows from this perspective that the prudent Christian owes a certain amount of respect to democratic political order and that political order in general is not necessarily opposed to gospel principles. Such a favorable view, however, carries with it a danger as real as the danger of the radical gospel. When the claims of political order are taken too seriously and when the gospel becomes comfortable, prudence shades into civil religion. The Church loses the distance from politics necessary to criticize it in the name of the gospel.

Prudence need not succumb to civil religion, for a more precise understanding of prudence builds up resistance. There are, I contend, two different kinds of prudence, which I shall refer to as "higher" and "lower" prudence.

Each is a legitimate form of prudence, and each form is recognized in ordinary language. Lower prudence is cautious and discreet. It is defensive, focused on survival and respect. These are important goods, reflecting proper concern with personal safety and one's appearance to others. Politically, lower prudence is conservative and realistic. It values political stability because it understands the fragility of order and the evils spawned by social chaos. It attempts to distinguish changeable conditions from those which, even though unjust, cannot be changed in the short run. It resists radical attacks on the latter, because they inevitably fail and generally produce greater injustices. Lower prudence is skeptical of all-embracing ideologies and plans for society. It recognizes the place of sin and self-interest in politics. Knowing that these cannot be erased, it devises and defends institutions such as capitalism and representative government, which minimize their effects and channel them into beneficial directions. Lower prudence appreciates the limits of political possibility and is open to compromise.

Lower prudence has a priestly orientation. In public life, it supports the status quo and cautious reform. In private life, it encourages those virtues making peace and stability possible. This kind of private support for virtue is, moreover, the most appropriate priestly role of religion. To give religion a *public* priestly role, as in civil religion, runs the danger of intolerance, incivility, and invasion of the political realm by religion.

Higher prudence, on the other hand, is active, caring more for justice than for survival, for love than respect. It takes risks in the interest of realizing higher values. While it appreciates lower prudence, it demands that the lower be governed by the higher, for it is less concerned with stability than with realizing love in concrete circumstances. More precisely, it follows the prophets in contending that the only genuine peace and stability are those founded on justice and mercy. Therefore, injustice and oppression are essentially unstable. They must be seen for what they are and their ugliness must be exposed, even though an attack runs the risk of promoting a violent backlash. The existence of higher prudence allows the New Testament to take an ironic stance toward lower prudence.

Higher prudence is prophetic. In public life, it denounces injustice and oppression. In private life, it encourages virtues like courage that enable personal change and personal resistance to public injustice. It can, indeed, be revolutionary. It is higher prudence that most often inspires the side of religion that challenges political structures.[42]

Higher prudence shares the lower's suspicion of ideology, because ideology claims ready-made solutions applicable to any society. Jesus' higher prudence is anti-ideological. He condemns injustice and oppression; he articulates the principles of a new order; but he leaves it to his disciples constantly to work out the particular institutions of that order in accord with the materials at hand.

Higher prudence, while not rejecting the importance of lower, comes closest to the authentic understanding of prudence in Aristotle and Aquinas, for whom prudence is not a cautious virtue, but one in which the highest things come alive in human action. The lawgiver must be prudent, but his prudence is directed by a radical goal. "The entire purpose of the lawgiver is that man may love God."[43]

Both Jesus and Paul exhibit lower and higher prudence. They do not directly challenge the political regime or attempt directly to overthrow an unjust order. They implicitly recognize, Paul more so than Jesus, the value of political order. But their message attacks the foundation of the Roman regime. When this message brings them into confrontation with the powers that be, they do not compromise it for the sake of life or reputation. Indeed, Jesus clearly recognizes that he will be killed by an unjust order on account of his demands. Thus the radical gospel joins prudence at the point where higher prudence demands that the actions necessary to fulfill loyalty to the Father and unconditional faith, hope, and love are actions that undermine the existing order and which provoke that order to defend itself through persecution. Jesus does not recommend love of enemies or justice for reasons of lower prudence—that is, because they might bring recognition or admiration. Quite the contrary: they bring disgrace and resentment. Lower prudence might practice love for its rewards; higher prudence will not.

Yet within the context of the higher, more radical prudence, Jesus frequently maneuvers with a lower prudence. He does not accept the futile Zealot revolt against Roman oppression. He simply leaves when the crowds try to make him king (John 6:15). He deftly avoids the traps laid by the tribute question (Matt. 22:15-22) and the question of his authority (Matt. 21:23-27). Lower prudence has its place.

Paul frequently practices the lower form of prudence. He seems to assume that the political order is just, or at least to act as if it were. He freely claims the rights of his Roman citizenship and defends himself against illegal and improper arrests and judicial proceedings.[44] Political order clearly has a value for Paul, as Romans 13 amply demonstrates.

But it is also amply clear that Paul considers that the Christian's loyalty is to Christ, not the political regime. Romans 13 is not a defense of unconditional obedience to the state, nor is it a declaration of the autonomy of secular institutions. Romans 13 is situated in the context of Paul's teaching of the same radical demands made by Jesus: do not be conformed to the world, be patient in tribulation, do not repay evil for evil, but do good to the enemy (Rom. 12) and love your neighbor as yourself (Rom. 13:8-10). In short, for both Paul and Jesus the demands of higher prudence always control the caution of lower prudence.

Stewardship

A concept that captures very well the sense of higher prudence is stewardship. Though "stewardship" today is often limited to the context of financial support for the Church, its actual range of application is the whole of life. The follower of Christ is accountable as a steward for the use of time, possessions, and talents. The steward must wisely administer all the gifts given by God, especially the grace of the gospel (1 Cor. 4:1-2; 9:16-17; Eph. 3:2; Col. 1:25; 1 Tim. 1:4; Titus 1:7; 1 Pet. 4:10). The highest things— love, faith, hope, forgiveness, patience, compassion, mercy, the good news to the poor—are gifts entrusted to his followers by Jesus, and his followers are stewards of these mysteries.

A steward must administer what he receives, using it for the master's benefit. Stewardship thus requires lower prudence, so that the gifts entrusted are not squandered or invested in foolish and unproductive enterprises. But stewardship also demands risk-taking, that is, radical action or higher prudence. It is not enough for the steward cautiously to protect the gifts of God; he must administer them so that they increase, and attempting to increase a thing of value is always risky. The person who invests money in new ventures takes greater risks than the person who hides it. This truth recalls the saying that the disciple of Christ must be a light shining in the darkness, not a lamp hidden under a basket. A light in the darkness is not only a guide for travelers; it is also an easy target.

Jesus, of course, tells a number of parables of stewardship, recommending the lower prudence of the "unjust" steward (Luke 16:1-9), but especially commending the risk-taking of the good steward (Luke 19:11-16; Matt. 25:14-30). In creative and risk-taking care to spread the gospel entrusted to him, the steward's left hand is not to know what his right is doing. The lender must not expect repayment. After all, Jesus did not worry about the ingratitude of the nine cleansed lepers who did not return; the faith of the one who did was worth the cure.

Such an idea of stewardship fits well with the role of religion to challenge political order. The prudent steward of the radical gospel might urge his nation to take the risk of cutting arms spending before its adversary does. Such a steward might not worry over much about abuse of income-support programs or about whether such programs are as efficient as possible. She will be more concerned about whether they are as compassionate as possible. Such a steward will preach and live her religious commitments in and out of season, honoring and encouraging the political regime insofar as it promotes human character and the common good through pursuit of freedom and justice. Insofar as the regime fails in these respects, it may be criticized and prodded by a steward church.

The lower prudence that forms a part of this understanding of stewardship must be exercised defensively, using common sense and political acumen, which it learns from its political interactions, to avoid the dangers of ideology. The steward who turns her charge over to a radical or to a conventional political program is an unfaithful steward and can be steward no longer, for she has nothing left to administer. The gospel has slipped through her fingers. These dangers may be illustrated by the fascination of the religious left with the Sandinista regime in Nicaragua and by the fascination of the religious right with laissez-faire capitalism.

The unique challenge offered by religion may be lost through the too great caution of lower prudence or the zeal of radicalism. Stewardship, the higher prudence, cherishes the gospel and so preserves it from loss; at the same time, the radical gospel goads the steward until she is free enough to risk herself in its service.

I have spoken of prudence from the religious side for economy of expression. Politics too has its higher and lower prudence, its New Frontiers and its "Don't make no waves; don't back no losers." Both are proper meeting places for religion and politics, but higher prudence is the more creative and exciting.

7

Narratives and
Institutions

Abstract ideals of brotherhood and harmony, of
love and union, must be translated into concrete
social practices.
—Rosabeth Moss Kanter, *Commitment and
Community*

This chapter continues the account of the border between public and private.
In it I discuss narrative (with the associated phenomena of history and
tradition) and institutions. These are tied to language and virtue, and their
portrait completes the picture begun in the last chapter. A long conclusion
draws the themes together. I argue that, though public and private life
connect through language, virtue, narrative, and institutions, their fit is
neither perfect nor perfectly harmonious. A tension between public and
private always exists, a tension, however, that is not undesirable; indeed,
creative tension is their best possible meeting place.

The preceding chapter reflected on virtue and tragedy. Tragedy and
conflict are among the hardest human experiences. They test commitments,
stir emotion, and challenge the dominance of reason. I argued that the
most satisfactory way to comprehend conflict and tragedy is to fit them
into the total pattern of life with its particular goals. Then these phenomena
can be interpreted as aiding, detracting from, or altering patterns and
purposes. MacIntyre says, "It is through conflict and sometimes only
through conflict that we learn what our ends and purposes are."[1] Of
course, conflict can defeat goals. Some persons even allow conflict to
defeat them, explaining opposition and tragedy as typical parts of a life
pattern of failure, the "poor me" syndrome. Apart from pattern and
purpose, conflicts and tragedies seem random and meaningless. With
pattern and purpose, they make some sense.

Conflict originates both internally (that is, different aspects of the self
struggle against one another; reason against taste buds, for example) and
externally (that is, self struggles against social expectations; honesty against

popular acceptance of income-tax cheating, for example). Human limits preclude perfect integration of internal and external life; tragedy and failure are inevitable. The virtues come into play as one confronts conflict, tragedy, and failure.

Description of pattern and purpose in life, individual or collective, often takes the form of a story. Triumphs, failures, and tragedies are woven into a pattern that, unlike an Escher print, has a beginning and an end. We tell the story of our public and private lives by recounting, reliving, mythologizing, and reinterpreting triumphant, shameful, and tragic events. Instead of defining our virtues and vices, we illustrate them in the story of our lives. These stories generate traditions, rituals, and histories interlacing public and private themes.

Narrative, History, and Tradition

The genuine unity of life is narrative. Such unity is unlike, and superior to, the idea of unity based on a plan for three reasons.[2] First, though characters in stories make plans, even the rational choice of a life plan is not created *de novo*. Makers of plans have histories, including previous plans with their successes and failures. Today's plan is part of the story of plans through a whole life. Second, plans sufficiently encompassing for an entire individual life, let alone a collective life, surpass the powers of human reason. We may set encompassing goals for our lives, but hardly plans, for life's contingencies demand considerable spontaneous adjustment and change. A successful life is more a Miles Davis improvisation on a given chord structure than a building erected according to an architect's schematics. Third, humans are time-bound. Triumphs and failures do not unfold whole, outside of time, but always in sequence, the remembered past dimly visible, the future only a hint. Successes and failures intertwine, forcing changed plans in midstream.

Even knowledge is narrative, contingent, and time-bound. Rational thinking, theorizing, and discovering, in all fields, including science, depend upon traditions, stories of knowledge and discovery by past and present colleagues, and already established goals. "The picture of the knower's situation is . . . shot through with time, history, place, and intention."[3]

Thus the account of the virtues given in the preceding chapter suits a narrative theory of character. Lives have themes, goals, and purposes that transcend rational planning and fixed agendas. We comprehend virtues and vices by their effect on the ability to follow themes, achieve purposes, and alter goals in terms of past responses and present circumstances. According to MacIntyre, "Every particular view of the virtues is linked to some particular notion of the narrative structure or structures of human life."[4] Character emerges from the story of a life; yet character strives to shape the story to fit its most important qualities. Character implies development, direction, and maturity. These also suggest narrative.

Though character, virtue, and narrative imply growth, they also set limits. They constrain the possibilities for speech and action. Ignorance of or refusal to limit desire by the prospects given in the past signifies megalomania. Therefore, narrative pertains to both the exclusive and the inclusive sides of private life. We should know well the story of our own greed, selfishness, and deception. Though stories can rationalize weakness, they are better used to explain it. And this is no mean feat. "Why did I say such a stupid thing?" we often ask. Awareness of our history illuminates, though it need not excuse, our tendency to cover up embarrassment or shame.

Do not confuse explanation with justification. Narrative does not by itself justify anything. Yet by connecting the fragments of life, especially the fragments we would just as soon forget or suppress, it reveals a pattern to life with shadows and brightness that can give meaning to life history and, therefore, contribute to both justification and repentance.

Although I have considered the narrative shape of life principally in individual terms, it is just as applicable to groups, communities, and associations, just as "at home" in the account of public life as of private. Pride, manipulation, thirst for power, imperialism, and impersonalism find their place in the stories of a nation's past, sometimes to a surprising degree, as in the Hebrew Scriptures. Though publics, just as individuals, try to suppress or ignore their history of failure and shame, the story is never completely distorted. The darkness awaits discerning eyes. As in private life, the story is not justification, though the public rationalizes as thoroughly as the private. The proper function of history is to explain, to fit the fragments of the past into a meaningful pattern. From this pattern a people can see the proper grounds for public pride and shame and learn ways to deal with present and future challenges.[5]

We make sense of public triumph, failure, and tragedy by fitting them into the story of the community's past. Therefore, politics cannot depend upon feelings alone, even benevolent ones. Sentiments of social benevolence rest on stories, myths, traditions, and history. These inspire cooperative political action when the participants do not feel like it, or when they are divided by current rivalry. The stories of their ancestors' common action help to direct them into cooperative paths.

Human life has an historical character reflecting its contingency and its narrative structure. Because life is contingent, surprising, unpredictable, and uncontrollable, blueprints cannot chart or capture its past or future. The past must be told in the form of stories or histories and the future in terms of intentions rooted in those histories. Therefore, concepts fundamental to individual and group life have an historical character. Attempts to express rights, justice, or equality in unambiguous, universal language founder on the shoals of historicity. A community's fundamental commitments, culture, idiosyncracies, and principles for ordering its internal and external relations depend on its past successes and failures in these matters.

The vital thing is that this past be a living past. Each generation must interpret and reinterpret its history and stories. Through such interpretation it renews itself and the meanings that constitute it. Memory thus is crucial to a culture as well as to individuals. Public memory is as critical as private.[6] Religions are especially rich in stories; indeed, stories often constitute much of the core of religious traditions. Witness the stories of the Buddha and of bodhisattvas in the Buddhist tradition, the epic poem of Hinduism, the *Mahabharata*, and the stories in the Bible. Hasidic Jews have stories of the *tsaddiqim*, the masters of virtue. For Islam the stories in the *hadith* supplement the Koran.[7] The narrative character of religion is largely what makes it so definitely both public and private.

Religious stories, therefore, have an important place in school curricula, a place more important than didactic courses in moral decision making, particularly at the elementary and early secondary levels. Moral education through sociology, economics, and quasi-philosophy cannot substitute for the importance of stories that involve the student in the midst of "thickly embedded" action quandaries.[8] Moral education, then, should draw on the stories from a nation's history and culture, as well as from those of other cultures. It is indispensable, moreover, that the stories selected reflect moral failure as well as success. History and literature, therefore, are vital parts of the "moral curriculum" as well as disciplines in their own right. But a crucial source of such stories is, in American culture, the Bible, which can be creatively used in the public schools as literature and religious history, its stories furnishing rich sources of material for reflection. Certainly, stories from other religious traditions can and should be introduced, but the Bible as part of the particular culture of this nation should have a privileged place when it comes to stories from religious sources.

Some religious groups, of course, would object to this "secular" way of handling the Bible and also to use of other religious texts. Indeed, the treatment and selection of such texts has been hotly contested in the courts in the 1980s. The point here is not to water down the public school curriculum, but to provide options for conscientious objectors to this curriculum. Such options suggest freedom for such groups to form their own, private schools, in which they could employ biblical and other stories in a different way and in which they could introduce the stories of their own, particular saints. Availability of tax credits or vouchers would make such schools feasible choices for all income groups in a pluralistic religious and educational culture.

The past forms the present and channels the future. Therefore, it is critically related to virtue and character. As stable dispositions, the virtues are clearly rooted in past actions and reactions, as are vices and bad habits. Virtues and vices, so rooted in history, constrain public and private goals and their achievement. A sense of the past anchors expression of individual and group needs. Narcissism results, unless needs and desires connect the future to specific past experiences of satisfaction and contentment. Free-floating desire signals loss of grip on reality.[9] Note how amnesia's devastation of self reinforces the case for the foundation of identity and character in narrative and history. Character is not the same without memory, without a past, even though a person may exhibit after memory loss the same personal qualities as before. This is as true of nations as of individuals. As Sydney Ahlstrom puts it, "A nation that is unaware of its past bears an alarming similarity to a person suffering from amnesia: a crucial element of its being is lacking."[10] The past, individual and national, resides in stories, but also in associated traditions and rituals.

Traditions not only solidify the past, as is commonly recognized, they also preserve future possibilities. They perpetuate different interpretations of stories, repositories of promise presently forgotten but available for revival.[11] Traditions are like the exoskeletons of shellfish. They must be rigid to protect the vulnerable life within. Most of the time we focus on the rigidity of traditions, failing to look inside to the life they preserve. Public and private groups need such structures to conserve their principles from the harsh effects of contingency, conflict, and tragedy.

Ritual, which seems even less adaptable than tradition, serves the same function of providing a channel for the narratives, stories, and traditions that preserve history and structure identity. The more familiar and seemingly innocuous a ritual, the more powerful its potential for transmitting meanings not formulable in universal definitions. Persons who participate in rituals fit comfortably within them, or they don't. Or sometimes one and sometimes the other. In the former case, they become imbued with the assumptions, traditions, and stories that underlie and support the ritual. In the latter case, their discomfort with the ritual drives them to rebel against it and thus, more or less consciously, against the underlying assumptions, traditions, and stories. In either case, the ritual and one's reaction to it has worked to fashion character and identity.

Religions are major repositories of stories, rituals, and traditions. These are constantly retold and reenacted, and modified as they are repeated. As Walzer and McWilliams have shown, biblical narratives and biblical lessons have inspired political action—particularly, challenges to easy political assumptions and oppressive political regimes—in the history of America and other nations.[12]

The perspective on narrative, history, and tradition just outlined has integral attachments to virtue and character, which themselves bridge public and private life. Similar connections could obviously be drawn between narrative and public-private life through the role of language in narrative, tradition, and history. These connections, however, are so far only indirect. It remains to trace the direct linkages.

Implications for Public and Private Life

I have demonstrated why private life displays a narrative character and why public life is similarly narrative. The narrative element of each, however, does not in and of itself couple them directly. There are public stories, histories, and traditions. There are private narratives and rituals. Public and private stories could be parallel, rather than intersecting. Only by intersecting do they bridge public and private life. What kind of intersections do we find?

Cultural diversity is one. Human historicity and contingency produce cultural diversity. Ironically, cultural diversity commonly provides ammunition against the unity of public and private. Human societies being so different, what ground can there be for generalization about public and private life? They exhibit sundry patterns across societies. Though linked in certain ways in some societies, they appear disconnected in others. Virtues and vices, and character, vary so much as to preclude a constant set of virtues tied in fixed ways to public and private life. Cultural diversity stems from contingency, history, and narrative. Cultures deviate, in great part, because they face novel circumstances as they evolve. Their histories diverge because their pasts branch uniquely. Because story, myth, tradition, and ritual structure societies, societies grow dissimilar over time. Only when their stories interact, as in the modern age of world communications, cultural diffusion, and cultural imperialism, do they begin to share a common history and to lose diversity.

Yet the very fact of cultural diversity provides grounds, within a particular culture, for public and private intersection. Budziszewski observes, "*That* [civic and intimate virtues] interact is a constant; *how* they interact is a cultural variable."[13] Constancy formed the subject of the last chapter. Here I wish to tease out the implications of the culturally variable "how."

Public and private do not interact according to some grand, universal scheme, but according to the unique patterns laid down in a culture's stories, traditions, and rituals. Narratives peculiar to each culture (and their embodiment in traditions and rituals) govern public and private in each culture. Narratives directly link public and private, because they function like border guards between the realms. They justify and explain "how we do things here." Thus a culture's stories illustrate proper ways to live on the border between public and private life, for example, the Roman story of Cincinnatus's laying aside the dictatorship to return to his farm. (Because stories can cross cultural boundaries, we have the image of George Washington as "the American Cincinnatus.")

Traditions and rituals serve the same border-defining and border-crossing function. Certain traditions in each culture specify the relationship between public and private. "A man's home is his castle." Rituals such as knocking before entering private space reinforce the tradition. In American culture the knocking ritual teaches and reinforces the boundaries. We knock to request permission to enter a private home, but not a restaurant. We knock before entering certain offices because an office has some characteristics of privacy and some of publicity. Though hard-pressed to specify all of the "knock before entering" rules, we can employ them skillfully, because they are ritualized so well. Such rituals help to define and govern the border between private and public life in *this* culture. Other cultures do not have such "knocking rules." The contours of the border are different, so other traditions and rituals govern the interaction.

Another quality of narratives interweaves public and private life. We are actors in each other's dramas.[14] The stories of private individuals and groups contain accounts of interaction with the public realm. These accounts may be positive or negative. Families among oppressed classes or races nearly always tell stories of harassment, brutality, or indifference by public officials toward particular family members. Stories of the same incident told from the other side, from the official's perspective, are different stories. I do not contend that the different perspectives are equally valid or that some stories are not better accounts of what transpired. (After all, some witnesses are better than others.) I only mean that different stories are equally stories and that the stories intertwine.

The stories interlock at the level of the particular story and at the mythic level. By the former I mean the level at which particular family members tell the stories to other family members or to friends and neighbors and at which particular public actors tell the stories to other public actors or to *their* families, friends, and neighbors. The separate dramas of cop and black teenager intersect at a particular place and time, and each tells the story of that singular meeting of public and private life. Their stories, however, merge with the larger, mythic stories and traditions that describe and govern interaction between larger entities such as the black family and the police. The totality of these myths and stories, and their associated traditions and rituals, structure the ways in which particular private and public persons interact and in which private and public in general interact in particular societies.

Though my specific example was negative, drawing on stories describing antagonistic relationships, examples of positive interactions in stories of cooperation could be used to illustrate the same point. The idea is not that narratives will always be of a certain kind, but that narratives of both kinds help guide interaction between public and private life. Religious traditions have rich depositories of stories about public–private interaction. Kings, priests, prophets, wars, gods, persecutions, and triumphs interact in the stories to form a tapestry of the public–private border.

Objections

A number of objections can be raised to the argument that public and private life intersect in narrative. Some of these objections apply as well to the previous chapter, criticizing the overall argument from virtue and narrative.

There are three important objections. I shall first state the objections and then respond to them all together. The first objection points to the relativistic implications of the argument from narrative and its associated concepts. The objection has two sides. The first side expresses a strong cultural relativism. Those who take this position might agree with my discussion of narrative, for its implications of cultural relativism fit nicely with their own assumptions. They would argue, however, that the relativistic implications run against my assertion of universal interaction between public and private. I have already considered this side of the first objection in the paragraphs above.

The second side of the objection finds fault with the relativistic implications of the argument from narrative. It might be made by those who advance certain varieties of ethical naturalism or moral absolutism. An ethical objectivism like that of Hadley Arkes exemplifies the position taken by proponents of this objection.[15] It contends that the narrative cast of arguments like MacIntyre's produces moral relativism. To allow narrative and its associated concepts to govern virtue and character and to define the relationship between public and private life, the argument goes, leaves these matters to historical contingency. Thus rules of reason and the moral principles derived from them would vary from society to society. Without a way of judging between narratives or traditions of morality, one story or tradition is a good as another; one society's institutions of privacy as good as another's. Therefore, no ground of judgment exists between them. This objection grants priority to public life, at least in-so-far as reason is public. That is, rational arguments are open to public debate, discussion, and modification. Only public reason and justification can uncover truth in morals. But if reason varies historically, there is no ground for truth in morals, let alone in defining public and private life.

A second objection, which draws on the first, contends that I am trying to eat my cake and have it too. That is, the argument from virtue in the previous chapter is implicitly naturalistic, the argument from narrative implicitly cultural. The two arguments do not comport.

A final objection to my argument from narrative contends that it is insufficiently liberal—that is, it does not adequately recognize and protect individuality. Narratives, traditions, and rituals, this objection runs, are inherently conservative in that they favor the group. Stories become fixed, traditions stultified. Rituals produce conformity. Although my argument may recognize cultural pluralism, the objection continues, it does not allow sufficient room for pluralism within a culture. Norm-setting narratives and behavior-defining traditions are not notably tolerant of dissent.

I cannot respond to the first two objections with the proper depth, for they come directly from ethical philosophy and require a digression into ethical theory that would be beyond the scope of this book. Nevertheless, I can indicate the direction of a proper reply without going too far afield.

I can respond simultaneously to the first objection (more precisely, the second variant of the first objection) and to the second. The value of my theory of virtue and narrative rests precisely in its explicit and direct recognition of both the constant and the contingent in human affairs. It does not contend that the variable content of narrative establishes the whole of morality. As Budziszewski says, "The narrative unity of a life or of a tradition is only a necessary condition for its goodness, not a sufficient condition."[16] If narratives, histories, and traditions (and their unity) were the only things, then objections based on narrative relativism would be sound, for there would be no way to distinguish unified, evil traditions from unified, good traditions. The theorists who join narrative and virtue are certainly aware of this problem.[17]

The very strong sense of history found particularly in MacIntyre, however, lends credence to the objection. His notion of a quest for the good is not sufficiently developed to deflect the criticism. Yet the sense of historical contingency in a narrative theory need not be as strong as MacIntyre's. What is needed is a "weak" sense of history sufficient to allow, as in Aristotle's account of the best practical regime, adaptation of the best in light of the realities of concrete, historical circumstances.[18] For it matters whether there is a good or a best beyond the reality of historically given traditions, rituals, and narratives. Traditions and rituals are authoritative, and defensible, only if they point beyond themselves to a reality to which they in some measure open access. The fundamental contribution of narrative to a theory of the virtues is the insight that in actual social conditions access to fundamental principles comes only through languages, traditions, stories, and rituals. Particular narrative traditions can be judged by the types of characters they produce and by whether the qualities of character in any given society fit together into a coherent whole. "By their fruits you shall know them."

Theories of "objective" morality, whether virtue theories or otherwise, suffer from a weakness corresponding to the temptation toward relativism evident in narrative theory. Such theories have the tendency to hang in midair, detached from circumstances bounding the possibility of their realization and detached from cultural settings fleshing out the meaning of abstract concepts such as honor, courage, wisdom, and diligence. These concepts are useless for judging particular persons or actions without reference to model lives, to which perforce cling the loose threads of history. Indeed, one of the most important functions of a set of moral principles, education of the young, cannot be accomplished without reference to models of appropriate behavior in contingent situations. History and narrative convey such models or patterns of behavior.

Thus the incipient relativism of the narrative emphasis balances the incipient abstract moralism of the virtue emphasis. The "naturalism" of virtue theory balances the "nurturism" of tradition and story. Each cries out for the other. Let the virtue of prudence illustrate. In the Aristotelian, natural law tradition, prudence bridges the distance between the constancy of moral principle and changing situations. Prudence depends on the practice of the other virtues, but also on long experience and reflection, both on moral principles and on various problems of living. It parallels facility in selecting and interpreting stories in the sphere of narrative moral theory. Stories do not apply themselves, nor are they told randomly. Rather, the storyteller, who acquires a certain moral authority with the ability to select and transmit stories, must choose, from the fund of available stories within a particular culture, the right story for the right occasion. The story selected must be appropriate to the audience, the circumstance facing the audience, the historical and cultural background of the circumstance, and the fundamental principles of the culture whose members form the audience. All these considerations parallel the questions facing the person of practical wisdom who attempts to discern appropriate courses of action.

The dialogue between principles and circumstances in prudential wisdom and narrative interpretation is analogous to dialogue between narrative traditions. Were there no reality anchoring traditions and stories, there would be no point to conversation between traditions. Conversation would be variations on, "You have your ways, and we have ours." The only responses available to such a statement are: (1) "So let's leave each other alone"; or (2) "So let's fight about whose we'll follow"; or (3) "So let's swap tales." Absent common reality to which each tradition refers, indifference or imperialism (the first two responses) are reasonable. If there were only circumstance, the best we could hope for is agreement to disagree. We leave each other alone and become interest-group politicians. Not a pleasant prospect, but a low enough common denominator, perhaps, to keep civil peace and avoid tyranny.

If, on the other hand, there is such a reality, then (with some effort) we can gain insight into each other's stories. Even if we cannot agree on the best version of a story, or of reality, we can, both within and between traditions, continue to discuss it as an open question. Reason, and therefore rational debate, though it cannot be divorced from the historical circumstances of a people, is principally public, open to objection and response. It must stand ready to give justifications in terms at least potentially accessible to all participants. Though the common good and justice may not be achievable, a participatory politics that debates these terms as though they referred to something substantive just might hold citizens to higher standards of speech and action, of virtue, than a politics of self-interest.

Such politics will also respect pluralism, and this is the answer to the third objection. Recognition that virtue is bound to history provides grounds for humility and for genuine toleration that might otherwise prove difficult in virtue theory. Failure to realize virtue is not sufficient ground for punishment, interference, or coercive regimentation, for all persons and cultures fall short, necessarily embodying virtue idiosyncratically.

It might be objected to this line of argument that it is precisely the emphasis on narrative and tradition that generates coercion. After all, narrative traditions easily provide a framework for closed communities. If all are heirs to specific rituals, traditions, and stories, then everyone within the story-formed community must adhere to its lessons and examples. Narrative might supply grounds for diversity between communities, but for rigid conformity within communities. This charge contains some truth. Strong traditions often suppress internal dissent.

Suppression is, however, not a necessary result, given that no tradition embodies the truth, but only approximates it. That is, the key to legitimate pluralism and tolerance is once again the balance between the different trajectories of the narrative and virtue emphases. Separated, they run to extremes. Together, they moderate one another. And, most importantly for my concerns, each shows the connection between public and private life.

Institutions

Narratives, traditions, and rituals, and virtues, coalesce in institutions. Institutions are relatively stable associations of social roles and expectations, providing important connections between public and private. Nearly forty years ago Robert Nisbet warned that institutions intermediate between the individual and the impersonal state were being weakened and destroyed. Their disappearance leaves a relatively unprotected individual to face the full power and resources of the state.[19] Institutions like religion, the family, and the workplace, which share in each form of life, can mediate between individual and political order. The problems of public and private life stem largely from the fact that in the modern world these realms face each other nakedly.

The public world structures the need for and the expressions of private life. The need for a place and time of one's own is universal, though particular forms of privacy are not. Rather, each culture gives unique shape to the need and develops social structures for its satisfaction. In short, social institutions play key roles in relating public to private life. In this section I shall not discuss institutions in general or long lists of institutions. Rather, I shall focus on those that manifest a particularly important union of public and private. These are family, work, voluntary associations, and churches. But first I should say something about social roles.

Roles

The idea of social roles with its suggestion of acting may seem artificial. After all, roles reflect the expectations of others, not the unique qualities of self. They are often seen as external impositions on the freedom to define one's own identity. Though roles *may* certainly be imposed, they are not necessarily so. Although fashions in clothing may be imposed on weak persons, others select clothing that, although conforming to social norms, also fits their personality. Historically contingent notions of what "fits," learned through socialization, constrain their choice, but this channeling of choice does not deny freedom. Rather, freedom's historical contingency gives definition to inchoate, meaningless choices.

Individuals play roles, so we never see abstract persons. But they do not simply play roles; interaction between person and role, person and social expectation, is constant. Individuals modify, shape, and adjust roles to fit. Roles define identity, but identity also alters roles to more personal dimensions. Roles are neither custom-tailored suits, nor suits put on from the rack. They are more like suits selected from the rack, but then tailored to fit one's unique dimensions and comfort requirements.[20]

So the dramatic metaphor is appropriate. Roles do involve acting. They do imply that life is at least partially theater, and necessarily so. As Saul Bellow observes, life is a "theater of the soul," each person striving to be unique, an individual. But the reality is that a person becomes unique only by imitating others. As we must emulate, why not imitate those worthy of it?[21] Such emulation is essential, not antithetical, to identity. Indeed, the idea of virtue and its distinctive role in relating public and private life does not make sense unless persons take on social roles through imitation.

Yves R. Simon, for example, argues that, despite the popularity of the idea of "moral man and immoral society" and of the idea that society cannot make people moral, the empirical evidence is clear that organized society has much to do with safeguarding good human behavior. Daily acceptance of ordinary social roles produces the result that ordinary people do not more often lie, insult one another, steal, and murder. Ordinary conventions and manners grease the wheels of social interaction. Roles, in short, channel behavior toward goodness when passions and instincts direct otherwise. Human beings are not born civilized; they become so through training, which includes role acceptance. To be civilized is not the highest of human goods, except in some circles, but it is nothing to sneer at. Simon also points out that besides conformity to roles as a way of forming persons, there is "sociability by way of inspiration," which helps to perfect freedom and uniqueness. Society can inspire a person to become better and even to change society.[22]

These features of roles have a clear bearing on public and private life. Roles are perceived by the person as outside, public. But they are essential for inner, personal identity, that is, for private life. As roles are accepted and then modified, public and private life mesh. This acceptance and modification of roles takes place primarily in social institutions.

Family and Voluntary Association

I cannot say much about these institutions beyond some (I hope) fairly obvious facts. Institutions like church, family, work, and voluntary associations are locations where public and private intersect. Language, character, virtue, and narrative are anchored in social structures, rooted in specific, historically and culturally shaped institutions. Thus, if language, character, virtue, and narrative and their associated concepts are points of contact between public and private life, then the institutions in which these concepts find concrete expression also constitute points of contact. I shall not try to design a theory of institutions in general or a theoretical description of particular institutions. Rather, I wish simply to make explicit the implicit status of institutions in all I have said about the overlap of public and private.

All institutions to some extent connect public and private life, but some do so in especially deep ways. Family and work probably have this function in all cultures. Voluntary associations certainly do in American culture. What can be said about these institutions is constrained by culture. My remarks are certainly derived primarily from the Western nuclear family and from Western experiences of work and voluntary association. Nevertheless, such institutions do play similar roles in virtually all cultures.[23]

The family, at least in American culture, is closest to private life. It aspires to be a place of intimacy, trust, and integrity, but it is also a location of secrets, guilt, and imperfection. This primarily private quality of family must be clearly recognized. Because it is primarily private, there is an inherent tension between family and public world, however that world appears in particular societies. Yet the family is also a connection between private and public life, a place where they blend and form new combinations, for what makes a family are certain kinds of shared stories, shared commitments, and mutual obligations.

First and most deeply, though the family is private, the individual family member confronts its public side.[24] There are intimate recesses of the person's heart that the family does not know, though it touches the hiddenness in ways that even the individual may not realize. There are secrets and mysteries of personal life that the family does not share. Individuals need refuge from the demands of family life from time to time. So family is public in profound ways with respect to the person. How the family appears as public and the way the person defines his private life vis-a-vis the public life of the family shapes both his own identity and the family's. Like all things that bridge public and private life, the family strongly affects identity.

Second, the family, though private, serves important public, even political, functions. Families are loci of traditions, both those particular to the family and those general social traditions played out in family life. Families develop their own unique stories, memories, rituals, and traditions. These define the family in specific, not abstract relationships. Daily living displays no generic mother-daughter relationship, only ties between specific mothers and daughters. The relationship between this mother and this daughter is defined by the memories and the stories of their past interaction and by the rituals and traditions that define their current association. But families also have their own versions of public stories, traditions, and rituals. Each family celebrates Thanksgiving and the Fourth of July in its own way; particular parents tell their children their own interpretations of the Revolutionary War, of cowboys and Indians, of encounters with public officials, and of political loyalties. These private versions of public stories socialize the young into the public world, but at the same time into this particular family with its identity-conferring narratives and traditions. Traditions and rituals protect the family from internal crises and external fragmenting forces.[25] Public-private narratives are deeply situated in family life. This is not their only place, but it is their chronologically first place.

Third, the family is the locus of virtue, as it is of narrative. Major figures in the history of political theory, especially Augustine, Aquinas, and Luther, but also major liberal thinkers, saw the family as the foundation of civic order, the first teacher of virtue, public as well as private.[26] The virtues linking public and private life are (most often) first learned in the family, if they are learned at all: responsibility, discipline, self-sacrifice, diligence, courage, toleration of differences, and prudence. The public has a crucial stake in child-rearing not only, as modern thought has it, because of children's potential as economically productive members of society, but more because of their potential as virtuous and responsible citizens.

So the public needs the family. This need is a source of attachment between public and private life, but also a source of tension. As the family crumbles (or, more charitably, changes) in contemporary society, there is an inchoate public awareness of the devastating effects—economic, political, and social—of children-become-adults who have little or no family grounding in tradition, virtue, and character. So a parade of "experts" on the family—

psychiatrists, educators, psychologists, counselors, therapists, physicians, social workers, courts—proposes and, frequently, enacts regulations, protections, and requirements that justify intervention in family life or turn child care over to experts. Many of these measures are justified, but they have side effects. One is the decreasing confidence of parents that they are competent to raise their children and to pass on private and public traditions, stories, and virtues without the advice of phalanxes of experts. This same effect then diminishes their sense of responsibility for passing on traditions and inculcating virtues.

Legitimate public concern for family life manifests the family's latent tensional connection between public and private. Public and private are connected in the family, yes; and the family can serve as a foundation for public order and decency. But there is also tension between the demands of public order, public traditions, and public role expectations and the way things are done in particular families. Because families are most fundamentally private, public demands on them produce considerable tension, both creative and destructive, in the families themselves and in individual family members, whose identities—at least partially—absorb these public-private tensions. School-textbook controversies dramatically illustrate this tension, as does the conflict between family roles and political ambition felt by politicians and would-be political actors.[27]

This discussion has important implications for public policy, child-care legislation, for example. Changed patterns of gender roles and work, as well as rates of divorce and remarriage have produced a clear need for public support for child care for working parents. The public world has its legitimate attractions; yet the public worlds of work and politics can undermine the strength of the family and stunt character formation in children. Moreover, the evidence is inconclusive on the effect of day-care arrangements on character formation in children and on family bonding. The following tentative conclusions, therefore, seem appropriate.[28] First, public support for child-care arrangements of all kinds is needed. Second, policy should seek to unite parents and children as much as possible, especially in the early years. Third, policy should seek to maximize parental choice in selection of child-care arrangements that fit different family traditions, roles, and commitments. Policy should not stint on support for parents who wish to remain at home or to use relatives and friends as care providers. Fourth, movements toward family allowances and home- based wage labor should be encouraged, so that in-home, both-parent child care might be more possible. Fifth, job-protected parental leave, flextime schedules, and job sharing should be encouraged by public policy for the same reasons. Sixth, in order to extend the range of choice, church-related child-care facilities should be as eligible for support as other facilities.

Finally, we may consider voluntary associations, including churches, which play so important a role in American culture. In discussing churches in this context, I do not mean to imply that religion is best understood from the perspective of voluntary association. I only mean to acknowledge that in American culture religion most clearly appears in the form of groups of believers in institutional structures.

Voluntary associations in this country are important linkages between public and private life. Labor unions, churches, civic clubs, bowling leagues, and business associations (to name a few) are private in that individuals join them freely and for their own particular reasons. They are public, however, because either by design or happenstance they channel public demands, challenge public decisions, and have public impact. Labor unions, for example, affect the economic health of a nation. Business associations lobby for public laws enhancing their private well-being. Bowling leagues petition city councils for zoning changes. Churches and civic clubs engage in public-service activities and sometimes become administrators of projects receiving public funds. In their tremendous diversity, voluntary associations are among the most fascinating intersections between public and private life. Churches are the most engrossing, because their relation to private life is the most intense and because their attention to public life is the most longstanding in our history.

Conclusions on Private and Public Life

Life on the border can be harmonious or tense, or, more likely, each by turns. Tensions in all areas of life wax and wane. Indeed, tensions, without intervention, always resolve themselves in some way. Even a steel bridge designed to last for decades, because it balances a series of tensions, eventually will collapse unless its components are regularly replaced. Similarly, tensions between persons or groups can be resolved (or transformed) by negotiation, violence, law, forgetfulness, or forgiveness. But they must be resolved. So with private and public life: their tensions must be resolved. Resolutions can be good or bad, creative or destructive. Yet they are always temporary, especially as public and private life contain essential components producing tension both within and at their borders. I shall first say something about internal tensions, then about border strains.

Tensions Within Private and Public

The two sides of private life are the clearest source of strain. The qualities of exclusion and of inclusion struggle against one another. Desire to be left alone contends with desire for intimacy. Shame and fear associated with guilt run counter to integrity and to trusting others with secrets. To search for the truth, to include others in the depths of personal life, and to trust others with the self's mystery require overcoming the pull of exclusion, which will not surrender without struggle. Giving up exclusive rights to part of myself in order to involve others in the depths of my life means risk.

The risks do not all run one way. Entering the realm of exclusion entails hazard. The circle of intimacy, contentment with trust and integrity, conceals personal secrets, shame and guilt, and imperfection. The values of inclusion draw one away from the uncertainties of exclusion, just as the fear of others pulls one away from inclusion.[29]

These tensions are creative if resolved creatively. Toleration of tension, taking risks, alternation between inclusion and exclusion are healthy ways to resolve tension. Denial, retreat to comfortable privacy, flight to the security of intimacy are self-limiting ways to resolve tension. The public can play a role here. Public tugging toward involvement with others makes it difficult to dwell solely within. Such contact opens possibilities for intimacy, for new private relations with those encountered in public. At the same time, public pressure on private principles forces reflection on imperfection, guilt, fear, and mystery.

There is tension as well within public life. The imperative of public trust encounters the impersonality of public bureaucracies and the power drive of public officials. Self-interest, imperialism, and the desire for rule frustrate loyalty and participation. It is hard to see oneself as an actor in one's own story, establishing one's own identity, when public life threatens to turn one into the thing acted upon, into a stereotype.

The imperious side of public life attracts strongly. It may grow in strength when the realities of collective life frustrate plans for the public interest or long experience turns to cynicism or the taste for power to thirst for power. As in private life, tension may be resolved in creative or destructive ways. The most obvious danger is triumph of tyrannical forms of public life. The unacceptability of that solution is evident. But ignoring the thirst for power is as perilous. Those who wrote the American Constitution understood this. Appreciating the importance of civic virtue and the attractions of public service, they also understood the necessity of "auxiliary precautions."

But there is another danger in stressing the virtues of public life, that is, its tension with private life. Even the proper attractions of public life conflict with the values of private life. Satisfaction derived from public interactions obscures capacity for intimacy and self-reflection. Many spouses (especially wives) have to remind their counterparts of their private responsibilities. This reminder raises the primary subject of this conclusion.

Tensions Between Private and Public Life

I have described at numerous points how public and private life complement one another. Public narratives intertwine with private; private virtue supports public; political language braids private with public concerns; institutions like the family look both outward and inward. Though all of this is true and must not be forgotten, in this section I want to emphasize the strains between private and public life, the lines of force putting them at odds. Political concerns become most relevant along these lines of force.

When public and private life harmonize, their borders are mostly invisible, like the borders between counties in the United States. Political issues seldom arise; there are no disputes to resolve; laws need not be passed. Life goes on, and it is unimportant to the participants whether they are in the public or private realm. There is tremendous value to this kind of harmony of interests and principles. Without it, ordinary life would grind to a halt. If every relation between public and private were fraught with dramatic tension, the strain would be unbearable. Crisis management or, failing that, open warfare would be the order of the day. Such conflict is frequent enough even under prevailing conditions of harmony. Absence of these conditions makes life (public and private) intolerable.

I do not wish to ignore or minimize the importance of the complementary aspects of public and private life. Politics, however, particularly concerns matters where issues are at stake, where there is conflict or disagreement, and where differences of point of view dominate. So a political theory of public and private must focus explicitly on their tensions.

Inherent tension between the two proceeds from the fact that *part* of the definition of each negates the other. Private life, in the form of privacy claims, means the right to resist incursion by various public realms. Public life stands outside and mediates, indeed enforces, settlements of claims among competing private interests. Moreover, the public must assert its prerogatives against the intrusion of illegitimate private claims. So stress is built into the association. Denying the stress lets potential conflict get out of hand. Yet overcoming the stress could only mean destruction of either public or private life, as their original equipment includes potential tension.

Public-private tensions take two general forms with many variations. First comes tension between the private person and the public. The public here can be any type of public, from a small group (public from the perspective of the person) to a business, a neighborhood, a local government, an economic system, or the national political system. The inclusive and exclusive sides of individual private life frequently conflict with these publics. Individuals claim rights to privacy from prying family eyes. Employers ask potential employees intrusive questions about their private lives. The economic system makes difficult certain ways of life—poetry, for example. Pacifists make claims against laws compelling payment of taxes for military spending. All of these examples come from situations in which there are legitimate competing claims on each side. Conflict also occurs through illegitimate claims on one side or the other (or sometimes both). Government agents employ torture to obtain confessions. Business makes an accepted practice of expense-account cheating. Individual property-owners demand special favors from building inspectors. All of these legitimate and illegitimate claims exemplify the inherent tension between the private person and various kinds of publics.

The second form of tension between private and public life features conflict between private groups and various publics. The McCarthy hearings, for example, placed pressure on persons faced with public punishment unless they testified against their friends. Families confront public institutions in zoning cases and fire-insurance claims. Most poignantly, family demands encounter public needs in hostage situations. Again, imagining confrontations between private groups and public bodies involving legitimate and illegitimate claims on one side or the other (or both) is hardly difficult.

Therefore, tension between public and private must be a permanent feature of the political landscape. This strain even becomes part of the internal life of each realm. Certain tensions internal to the private realm, mysteries of evil and pathologies of privacy, call for public intervention—for example, child abuse. Similarly, the public world reveals its own internal tensions, its inordinate demands, summoning private counterweight—for example, the exclusionary rule in search and seizure cases. The lines of tension run in multiple directions and cross each other at sensitive points. Certain institutions, as I have emphasized, occupy these points—family, work, religion most especially. Thus the tensions can be examined very directly by attending to these institutions, which I shall do with religion in the next chapter.

Private life has a certain primacy over public. Their most important point of tensional intersection is the individual soul, the focus of competing claims on time, energy, attention, and commitment. The solitude of private life and the intimacy of treasured others are essential for arriving at principled resolutions of competing claims. Moreover, the conditional primacy of the private is indicated by the fact that one can legitimately opt out of politics, the purest form of public life, but one cannot opt out of self-knowledge, the purest form of private life.

Yet the primacy of private life is sharply constrained. One may not opt out of all forms of public life; exclusively private life is pathological. The claims of justice outweigh all but the highest claims of private life. This statement is obscure. Though I have said some things above about the claims of justice and the highest private things, I have not dealt with them systematically. Indeed, I shall not be able to do so over their entire range. But I hope that detailed discussion of religion in public and private life, which necessarily involves justice and the highest things, will clarify the above statement.

The very particularity of the private world constitutes its strength and weakness vis-à-vis the public and becomes a source of strain between public and private. The private world is rooted in specific persons, places, interests, stories, and traditions. Its particularity, its boundedness relative to the more cosmopolitan public, ensures that those entering or coming into confrontation with the public from private life will have different voices and interests from others so entering. These differences stimulate conflict, but they also form the basis for politics and for political justice, freedom, and participation. Yet the particularities of private life also provide shelter from the demands of public life with its drive toward consensus and conformity. By serving as a refuge from the public, private life supports public by providing temporary respite from its intense demands, a place to lick one's wounds before entering the fight again.

Private life could not do its work if it were not particular. But universal ideals and principles also have a claim against the particular. The particular traditions of a family may include child abuse. The particular angle of vision of an entrepreneur must give way to general justice. A sense of truths beyond the narrow range of family traditions leads a child to break with family. To say this is not in all cases to exalt the relative universality of the public over the particularity of the private. What I have said about the primacy of the private still holds. The universal versus the particular, however, creates another tension between public and private.

The particularity of the private, however, engenders an objection to my entire enterprise of setting public and private on different, but connected, bases and of establishing a necessary and permanent tension between them. Certain moral theories see in the universality and necessity of moral principles justification for folding the private into the public or at least for the primacy of the public. I shall argue, through a case study of one such theory, that of Hadley Arkes, the error of collapsing private life into public.[30] Arkes argues against moral relativism in favor of universal moral first principles based on the logic of moral justification. These first principles, though few, have broad sweep, being decisive in a "surprisingly large amount of cases."[31] They are set against moral subjectivity and relativism, which Arkes identifies with private moral criteria. All moral argument, he contends, must be based on moral principles and objective arguments open to the reason of all persons; therefore, moral argument must be public. Given this perspective, it is not surprising that Arkes contends that the full sweep of the law need not honor the distinction between public and private, that neither philosophical nor religious grounds for conscientious objection give reasons for exemption from draft laws, and that privacy covers legitimate acts only. Public and private are irrelevant when a wrong has been committed.[32] Indeed, Arkes's position implies that, though public and private might form a useful practical distinction in some circumstances, private life has no inherent foundation. The public subsumes the private, and any private rights or claims are public concessions.

Arkes's relentless moral logic counterbalances the kind of easy moral and legal relativism that draws sharp, fixed, and impenetrable borders between private and public life or that makes public life simply a subcategory of private interest. But Arkes goes too far, ignoring the indispensable lesson that the heart of the law is not logic, but life. For Arkes's argument not only objects to the particularity of the private, it also denies inherent value to private life as such. Private life, for Arkes, only derives value from public life, indeed from the concessions of public reason. Arkes would be on solid ground if he simply argued that the public-private distinction is not sacred, that is, that it does not *control* moral and legal principles. Instead, he advocates the moral dominance of private by public life.

Public and private do form a border, but, as I have argued, a penetrable one. The particularity of the private realm, though a weakness from Arkes's point of view, is in fact a strength. Indeed, my discussion of historicity should have made clear that public reason, though less particular than private, is also contingent. Because of inherent limitations on the ability of public order to achieve the good, it must never absorb the private. "Politics [and, I would add with reference to Arkes, law] should keep away from those matters whose privacy at the time seems most important to strengthen the individual's capacity to transcend the experience of his age and his group and to initiate experiments in humanity."[33]

The odd place of prudence in Arkes's argument reveals the argument's limitations, particularly for one who claims the Aristotelian mantle. Arkes is not sufficiently sensitive to the distance between first principles and concrete situations. Though he acknowledges briefly the importance of prudence,[34] that virtue makes few appearances in the second and largest part of his book, which is given over to discussing specific moral and political issues in detail. If ever a discussion cried out for prudence, judgment, or practical wisdom, this is it, but these ideas seldom surface in Arkes's analysis. Indeed, he says little about any virtues, certainly not those crucial in linking public and private life, such as tolerance, civility, responsibility, prudence, and judgment. And there is nothing about the tragedy of public and private life.

The absence of these concepts points to the weakness of a theory that ignores the distinction between, yet interpenetration of, private and public. Because he subsumes the former into the latter, Arkes is largely blind to these fundamentally political and moral concepts. A theory such as the one I have developed, which recognizes both the particularity and the universality of moral reasoning in public and private, necessarily makes a prominent place for the concepts ignored by Arkes. Ironically, Arkes imitates the liberals he so vehemently criticizes. For one of the goals of liberalism was to place passion and interest in the private realm and reason in the public, and then to define the terms on which private interests might enter the public. It was this effort that spawned moral relativism and contributed to the strange haunting of the public world by excluded passions.[35]

So, I contend, public and private are distinct realms of life, but related partly through harmony and partly through tension. Their relations are multidimensional. Language, particularly political language, virtue, narrative, and institutions are the principal features defining the border between their worlds. These features are also the principal focuses of tension and of commerce between the two territories. Yet, as I have argued, the essential question to ask with respect to tension is how it is resolved. Though tensions such as those between public and private are never finally resolved, they must have periodic release. So far I have not addressed this vital issue in any detail.

It is beyond my capacity to examine the issue in general or in all of its possible, or even its important, manifestations. For the issue arises wherever substantive commerce between public and private occurs. Therefore, I shall attempt to address tension resolution in detail in one crucial area of intersection, religion. For religion, as I have suggested, is one of the most important stations on the border of public and private life. Sometimes it seems to facilitate peaceful commerce between the two, constituting a point of mutual support and complementarity. At other times, religion is a lightning rod for strife.

Religion at the Border

Direct implications for public and private life flow from the meaning of religion. Earlier I argued that language is one of the important means for shedding the illusion that the world revolves around the self. Religion contributes to this struggle by generating private and public language orienting self to the transcendent. Even though a religious person may believe that she has a special relation with the sacred, she at least knows that she is not the sacred. If the world revolves around her, it is only with the permission of the divine. Not major progress in shedding illusion, but some progress.

Religious language helps define various terms that arrange private and public life, that establish relationships between self and other. The idea of "illusion," for example, is filled with religious meaning in Hinduism and Buddhism. "Nation" and "people" contain pivotal religious value in Judaism. "Duty," "self," "body," "family," and "community" possess religious denotations and connotations in Christianity and other religions. In other words, religion suffuses the very language defining the private–public border.

Religion similarly effects virtue and narrative on the boundary. When religion shapes character and virtue, it plays a public and private role. Analogously, religions embrace narrative traditions, stories of founders, heroes, and villains, shaping the private and public lives of believers. Religion does not correspond to either the public or the private, but intersects their border in different places. Yet narrative, virtue, and character only establish religion's indirect public consequence. What kind of direct public role does religion play? And how does religion contribute to tension and resolution of tension on the border between private and public life?

We cannot make too many presumptions at the outset. As Luckmann warns, both those inclined toward traditional religious belief and those antagonistic to it must moderate their passions in order to understand the social place of religion. "One must not avoid seeing [the contemporary trend of religion] because one clings to traditionalist religious illusions. Nor must one ignore its implications because one may be inspired by secularist optimism."[36]

The passions of religion are real. We cannot ignore them in calmly, rationally, academically discussing religion and politics. Religion exists, among other things, to control, channel, direct, release, and moderate passion. Religious passions sometimes create tensions and explode in destruction on the private-public border. Its partisans must not ignore this side of religion. (Its opponents never do.) Yet border conflict may come from other passions, from individual emotions or political battles. Sometimes religion's ability to sublimate emotion, to channel passion, to stimulate forgiveness can resolve battles on the private-public border and clarify the boundaries and the kinds of commerce across them that helps to maintain peace and justice. The opponents of religion should not ignore these qualities. (Its supporters never do.)

8
The Distinctiveness of Religion

Government seems to me a part of religion itself, a thing sacred in its institution and end. For if it does not directly remove the cause, it crushes the effects of evil and it is as such (though a lower yet) an emanation of the same divine power that is both author and object of pure religion. . . . But that is only to evil doers, government itself being otherwise as capable of kindness, goodness, and charity as a more private society. They weakly err that think there is no other use of government than correction which is the coarsest part of it. Daily experience tells us that the care and regulation of many other affairs, more soft and daily necessary, make up much of the greatest part of government and [this] must have followed the peopling of the world had Adam never fell and [it] will continue among men, on earth, under the highest attainments they may arrive at by the coming of the blessed Second Adam, the Lord from Heaven.

—William Penn, *Preface to the Frame of Government of Pennsylvania (1682)*

Penn's rather sanguine view of government assimilates it to both religion and private life. Yet there is something to be said for it. Government does outlaw (some) sin, and it does regulate (not always softly) matters of food, clothing, and shelter. Government acts on the border of private and public life, yet it forms its own border with religion. In this chapter I shall examine these borders in some depth, mapping their contours and the legal and illegal transactions across them.

In the first section I consider contributions that religion can make to public life that are unique to religion, particularly respecting sin and evil, the fear of death, and the fragility of public and private life. The second and third sections take up the contributions of religion to political life and the contribution of politics to religion, respectively. Throughout this chapter I am concerned to demonstrate how keeping religion and politics in connection through tension balances the strengths and weaknesses of each. In particular, a life of tension avoids four perversions that occur when the tension is relaxed. Religion without the tension afforded by political life degenerates at one extreme into a fanaticism that tries to bring heaven to earth and at the other extreme into disengagement from the world ("pie in the sky in the sweet bye and bye"). Politics without religion exhibits analogous debasement. At one extreme is a "realism" that rejects all hope of principled reform; at the other a political fanaticism as dangerous as religious, in which earth must become heaven.

The Unique Contributions of Religion

Religion is a constant reminder of the unity of public and private, but also of the boundary between them. Private and public life need each other, but they are different realms. The validity and the distinctive character of each contributes to a healthy society. Religion affirms the public–private distinction, but also the need to cross the boundary.

As a system of belief, behavior, and emotion relating to a reality beyond human control or achievement, religion suggests to the sensitive participant in culture just what is at stake in public–private border controversies. Culture is first of all public; its beliefs, customs, traditions, stories, and emotions are the common possession (willy-nilly) of citizens who need share no significant private life. Culture's material and spiritual goods attract and (sometimes, perhaps often) repel, just because they are part of a deeply ingrained heritage.

Because religion suggests that ingrained culture is not divine (at the most, it is the direct will and creation of the divine), religion more directly than other systems of value insinuates the tension between culture and something higher than culture. Although religion is linked to culture and frequently coopted by it, the "higher" religions and religions with more reflective traditions emphatically suggest tension with culture. The inherent dynamic of religion's orientation to a transcendent source of being, independent of human control, opens the path toward cultural conflict. As much as culture takes on itself divine color, it cannot hide its human roots.

Though the tension between the divine and the mundane sometimes manifests itself as stress between private and public life, the individual person, where the competing attractions of culture and the sacred intersect, is the locus of tension.[1] Machiavelli, for example, denouncing Christianity's public effects, clearly understood that the strain was not between private religion (Christianity) and public good (the republic), but between the different public demands of Christianity and the republic. Machiavelli rejected Christianity for its cultural consequences. The unique perspective of religion reveals the person as a field of cross-cutting tensions between the divine and culture in private and public life.

Political and economic conditions can pose a threat to spiritual and mental health. The converse also holds. Spiritual conditions can threaten political and economic health. These threats have no fixed source. Their origin may lie in private life or in public—in particular individuals or in culture itself. Martin Marty expresses well the private and public dynamics of (particularly Western) religion:

> Religion in the Western world delicately balances its private and public faces. The impetus of biblical thought is to keep the two in tension. People will not respond to the sacred or be faithful to what they experience as the divine if they do not find their inmost needs addressed. . . .
> The religion that has predominated in the West, however, . . . has always seen that purely private faith is incomplete. Worse than that, because it serves only the purposes of those who hold it and comes under no scrutiny of judgment, it can easily become idolatrous.[2]

We must go beyond Marty's insight, however, to see that these are not separable concerns, for the demands for private meaning and public interchange take place in the same persons and the same religious institutions. Private sorrows and public conflicts compete for attention in the same hearts, as do religious principles and economic realities. Religion furnishes distinctive insight into these tensions.

Although I emphasize cross-cutting tensions within the human heart, I do not mean to suggest an individualism focused on how persons experience and cope with such tensions. Private and public groups, too, such as families, associations, neighborhoods, businesses, legislatures, and courts experience these tensions as well and seek collective resolutions.

Surprisingly, as sensitive as he is to the interrelatedness of public and private, Michael Walzer misses this point. Though *Spheres of Justice* is remarkable in explicitly considering divine grace in a theory of justice, Walzer devotes only six pages to grace and seems to regard its place as (theoretically) simple.[3] Walzer's realm of grace is a purely autonomous sphere, and he invokes the metaphor of the wall of separation. This sphere is autonomous because he regards it as a matter of freedom, of individual choice. Therefore, as I read him, the realm of religion is purely private.

Walzer recognizes that parents try to pass grace to their children, and this fact is for him the proof of its privacy, for sons and daughters often choose not to believe. But religion is not simply the private choice of belief or unbelief, acceptance or rejection of grace. It comprises as well the consequences, private and public, of belief and unbelief. Moreover, other spheres of life affect religion, shaping the content and manner of belief and unbelief. To say that grace is purely private is to ignore religions such as Islam in which the idea of purely individual or familial grace would be quite foreign. Moreover, even in religions that tend strongly toward privatized grace, such as evangelical Christianity, this grace often has been a primary motivator to public action. Indeed, public action can seem to be demanded if the individual is to remain in a state of grace.

Because religion touches (sometimes unconsciously) the core of a believer's character, it bears on the moral boundaries of public and private life. The role of politics in creating social peace and justice depends on personal interior peace and justice. Government and politics can contribute, as Penn argued, but it cannot bring men and women to virtuous living or inner tranquility, for they cannot prescribe all virtuous actions or proscribe all vice. Moreover, political life cannot bring final beatitude.

Because it influences moral virtue and individual well-being, therefore, religion can powerfully assist the state by inculcating and nourishing a moral foundation for culture. Yet this role is easily misunderstood and often converted into either theocracy or civil religion.

One final general consideration is in order at this point. Although I have stressed the intersection of religion and public life, religion, nevertheless, fundamentally reminds us of the limits of politics and of the nonequivalence of politics and public life. Because religion intends transcendence, it relativizes and thereby limits all other spheres of activity, including politics. Religion points to a sovereignty beyond state sovereignty.[4] In the American tradition, for example, the Bible has reminded us "that public spirit will always be opposed by private interest," that law and coercion must supplement public virtue and participation, and that "the larger the political society, the greater the tension between body and spirit, private feelings and public duties."[5] Religion need not disdain interests, but it urges elevation of interests. For example, Jesus makes "You shall love your neighbor as yourself" the second great commandment. Self is not denied, but the interests of the neighbor are to be elevated to the same level of intensity that we innately feel for our own. The elevation transforms them. Thus, religion can recognize self-interest in politics, but work to transform it. There is an analogy here to Tocqueville's comments about "interests rightly understood" in an educated democracy.

Yet we must remember that religion points resolutely to life beyond politics. Interests elevated or transformed do not equal salvation. Religion reminds us that public problems and their solutions are not entirely political. Indeed, the distinctive contribution of religion to public and private life, to individuals and to culture, is to refer them to what is beyond politics. The following pages discuss some of these things—sin, evil, death, tragedy, forgiveness, promise, and trust—and how they appear on the border between public and private life. Because their connection with religion on the private side is nearly universally acknowledged, I focus principally on their public appearance.

Sin and Evil in Public and Private Life

A persistent delusion in contemporary culture, an emanation of Philip Rieff's "therapeutic society,"[6] makes obsolete sin and evil, and therefore guilt. The delusion pervades the contention that education and counseling, plus appropriate doses of technology and money, can cure major social and psychic ills. AIDS, teenage pregnancy, urban decay, drug abuse, joblessness and homelessness, crime, and racial and sexual discrimination could be cured or greatly alleviated if society, and the particular individuals most concerned, could only receive appropriate education and compassionate counseling and if enough money and high technology were devoted to solutions.

This delusion cuts across the public-private boundary, involving weight-loss fads, psychological nostrums, and self-help books as well as public programs. By labeling as delusions such approaches to social and personal problems, I do not contend that education, counseling, technology, and material resources are irrelevant. Rather, I insist that we acknowledge, privately and publicly, the role of sin in creating and perpetuating what are as much evils as ills. Attacking them requires methods suitable to combating sin as well as the methods for fighting ignorance, psychic disturbances, and lack of material resources.

What we call something reveals our sense of its causes and suggests how we think it might be attacked. To speak of social disturbances or crises as ills suggests medical and psychological causes and the ministrations of science, technology, and counseling. The language of problems suggests rational solutions. To speak of them as evils suggests religious or philosophical perspectives, and to speak of crimes suggests legal, penal, and coercive approaches. I submit that to understand and attack social ills–problems–evils–crimes requires all these perspectives. No single approach suffices, certainly not the rationalistic educational-technological.

Religion reminds us of the role of human volition, and the sins and crimes stemming from it, in creating and perpetuating personal and social evil. There is a clear connection between this point and my earlier assertion of the role of religion in promoting the morality necessary for public peace and justice.

I do not argue that all religions stimulate the sense of sin or that they do so in the same ways or to the same degree. But certainly Judaism, Islam,

Christianity, Hinduism, and Buddhism recognize the deep roots of sin in the orientations of the human heart, and they contain stories explaining its origin, accounts of how to resist it, and rituals and disciplines for cleansing the soul.[7] Some methods are more passive than active, but the point is that private sin is recognized, as are its public consequences, and that public sin is also recognized with its private consequences. These religions discern not only "moral man and immoral society," but the reverse as well.

Guilt effectively links public and private life. To acknowledge guilt is to make contact with a world outside one's own delusions. Guilt ties the agent to the world through admission of the consequences of choice. Those without a properly proportioned sense of guilt (I am not, therefore, speaking of those burdened by generalized guilt and a sense of worthlessness) lack firm connection to the world. They float through it like jellyfish on the tide, taking their nutrients, heedless of their victims.

What is true of individual guilt holds for nations and other public bodies. Religious sensitivity to guilt can call the public, especially politics, to awareness of responsibility vis-a-vis citizens and to surrender delusions of innocence or grandeur. Such constitutes the public role of religious prophets. The prophet as public critic parallels the priest in the private world. (It is dangerous to reverse the two roles. The priest in public underwrites the regime; the prophet in private becomes a cynic.)

Because religion has a special link to guilt and sin, the public, through the state, may profitably use religious institutions to address public problems such as crime and drug abuse particularly involving guilt and shame. It should not do so by making such things matters of public sin or involving religion directly in the definition of crimes or by making the struggle against crime or drug addiction religious crusades. Rather, the proper role of religion lies in rehabilitation efforts, service to victims of crime and drug abuse, and preventative education programs. I have specifically in mind here public employment of chaplains in prisons, youth detention centers, drug-abuse treatment programs, and the like. I also have in mind public funding of private religious (on the same basis as nonreligious) youth programs, detoxification and recovery programs, counseling centers, halfway houses, and literacy and job training programs.

Fear of Death

If the public, especially political, significance of religion for the sense of sin is crucial, the importance of religion in the face of death is doubly so. Evil may be accounted for, and even dismissed, in a variety of ways, but death is more difficult to deny.[8] Few deny that religion does and should deal with death, but privately. Individuals face death alone or with their families, and they deal privately or in small groups with their fears. Religion, for believers, involves the encounter with death, but what relevance is that to politics?

Public life and death are not unacquainted. Think of the public funerals of heads of state or major public figures such as Gandhi, Robert Kennedy, and Martin Luther King, Jr. These are occasions, heavily laden with religious and political symbolism, in which the public ritually and collectively confronts death. Even more pointedly, think of the significance of the public display of Lenin's corpse and of the political crises in Argentina occasioned by disputes over the embalmed body of Eva Peron.[9]

These illustrations pale, however, before the fact, not simply that polities hold the power of life and death, but that they claim legitimately to hold it. In the modern world at least, only the political order is allowed, legitimately, to take life through capital punishment and to wage war. This latter activity involves ordering citizens not simply to risk their lives, but also to take life. Moreover, polities have the responsibility to ensure that citizens are guarded as much as possible against the threat of death from starvation, drought, disease, and natural disaster, and their efforts to do so sometimes threaten the lives of citizens of other polities.

Recognition of the link between death and politics and, therefore, of the connection through religion between private and public life is not unknown in the history of political theory, but lately it has been rarely expressed. Plato, of course, saw these connections: he began and ended the *Republic* with the theme of justice and death.[10] Hobbes recognized how problematic is the sovereign's power of death. Therefore, the little-read second half of *Leviathan* on the Kingdoms of Light and Darkness binds the book's whole argument. According to Hobbes, successful political order requires readiness to die, but self-interest cannot motivate such willingness. Only religious belief can.[11]

This insight into the links between death, politics, and religion deepens earlier points about morality and sin. Reflections on public and private life apart from religion could help explain the importance of character and virtue and even motivate citizens toward them, but what about death? How, apart from religion, can one motivate a person to die?[12] Religion does deal with the private and public meanings of death, so every society, every public order, must have a religious component of some sort, for every society must deal with both dimensions of death. Natural reason and political history need, in the face of death, sacred history and supernatural religion. Hence, the excitement and the risk of religion and politics. They seek to instruct us in death.

It might be objected that this argument is merely a subtle rationalization of the utility of religion to politics. Religion is useful because it provides a way to justify a regime's life-taking. Hobbes's account is certainly open to this objection, as is mine up to this point. My response will have to be twofold, and it can only be developed over the entire course of this chapter. First, I have not yet said anything about *how* religion must interact with politics. Some ways of interaction certainly do improperly make religion the servant of politics. Mine does not. Second, I shall address explicitly the question of the utility of religion to politics in the discussion of civil religion in chapter 9.

One final thing, however, should be said about the importance of religion for death and politics. Absent religion, politics is deformed in two different ways by death. The first deformation specially tempts liberal democracy.[13] Death trumps the pursuit of happiness. Indeed, death openly acknowledged moderates the excesses of individual or collective happiness-seeking. Therefore, it moderates their deleterious impact on the poor and the marginal and on the fabric of communal cooperation and solidarity. Awareness of death may lead one to cling to life as long as possible or to insist on enjoying it selfishly; yet "I've got mine, Jack" sounds hollow when death knocks.

Religion can keep liberal societies aware of death and, therefore, of human limitation. Thus for liberal society to succumb to the temptation to relegate religion to the private sphere is to support its ready tendency to deny death. This denial unleashes liberal society's most negative inclinations. Therefore, the public-regarding, communal side of religion has a value for liberal society in counteracting these negative inclinations and directing attention to the importance of high aspiration and sacrifice. Though it might be argued that reason can substitute for religion to address the problem of death, this solution will not work. The sources of our fear of death are too deep for rational analysis.[14]

The second deformation is the path taken by nationalist and totalitarian ideologies. Ultimately, the power of life and death needs legitimation, which pseudo-religious ideologies seek to provide. Replacing the sacred with the trans-human value of the nation, history, the race, or a utopia, they seek to justify death in the present in the name of these values. The proportion of believers in a society is always large and relatively constant. When they cease to believe in the gods, they make gods of what they believe in. The horrible costs of this route in human life and dignity are only too well known. The desire of ideologies to become substitute religions is nowhere more powerful than in the encounter with death. The political role of religion might be justified for no other reason than to guard against totalitarianism. Yet religion itself has been put to the service of totalitarian and authoritarian justification of regimes of death. This service usually takes the form of theocracy or an oppressive civil religion, which I shall explicitly criticize in the final chapter.

The Frailty of Public-Private Life

The death of a citizen is both a public and a private event because it sets the limit to character development. How and when a citizen dies says something about her identity, providing a unique perspective from which to view her virtues and character and their public implications. Virtues and stories make sense of death; abstract moralities cannot. Thus death puts an end, tragic or fitting, to public and private responsibilities. Death is also the greatest teacher of the fragility of public and private life and especially of the bonds between them.

Friendships die not only when friends die, but also when friends hurt or neglect each other. But public bonds also are frail. Betrayal, violence, and rampant self-interest rend polities as well as marriages. The links between public and private are fragile. Conflicts over the proper domain of each end in broken trust, recriminations, and hostility. New fences replace the old, broken boundaries.

None of this is surprising or uncommon. What is unique is the position of religion among the broken fragments of private and public life. Just as religion provides understanding of death, it explains the fragility of human relationships. Used to dealing with frailty, its picture of the moral order has a place for fragility and broken relationships. It channels anger and hostility; it points to new possibilities within the shards; it reconciles and forgives hurts; and it supplies justification for retaliation. No human relations, least of all those on the public-private border, offer any guarantee of solidity.

Arendt discusses movingly the brittleness of public space and how the uncertainty and irreversibility of action undermine it. Only the human capacity for forgiveness and promising overcome this frailty. Although Arendt emphasizes the secular sides of these experiences, she acknowledges their religious origins.[15] Justice too is prone to fall short. Self-interest, human weakness, natural calamities, and differential individual capacities, needs, and desires upset the temporary balances of justice, producing injustice and demands for a new balance.

In the midst of the conflict, which is frequently the violence spawned on the private/public border and in political life by the failures of justice, often only the admission of guilt—with corresponding forgiveness and promises of reform—can defuse violence and work political reconciliation. Although it is certainly possible to offer forgiveness and to make promises from nonreligious motives, historically speaking, religion—especially the religions of Judaism and Christianity—has introduced forgiveness and promise (covenant) to the public stage.[16]

The question of how, when, and in what form forgiveness may be introduced to the public stage is difficult. Appeals to forgiveness may be masks for self-interest. These appeals are also most open to rebuttals from the perspective of justice, the principal political virtue. To forgive a wrong or to give up enforcement of a contract, it is argued, will be unjust to the wronged or to the other party to the contract. Moreover, it will encourage the same old behavior that created the situation in the first place. There is no abstract answer to such objections. Sometimes justice must take precedence. Forgiveness is not always the appropriate response to a political problem. Nevertheless, appeals to forgiveness can be powerful, and they can be healing. The difficulty of making any fixed "rules for forgiveness" is illustrated by three highly publicized instances: amnesty for Vietnam-era draft evaders, forgiveness of massive Third World debt, and former House Speaker Jim Wright's impassioned appeal to end the "mindless cannibalism" in congressional ethics investigations.

Often admissions of guilt, forgiveness, and promises are smoke screens for continued pursuit of self-interest. But this fact does not detract from the deep necessity in political life of genuine forgiving and promising. Indeed, all-too-familiar deceptions generate the need for sacred support for acts of forgiving and promising. Without such roots, trust too easily gives way to cynicism. The pains of public life—conflicting interests, false promises, and false images of ourselves and others—are only too real. It is precisely the surprising power of the gift of forgiveness when it is offered and of the promise when it is kept that make it possible to keep forgiving and trusting in the face of so much evidence to the contrary. Here, according to Gilbert Meilaender, is the role for religion. "The churches and other communities of virtue do not 'possess a moral superiority' so much as they witness to the gift-like character of the good."[17]

I have spoken so far in this chapter of the vital importance of religion to public and political life. Religion uniquely deals with sin, death, and the fragility of public life. It supports and sustains the continuation of politics when evil, death, and broken promises threaten to overwhelm public life and transform it into coercion, violence, or simple self-interested manipulation. It is now time to address even more explicitly the ways in which religion and politics can interact creatively to resolve tensions on the border between private and public life.

Two (or more) forces pulling in different directions define a tension. Sometimes its stress holds things together, as with a rubber band. But sometimes it causes things to break apart, as when a spring snaps from being wound too tightly. To understand the religion-politics tension, we must define the directions in which each pulls. We must also show how tension between them permits each to work better.

Religion brings politics to awareness of the highest, lowest, and most mysterious features of life, especially of the lofty and the mysterious. Politics, better acquainted with the lowest, brings religious passion and self-assurance to awareness of the middle ground between the highest and the lowest—that is, it teaches religion the necessity and the art of compromise. Moreover, some of the highest and lowest things are already at home in politics—honor, bravery, lust for power, and the passions of blood and soil. Politics can make religion alert to these, and to their danger.

Religion pulls toward the transcendent, toward principles, virtues, ideals, and perfection. Unrestrained by tension, this religious dynamic produces fanaticism. Religious passion finds it difficult to compromise, to acknowledge how striving after perfection founders on human weakness. Politics, however, demands compromise, for the key fact of politics, especially of participatory public life, lies in confrontation with the ideas and the interests of others, with the mosaic of human frailty and plurality.

Just as religion would avoid compromise, politics would avoid righteousness. Politics pulls toward the vague middle ground, toward indifference and cynicism. Left to itself, politics seeks the easy, painless way. High principles make for difficult political choices, for it is painful to confront higher things, to acknowledge the possibility of something better and to accept the discipline necessary to reach it. Religion in public life can teach politics about the higher things and stimulate, even embarrass, politicians and citizens to discover them.

The tension produced by these conflicting natural tendencies defines their relationship as both competitive and cooperative. The danger of misunderstanding the relationship between religion and politics comes when we forget that it must include *both* cooperation and competition. When the tension is lost, the two either fly apart or, worse, collapse together. The latter is the world's too frequent condition. As Roland Robertson observes, "Religion is being politicized and politics (as well as economics) is being sacralized intrasocially and globally."[18] The Unification Church worldwide and fundamentalism in the United States and Iran currently exemplify politicized religion; sacralized politics takes form in totalitarian ideologies. Both of these forms of lost tension obscure the border between religion and politics. These territories should remain distinct but mutually interactive. The next section considers the way religion should act upon politics; the following section the way politics should act upon religion.

What Religion Teaches Politics

In a skeptical and relativistic age religion challenges easy moral relativism and indifference. Religion contests the cynical and egoistic political consequences of this relativism by advancing in public debate principles claiming sacred roots.

Thus, despite the exaggerated claims and extreme lengths to which some religious groups have gone in policy debates, it is healthy for a political system (and for citizens) dangerously close to "interest-group liberalism" to face demands for unilateral disarmament, for feeding the hungry and taking care of the sick, for full employment, action against pornography, cessation of abortion, and an end to capital punishment. The debate sparked by religious campaigns to confront the political system with these issues is uncomfortable, but the debate at least revives substantive political issues and principles and pushes fundamental questions of justice and peace to the forefront of attention in a system characterized by self-satisfied, cynical boredom with any issues but self-interest.[19]

The abortion debate in its present form has certainly been shaped by the political activity of religious institutions, though not only by them even on the "pro-life" side. Yet the role of such institutions is not to be regretted, still less ruled unconstitutional. No matter what position one takes on abortion, the key point here is that serious debate, even sharp disagreement, over issues of life and death and of fundamental justice are the most genuine stuff of politics. Prior to the *Roe v. Wade* decision in 1973, that public debate had hardly begun. To make abortion a matter of constitutional law was, in the context of American political and legal culture, to take it out of the realm of public discussion. The involvement of religious groups, particularly on the anti-abortion side, has performed an important role in challenging the tendency of professional politics to relegate such issues to specialized agencies and away from public life.

Abortion is fundamentally a public issue to be addressed by public, political means for good historical reasons. The state has increasingly reserved to itself questions of life and death and the definition of the rights of persons (for example, war, revenge, child abuse, and rights to employment and enjoyment of public accommodations). Therefore, government has the duty to define and to protect life and to establish the principles of due process according to which life may be taken.[20] To say this is not to say that the abortion debate should be conducted in religious terms. Far from it; indeed, that debate must be conducted in public terms of life and death. The role of religion has been to make sure that the debate takes place. The temptation, and the potentially destructive role, of religion will be to carry that debate out religiously. My earlier discussion of the role of religious language should make clear that allowing or restricting abortion should not be debated in the language of biblical norms or religious beliefs, but in the public language as much as possible. Politics must begin to teach religious groups how to do this, even as such groups forced politics to confront abortion.[21]

Neither politics nor political theory is to judge the truth of competing religious claims. I recognize that religious groups disagree on matters of principle and policy and that they themselves pull in multiple directions. However, even their advocacy of conflicting principle is vital, for genuine public life depends on matters of character and virtue and pertains to substantive issues over which citizens create a common good out of conflicting interests and principles. Politics must not deplore or dismiss religious competition, but rather moderate its worst passions.

The approach to justice in the 1986 pastoral letter on the economy issued by the United State Catholic Conference illustrates my point. I do not intend to analyze the strengths and weaknesses of that statement or the debate it occasioned, or even to reveal my agreement or disagreement with its positions. The point I wish to emphasize is Gerald M. Mara's contention that the letter contains an account of justice superior to such liberal, political treatments as Rawls's, for the letter addresses the urgency of justice.[22] Political theorists' accounts of justice tend to be abstract and categorical. They supply no urgent motivation to act against injustice. The bishops' statement is substantive and sensitive to historical conditions. Moreover, it furnishes for those who agree with it urgent motivation to political action.

The bishops' theory of justice is not philosophically unchallengeable. Yet their account of justice, like that of the Hebrew prophets, resonates with the passion for justice. A religious dimension advances in policy debate the passion for justice neglected by "neutral" theories and interest-group politics. Justice touches the feeling heart as well as the calculating head, and religion can push the public to take that fundamental emotion into account. The story of Naboth's vineyard (1 Kings 21) is more effective than the difference principle in motivating ordinary citizens to reflection on justice in income differences and land tenure.

Similarly, the radical activity of those religious groups and individuals acting outside ordinary politics—such as Gandhi, Mother Teresa, Dorothy Day, Mitch Snyder, and Dietrich Bonhoeffer—can goad formal, bureaucratic political institutions to take account of a higher spirit and a good greater than rules, efficiency, and the letter of the law.[23] Sparks often fly in such encounters, just as they fly in the creative tension of a steel blade pressed against a sharpening stone. They force liberal society to address substantively issues such as civil rights and abortion that it would rather handle procedurally.

Let me advance an even more controversial example of the kind of contribution religion can make to politics in a liberal democratic society, one itself in some tension with the preceding paragraph. Though religious groups may take obedience too far, liberal society needs religion's lessons in obedience. For liberalism tries to abolish obedience by making the legitimacy of rules depend on the satisfaction of interests. Rousseau, no liberal but here in the liberal spirit, wanted to find a way to make it possible in civil society to obey only oneself.

Liberalism tends to undermine the public grounds of obedience, leaving it only, for example, for the private life of the family. Even in private life, however, increasing public requirements for procedural rights hedge obedience. Yet, as Milgram's experiments show, a deep human propensity to obey authority remains even in liberal society.[24] "Blind" obedience, frowned on by liberal principles, goes underground and emerges in strange places, not least of which are cultic forms of religion, such as that of the reverend Jim Jones, and claims of obedience to demons in cases of strange, often violent behavior. Though I realize that these brief illustrations do not constitute proof, traditional Western religions could perform a public service in reemphasizing discipline and obedience with respect to religious principles, rules, rituals, and behavior. Bringing obedience above ground makes it more likely to find appropriate outlets.

Oddly enough, obedience in certain contexts can contribute significantly to public debate. "Obey" derives etymologically from the Latin *ob audire* meaning "to hear." To obey is first of all to listen to another, to enter into a relationship in which it is vital to hearken to the heart and will of another, rather than solely one's own. Generally speaking, religious traditions emphasize this kind of listening to certain voices—god, prophet, and religious leader.

Obedience in this sense has two important consequences. First, it can inculcate a habit of listening to others that becomes useful in public discussion. Though such discussion is not about obedience and should not be a matter of obedience, a habit of listening to the heart of another makes contribution to such discussion. Second, a habit of obedience need not mean unquestioning submission, especially to political authorities. "We must obey God rather than man" is an important refrain for political life. Moreover, it is precisely the habit of ordinary obedience that makes civil disobedience an important political means of challenging regimes. The willingness of fundamentally obedient persons publicly to disobey law and to go to jail forcefully raises to consciousness the substance of what is at issue in, for example, segregation laws or nuclear warheads. Religious obedience frequently motivates civil disobedience.

If it enters policy debates on politics' terms, religion gives up its claim to uniqueness, becoming one more interest group trapped within the limited alternatives offered by modern ideologies. It must never completely surrender to political language or forget its own discourse. To accept these alternatives would be to resolve the tension between religion and politics by surrender. It would abandon the cold, lonely marches of religion's border with politics for the warmth of the political capitol. I contend, on the other hand, that religion must maintain its claim to a truth higher than politics. This perspective does not mean that politics can or should judge that truth, only that religious claims should force politics to a higher level than it otherwise would discover. Its truth claims do not relegate religion to the private sphere. The proper ground of these claims is the public-private border, not the heartland of private or of public life.

This argument suggests that religious persons should approach politics from their particular faith perspectives, from their own truth-claims. Politics will water down those claims sufficiently without religious groups themselves attempting to find a lowest common denominator set of religious or moral beliefs. Religious groups become properly political and place the necessary pressure on politics when they advocate their distinctive principles on matters of public concern (this latter phrase is vital) and when they live faithfully their distinctive beliefs about the transpolitical.[25] Religious persons or groups that wish to engage political life must learn to become bilingual, to speak both the language of politics and that of their own particular tradition. To speak only one would be to succumb to the dangers of ideology or of theocracy.

Religions should not promote all of their beliefs in political debate. Doing so confuses the territory of religion with that of politics. Rather, those religious beliefs and principles that most touch public concerns—for example, justice, freedom, respect for life, peace, the place of sin, death, and the meaning of human sociability—should enter political debate in order to draw politics beyond the level where it otherwise would settle. Privatization of religion is dangerous, because it allows politics itself to become privatized and self-absorbed. As George Armstrong Kelly observes, "If privatization has pushed religion out of the public sphere, it is currently turning politics into an I-Thou relationship or a sphere of indifference."[26] Reduced to administration and interests, politics becomes as secularized and squeezed of meaning as private religion. Politics without high principles is a dull but dangerous business for anyone not driven by consuming ambition, greed, or need for recognition.

What Politics Teaches Religion

But religion without politics is also dangerous. I have previously alluded to religious fanaticism. Messianism without a messiah sweeps all principle before it. Religious persons often divide the world into two camps, fellow believers and those outside the faith. Toward the former the appropriate attitude is familiarity and community, including both affectionate feelings and (at times) discipline. Attitudes toward the latter, however, include attempted conversion, conquest and enslavement, and withdrawal. Relationships with outsiders governed solely by their lack of faith allow no public bond between believers and nonbelievers. What remains are only the deadly, dichotomous categorizations: us and them, believers and heathens, friends and enemies.

Public life creates other possibilities. The first is "stranger."[27] The fellow believer is known as one of the group, and the heathen is known through stereotypes. The stranger, however, is mysterious and unknown. He may be one of us or one of them, a potential friend or enemy. Or, the most radical possibility of all, he may just be himself, different from us, but related none the less. Public life, especially in the form of politics, requires interaction with strangers. For politics is full of strangers, people with ideas, customs, interests, emotions, and beliefs different from, and sometimes at odds with, our own. Entry into a political relationship with strangers dispels some mystery, but does not eliminate it. Strangers still remain different. Nevertheless, politics opens a middle camp between friends and enemies, and, because both friends and enemies trade with that camp, the world seems less black-and-white, the grounds of fanaticism less solid.

Indeed, politics requires everyone to spend some time among strangers and to discover their own strangeness. Politics is self-discovery as well as self-display. Believers who enter politics enter the strangers' camp and discover things about strangers and about themselves that alter their frame of reference and call for less single-mindedness, for more tolerance and civility. Ultimately, believers might even learn that they are strangers to themselves and that God is also a stranger, for the God completely known does not transcend human control. Politics can teach religion humility and the tolerance that is humility's natural partner. It may teach the believer the limits of her belief.[28]

Politics can teach religion how to live with pluralism. As religion can reconcile politics to mysterious forces beyond its control, so politics can reconcile religion to facticity, to the hard places against which the tide of religion crashes.[29] Religious ideals meet recalcitrant political reality and the strangers who live there. The principles, values, excellences, and virtues of religious life cannot suffuse public or private life with the wave of a wand or a word of blessing. Use of coercion is always a temptation for frustrated virtue, a temptation to which even the most perceptive (witness Augustine) can succumb. In authoritarian, totalitarian, or oligarchic regimes, use of coercion finds ready justification. A political regime, however, supports resistance to imposed religious ideals, blunts the weapon of coercion, and teaches religion other methods for dissemination of belief. As William Penn suggested in the headnote, coercion is the coarsest part of government; so political regimes restrict its availability.

When politics involves the encounter of strangers on a common ground where they must interact peaceably, it learns compromise. Compromise is a lesson religion too must learn, though it does not like the name and tries to find synonyms, like "prudence" or "pastoral solutions." The full excellence of religious ideals is seldom achieved. As J. Budziszewski argues, "Real excellence is apt to be a rare item, more like leaven than like flour. Cultivating the excellences will always be of the first importance, but we should also be prepared to curb and channel the flows and eruptions of passion."[30] Compromise is one way, a distinctively political way, of resolving the tensions between religious ideals and recalcitrant facts.

This role for politics allows religion to be religion; it allows all religions to advance their views strongly. Religion entering politics should not be wishy-washy. But politics and the necessity of compromise force religious groups to recognize the plurality of the political world, especially the plurality of religious groups strongly advancing distinctive views. The point is not for religious groups to compromise their principles in order to enter the fray, but for politics to force compromise at the level of policy.[31] When religious groups recognize and acknowledge both politics as a form of public life and the recalcitrant facticity of political life, they can begin, not to change their principles, but to find ways of applying them to policy that are acceptable to other citizens. They can begin to learn political civility, tolerance, and the art of compromise. They can begin to learn the subtle arts of civil rhetoric, to learn how to speak political language without abandoning their principles or their own religious language. Observe the course of Reverend Jerry Falwell in moderating his policy proposals on abortion and other agenda items of the new religious right from the late 1970s to the late 1980s.

In the previous section I used the example of the Catholic bishops' pastoral letter on the economy to illustrate the contribution religion can make to politics in introducing high conceptions of justice into political debate. Let me use the same example to illustrate what political life can teach religion. The bishops' letter is particularly vulnerable to criticism in light of the social and economic realities of modern, postindustrial society. The pastoral letter does not address these realities creatively, nor does it reflect the limitations of social and economic resources for realizing the principles of justice.[32] It fails to engage social science policy-evaluation research relevant to its recommendations for employment programs and welfare reform. It is naive on international trade issues. The passionate concern for justice that is the bishops' special contribution must meet the social realities that are politics' special concern. The relevant strangers here (as far as religious leaders are concerned) are economists, policy researchers, bureaucrats, elected officials, and political groups of the left and right. Both the passion for justice and social realities are necessary for creative policy-making.

I have frequently mentioned two fundamental dangers of public religion: religious domination of public life and the affiliation of religion with political ideology. Both dangers stem from religious passion. The first occurs when religion is able to use government as a means for realizing its vision. The second occurs when religious passion is coopted (often willingly) by a political ideology and used for the ideology's ends.

The realities of participatory politics moderate the proclivity of government and political ideology to inflame or coopt, and sometimes to be coopted by, religious passion. First, politics tames religious passion for reasons suggested above. Passion must put on decorous clothes to appear in public. Moreover, religious passion encounters the seawall of interest-group reality and of counter-passions in other religious and nonreligious groups. The garb of moderation and the confrontation with other interests and passions mean that religious passions must actually become moderate or, more precisely, seek more moderate, tame expression and more limited goals. The realities of pluralism make it less likely that government or ideologies will be able to enflame religious fervor or to be coopted by such emotions more than temporarily.[33] There are too many influences on the state for religion to dominate more than briefly.

This is as it should be. Religion should expect to be only one voice (though it actually is many) in political life. It can help to move policy in certain directions, but it cannot expect to determine the outcome of political debate.

One unfortunate, but unavoidable, consequence of the political taming of religion is that both good and bad religious passions are tempered. Politics is, in this sense, indiscriminate. Given politics' haphazard effect, what counts is the character of citizens. Ultimately, the people must separate the wheat from the chaff of religious ideals and passions.

There is no guarantee of popular virtue, but preservation of the good and discarding the bad finally depends on it. The mechanisms of public life cannot make such judgments, but only furnish the space, time, and civility needed for character to work. The many political devices for channeling passion known to the ancients and moderns are prone to fail, to lose sight of excellence.[34] Compromise itself cannot be a final ideal, for compromises must be judged better and worse. We come full circle from what politics teaches religion to what religion teaches politics. Religious vision can help to judge and call to account political compromise, keeping the aspiration toward excellence before citizen attention.

It seems to follow that, if religion is public in the ways I have specified and if it makes the political contributions I have described, then it should be admitted to political life on precisely the same terms as other groups. Yet an important consideration militates against this simple conclusion. Religion is fundamentally private as well as public. Religion is a distinct realm from politics. Inviting it too far into political territory runs the many risks of politicized religion and may produce dilution of its distinctive qualities.

Religion should not be excluded from politics, but kept at arm's length. The relationship between religion and politics should imitate that of partners in a dance of approach and flight, a ballet expressing the tension between attraction and repulsion. Neither partner must dominate, if the dance is to continue. Religion and politics challenge and test each other; that is their special dynamic.

Religion beckons from the periphery for politics to come seek its ideals; politics cajoles religion to shed its unrealistic ideals and recognize the goods of plurality, civility, and tolerance. Such transactions produce just enough knowledge for mutual repulsion. Religion knows well the temptations of power.[35] Politics recognizes the fanaticism of religion and flees it.

Religion lives with a double border: the boundary between private and public life and the boundary with politics. Life on the border is never easy, but religion should remain there. To confront politics wholeheartedly, though not to enter it fully, constitutes its political mission. To abandon either private or public life is to betray its essence.

The lines of influence between religion and politics do not run one way. Politics—and culture generally—shapes religion as much as religion shapes politics. Not every political influence on religion is beneficial. Evidently, religion can learn the worst aspects of politics as well as the best. The point is that the debate about religion and politics, and the speculations of political theorists, have neglected the positive influences in each direction, the creative tensions characterizing this encounter. The debate and the theorists have, in fact, tended to develop standard, but false solutions to the relation between religion and politics.

9
Passion and Civility:
Religion in Politics and Policy

> Know that you can have three sorts of relations with
> princes, governors, and oppressors. The first and worst
> is that you visit them, the second and better is that they
> visit you, and the third and safest that you stay far from
> them, so that neither you see them nor they see you.
> —Abu Hamid Muhammad al-Ghazzali
> twelfth century Muslim theologian

The challenge of practical politics is to combine the passion of religion with the civil tolerance of democratic pluralism. The magnitude of the challenge is drawn by al-Ghazzali's warning to believers to stay away from rulers. Princes are dangerous for the faithful, no matter how the relationship is formed. Better to avoid the entanglements of politics than to be coopted by them.

Al-Ghazzali stands as a warning, but the challenge must be accepted. Religion neither can nor should remain within the confines of private life, abandoning public business. Religion needs the influence of politics, and politics needs the challenge of religious belief. A "tensional" model of religion and politics best meets the challenge.

I shall not lay out a set of policies or a political or ideological program, but rather try to think through the most critical implications of the tension between public and private life and between religion and politics. If the argument of the book possesses validity, specific policy issues must be addressed from within particular political or religious traditions. Because principles are embedded, policy conclusions and recommendations cannot be determined by religion in general, but only by specific religious traditions. It is outside the scope of this book and the competence of its author to articulate Catholic policy on welfare reform, Jewish policy recommendations on capital punishment, or the proper Methodist approach to energy policy.

Similarly, I do not consider, except tangentially, questions of constitutional law. Occasionally, I shall have to mention a particular case or principle, but my aim is not to interpret the First Amendment. In some instances, the conclusions dictated by the argument of this book fit within contemporary constitutional interpretation; in others they do not. To the extent that separation of church and state is the guiding principle of American constitutional law, my conclusions diverge, for separation of church and state is too constrained a perspective. I shall go where the argument leads, for political theory, unlike political institutions, need not be bound by constitutional law.

What I can do, however, is address the kinds of transactions appropriate to the border area, though not the specific goods transferred or the precise exchange rates. After considering some inappropriate mixing of religion and politics, I describe the permissible political activities of religious groups.

I argue that three common models of religion and politics do not meet the principles developed in earlier chapters. Secularization is imprecise theoretically and inaccurate as a predictor of the public influence of religion.[1] Theocracy and civil religion eliminate the tension between religion and politics: theocracy by eliminating politics, civil religion by attributing religious qualities to the political order.[2] Advocates of this position forget that theocracy subtly unfolds into caesaropapism. Finally, separation of church and state has much to recommend it, but ultimately it too eliminates the religion-politics tension by allowing no transactions across their border. Moreover, it is too institutional in its focus. Public policy is never as religiously neutral as the separationist position imagines.

Kenneth Wald reminds us of a simple but highly consequential truth: "Conflict and interaction is inevitable, because the two institutions involved, church and state, each claim authority to regulate human behavior."[3] Each side often forgets this truth. Religious groups believe they have a lock on morality, giving them the right to define (and dictate) it for society as a whole. Morality is not private. Justice is a moral and political term. Religion too often forgets this. But politics also can be forgetful, ignoring important moral claims in the search for power or the rush to accommodate interests.

A tensional model recognizes the claims of each and that these claims are not fully synchronized. Yet their tugging and straining can keep each wary of stale dogmas, provide a critical distance on the other, and counterbalance totalitarian temptations on either side.[4] Religion in its relation to politics is certainly not the only point of tension in civil society. There is indeed a tension among the ideals of participation, loyalty, and privacy inherent in the Western idea of citizenship itself. As H. Mark Roelofs argues, "The citizen, in our Western heritage, is held to be both a public person and a private person, to be both in and yet also out of society."[5] The impact of faith on the ordinary demands of citizenship reinforces this creative tension. Indeed, the history of the Christian faith in the West has helped to produce this tension.

To this extent the separation model has validity. A tension between religion and politics can only exist in a culture in which there is some degree of institutional specialization of religion, in which sacred world views are partially differentiated from the rest of society, specifically from political power. The "church" in the Western tradition represents, in Luckmann's words, an "extreme and historically unique case of institutional specialization of religion."[6] Such specialization creates, in a situation of religious pluralism, an especially likely context for creative tension. Creative tension, however, does not occur only in Christian societies with institutionalized churches and a high degree of separation of church and state. Ancient Judah had neither; yet the prophetic office was sufficiently separated from priesthood and kingship to challenge rulers in fundamental ways.

False Solutions to the Issues of Religion and Politics

From one point of view my reflections concern the legitimacy of religion's involvement in politics. At the same time, they concern the legitimacy of politics itself. Political legitimacy today is problematic because the boundaries of public and private life are confused. Giving the state the right to intervene in certain areas of life—reproduction, say, and moral education—disturbs those who regard these as private matters and pleases those who regard them as vital public issues. Some regard the appearance of religion on the political scene as timely, for it might yield the moral and cultural legitimacy needed by modern politics. Others, however, though recognizing that religion in the past has addressed the question of political legitimacy, regard it as improper in a secular society. Therefore, they assign religion to the private realm, preventing it from addressing the question of legitimacy.

The problem thus presented resolves itself into this: on what grounds does religion, particularly in the form of a church, legitimately concern itself with politics, and on what grounds does politics legitimately concern itself with issues of transcendent importance? My arguments in previous sections have not explicitly asked or answered these questions with respect to the institutionalized forms of religion. It is one thing to acknowledge the value of generalized religious principles in politics, quite another to describe the proper role of the Lutheran Church in foreign policy. The question of the relation of church to state is only part of the domain of religion and politics, but it is the most contentious. Picture the border between religion and politics as a river with currents in some places calm, in others swift and dangerous. There are shallows and deep pools, rocks, rapids, and sandy beaches. Therefore, the placement of bridges, fords, and scenic overlooks is critical. The parts of the river that pass church on the religion side and state on the political side are swift, rocky, and dangerous, because church and state are heavily institutionalized. Issues of church and state, then, present the most difficult test of the tensional model. I want to address four possible orientations to the issue of organized religion and politics, each of which has important advocates, but which are fatally flawed from the perspective I have been working out. These are: secularization, theocracy, civil religion, and separation of church and state.

Secularization

The theme of secularization, of course, is popular in journalism, religious studies, and sociology, where for a long time secularization theory represented something like the conventional wisdom. Thus the literature addressing the theme is massive and diverse. I shall not cite much of it, nor shall I try to do justice to the arguments, though some of the works I shall cite can be consulted for reference to the fuller debate. I shall also not deal with the empirical questions of whether secularization is really occurring or whether this nation or that represents an exception to secularization. Rather, I take up here only the question of whether secularization represents the proper relation between religion and politics. Such a view has been advocated as best both for politics and religion.

Secularization has widely variant uses and broad referents. It might be thought of as religious decline (either decline in individual religiosity or in religious institutions) or as religious transformation from church-oriented to individual-oriented religiosity stressing autonomy and self-realization. Whichever is meant, there are four aspects of secularization.[7] First, secularization involves institutional differentiation. Religious institutions are detached from other institutions and confined to those areas of life, usually considered private, most directly concerned with the sacred. Second, pluralism presents to religion competing validations of different ways of life, individual or collective. Third, the world is "disenchanted" and rationalized. Means–end rationality triumphs. Fourth, the self is privatized and identity located in the private sphere.

Diverse forces account for these developments (to the extent that they really are characteristic of modernity).[8] Religious pluralism itself, the diversity of religious groups, suggests withdrawal of religion into its own sphere. Liberal political thought also advocates differentiation. Technological forces, representing positivistic, scientific methodology, pervade business, academy, media, and politics, displacing religious perspectives. Finally, modernity's individualism suggests that matters of fundamental belief are the prerogative of the individual person, to be decided in the privacy of heart and mind. As Bryan Wilson says, "It is the increasing dominance of the intellectual, scientific, technical, and practical over the emotional and moral which is the basic premise of the inherited model of secularization."[9]

Secularization may be viewed as a force within religion as well as a separation of religious institutions from others. In this form, secularization supports religion becoming more and more private as public and private life increasingly diverge. I have alluded to this idea previously. Here I want to focus on its advocacy.

One major problem with the theory is that the idea of secularization within religion seems to take two different and contradictory forms. The first form, especially advocated by some religionists, views secularization as a purification of religion. Religion, in this view, has been historically contaminated by its alliances with politics and culture. Power, wealth, duplicity, bureaucratization, and a host of other evils have corrupted the true spirit and purpose of religion, which is to orient the individual to the sacred. Accretions of culture interfere with that task. Once secularization of society is complete, religion can serve as an alternative (private) culture where emotion can flourish as a refuge from the desiccated rationalism of the public world. This idea recalls the theme of religion as a refuge from liberal political culture.

In the other view of secularization, however, secularization within the churches means that religion itself takes on the forms of modern culture— that is, it becomes more rationalistic, more organized and bureaucratic, more individualistic, and more formal. If these internal developments seem paradoxical, they only reflect the paradoxes of secular culture. In this second view, religion is secularized because it mirrors secular culture.[10] If secularization means the invasion of religion by secular culture, how can religion serve as a refuge from that culture?

Another problem is that secularization theory is usually expressed in linear form. Secularization is modern and irreversible. Evidence is substantial that modernized societies lean toward the secular, at least in the sense of religion being differentiated with institutional religion declining in importance, and that the more modern a society, the less important institutional religion. Yet there is little reason to believe that this is only a modern phenomenon or that it is irreversible. Ahlstrom, for example, points out that the church of the late Middle Ages and the Renaissance was itself highly secularized, in the sense of performing secular functions and of being in its internal life "worldly."[11] Can it really be said that, say, the Episcopal Church is more internally secularized today than the Catholic Church of the late Middle Ages? Moreover, nations can turn from the path of modernization and secularization to theocracy, as the case of Iran suggests.

Finally, secularization may very well be self-limiting, a normal part of the cycle of religious group development. Churches lose their vitality as they become too worldly; then they split or transmute through revival into more sectlike, less worldly groups. And then back again.[12] Secularization theory also runs into America, and a good deal of the literature attempts to explain the seeming exception of America to modernization leading to secularization. America is arguably the most modern nation, but also the most religious, at least institutionally speaking, in the developed world.[13]

None of this is particularly original; so I have tried to say it briefly, but without (I hope) distorting the arguments. The conclusion I draw is this. First, secularization theory is too confused to provide by itself coherent grounding for recommendations about the relation between religion and politics. Its lack of specificity dooms it. Some forms of secularization theory, however, have affinities to the concept of separation of church and state. When secularization advocacy takes this form, it contains enough specificity to serve as a challenging theory of religion and politics, a theory I consider below.

Second, secularization theory attempts to solve the relationship between religion and politics by making the former private and the latter public. It confronts, then, all of the objections I have offered throughout this book to the privatization of religion and the separation of public from private life. Incoherent as it is theoretically, it is not in good enough fighting trim to meet these objections, which (mercifully) I shall not repeat here.

Nor can secularization theory answer, for all these reasons, the question of religion's legitimate involvement with politics or the legitimacy of politics itself. Two other false solutions to the relation of religion and politics, however, do tackle legitimacy head on. These are theocracy and civil religion.

Theocracy and Civil Religion

Though the section heading might suggest otherwise, these are not equivalent terms. Assessing them in the same section does not imply correspondence. Each, however, does address the issue of legitimacy, and I discuss their answers together.

Theocracy, the direct rule of society by God through divinely selected spokesmen, goes directly to the heart of legitimacy and proposes a simple solution. (When I use "theocracy" in this section, I mean also to include theonomy, the rule of society, not directly by God, but by divine law.) The political regime is legitimate because it is structured in strict accordance with God's law or, in some versions, ruled directly by him. Why should laws be obeyed? Because God is to be obeyed. Similarly, the entry of religion into politics is legitimate because God wills it.

Examples of pure theocracies or theocratic theories are difficult to find in the modern world. Saudi Arabia and Iran in different ways come very close. Israel's religious parties promote strong and growing theocratic tendencies. Solzhenitsyn's rejection of modernity in favor of Orthodox religion has a strong flavor of theocracy. In the United States, the Christian Reconstructionist Movement, which advocates rule by Christians on the basis of biblical law, is theocratic. This movement, which is relatively small and not identical with conventional fundamentalism, believes that the law given for the political and legal ordering of ancient Israel is intended by God for all peoples at all times; therefore, democracy is to be rejected as a heretical ideology.[14]

The appeal of theocratic ideas is but the reverse of the appeal of Hobbes' caesaropapism. Certainty of law and social order require clear guidance from a sovereign, human or divine. As Hobbes says:

> But seeing a commonwealth is but one person, it ought also to exhibit to God but one worship; which then it doth, when it commandeth it to be exhibited by private men, publicly. And this is public worship, the property whereof, is to be *uniform*: for those actions that are done differently, by different men, cannot be said to be a public worship. . . .
>
> And because a commonwealth hath no will, nor makes no laws, but those that are made by the will of him, or them that have the sovereign power; it followeth that those attributes which the sovereign ordaineth, in the worship of God, for signs of honour, ought to be taken and used for such, by private men in their public worship.[15]

The obvious failure of theocracy as a political theory (it also fails theologically in many religious faiths) is that it eliminates politics and public life. Theocracy is all rule, regulation, and administration. It has no place for public space, strangers, differences of idea and interest, or political language. Theocracy easily solves the problem of public legitimacy, because it eliminates the public! The interpreter of God's will or law is the only public figure; everyone else is a private person. Therefore, theocracy is clearly unacceptable as a political theory. I address it here, albeit briefly, only because it does have important modern manifestations and because it represents one end of the ideological spectrum anchored at the other by that form of secularization theory divorcing religion from all other areas of life, relegating it to an entirely separate private sphere.

The idea of civil religion, on the other hand, is popular and intellectually respectable, and it too holds promise of addressing the legitimacy problem.[16] Secularization really poses the problem of civil religion, for, according to Rousseau who seems to have coined the phrase, isolation of Christianity in the private realm leaves the *citizen* without a religion. Some kind of public religious ideas and practices are a functional necessity of politics for Rousseau, as well as for Robert N. Bellah and other civil religion advocates. Politics needs legitimacy, a "sacred canopy" to use Peter Berger's phrase, from a source outside itself; it receives it most powerfully from the sacred realm.[17] Civil religion expresses in belief, ritual, tradition, and story the sacred foundation of the political order. Religion relates to politics by (the metaphor varies) supplying it a transcendent foundation or a sacred canopy.

Civil religion attaches the characteristics of religion(such as transcendence, worth, dignity, loyalty and trust, meaning and identity, behaviors and practices) to the political order. Civil religion does not go so far as to identify the political order with the transcendent (in some forms, the ideology of nationalism; in others, theocracy), but it does place the political order in some specific relation to the divine. Civil religion is necessary because political society must cultivate loyalty and unity; neither utility nor self-interest can accomplish this. Something greater than the person, but also greater than the society, must ground loyalty and unity. Hence the importance of supplying politics with a specific relation to the divine through civil religion.

The most well-known recent version of civil religion advocacy is Neuhaus's *The Naked Public Square*.[18] Neuhaus argues, in effect, that secularization has stripped the public square of sacred legitimation, leaving only the bare clash of interests. The cause of the stripping is not a conspiracy of secular humanists, but a powerful "myth" of America as a secular society. "Religion and politics," he says, "are today engaged in a struggle over culture definition and culture formation" (132).

The central issue for Neuhaus, and, I contend, for any civil religion position, is the moral legitimation of society (chaps. 4 and 5). Society requires moral content. The fact that liberal attribution of guilt to America for the world's evils is mirrored by conservative defense of America's moral goodness, proves for Neuhaus the importance of moral backing for society. Both positions depend upon the notion of collective responsibility; praise and blame of America make no sense without a notion of shared moral responsibility, which lies at the heart of democracy. If there is any communal character to a nation-state, there must be collective responsibility. But what is the source of collective responsibility? It can only be a shared moral vision and commitment, a civil religion if you will, though Neuhaus avoids that term. Loyalty and patriotism are important as forms of piety supporting and expressing that shared vision (73ff). If the public square is naked, then there is no source higher than the community itself to judge it (76). The public square, however, cannot remain naked (chap. 5)—that is, without legitimacy—for then law would lack legitimacy. Public responsibility would be meaningless. Without religious legitimation, ersatz religions, forms of totalitarianism, move in to cloth the naked public square. Therefore, democracy needs a limited and humble civil religion, like Christianity, that admits diversity and compromise (chap. 7, esp. p. 124) in order to resist totalitarian, fanatical invasion of public life.

Neuhaus argues persuasively that the new religious right is best interpreted as an attempt to clothe the public square left naked by secularization. Though he is critical of the religious right's efforts in this respect, he appreciates their awareness of the problem and their recognition of America as a force for good in the world. The fundamental source of the problem, Neuhaus argues, is that the mainline Protestant churches that hitherto provided legitimation of public life no longer are willing, for they no longer believe in the triumph of America, of civilization, and of Christianity itself. Much of the mainline is now part of the "new class" so critical of American culture (chaps.

13–15). The religious right does believe in the ultimate triumph of Christianity, and America is the chosen vessel of the triumph. Oddly enough, both the religious right and the old Social Gospel movement share a belief in America's special role in the world, the idea of a Christian civilization matched against others to work God's will for human progress and salvation (209ff). The new religious right and liberal Protestantism each represent a curious blend of pietism and politics. The religious right takes the pietistic, salvation-oriented stance, but also wants government intervention in certain areas of life—sexuality, for example. The religious left, on the other hand, stresses individual conscience, but still wishes government intervention for its agenda on child care and income support. Neuhaus believes, however, that the fundamentalists will not successfully form a new civil religion, for the fundamentalist churches at the core of the religious right have tradition-ally been ambivalent toward America, alternatively exalting its special role in God's plan and condemning its moral corruption. Moreover, these churches possess a strong strain of individualized, privatized religion.

The most persuasive argument for civil religion's legitimation of public life flows from the case made by MacIntyre against the moral fragmentation of contemporary culture. If MacIntyre is correct about the collapse of a moral foundation for the contemporary world, then religion has been necessarily involved in this whole project at a profound level.[19] Civil religion and Neu-haus's cultural legitimacy argument constitute a response to MacIntyre's discovery. Among the moral fragments of modernity, none retain enough power to serve as a unifying or legitimating force for collective moral respon-sibility. Though religion has been thrust aside, for reasons MacIntyre men-tions, it must displace secularization and work its way back into a position of public responsibility, if the modern, democratic polity has any hope of moral legitimacy.

This argument is the whole appeal of civil religion, and it is a significant appeal containing a limited truth. Legitimacy *is* a moral problem in moder-nity; rational self-interest and abstract individualism cannot provide the required moral weight or motivation for justice and the public good. Some-thing else must morally support liberal, democratic public institutions. Per-haps religion can (must, in the strongest form of civil religion) support and nourish the moral aspirations that define law's goals. Perhaps religion can be part of the polity's public narrative, part of its stories and a source for its rituals, directing the polity from what it is to what it might, at its best, become. Perhaps religion can furnish content and inspiration for public and private virtue. And perhaps an "ordering" civil faith can take its place around the republican banquet table with the particular, "saving" faiths and contribute to the discussion of how to achieve public aspirations.[20]

In other words, the idea of civil religion responds to a real problem with a limited truth. I contend that my earlier description of religion's entry into political life from its position on the border is a fuller truth and a more adequate account of religion's contribution to politics, and vice versa. Civil religion brings religion too close to the heart of politics, reducing its necessary critical distance.

The first major problem with civil religion is precisely that it blunts religion's challenge to politics. As an honored guest at the banquet, it would be impolite of religion to criticize the food. The role of the honored guest is to speak politely to everyone, look interested, and express gratitude. Invited to the heart of politics and lulled by its religious aura, religion would simply accommodate and reflect culture as, for example, the Baptists and Methodists did during the post-Civil War era of industrialization or as virtually all the churches did with the conduct of World Wars I and II. The inability of civil religion strongly to challenge political culture is captured in the widely quoted statement of President Eisenhower that "Our government makes no sense unless it is founded on a deeply felt religious faith—and I don't care what it is."[21]

The deepest problem of civil religion, however, is that it is a cop-out. Instead of confronting religious claims directly, it relies on the utility of religion. As Hauerwas says, "We should not want to know if religious convictions are functional; we should want to know if they are true."[22] The strongest denunciation of advocating religion for its utility is Leszek Kolakowski's:

> There is something alarmingly desperate in intellectuals who have no religious attachment, faith, or loyalty proper, but who insist on the irreplaceable educational and moral role of religion in our world and deplore its fragility—to which they themselves eminently bear witness. I do not blame them for either being irreligious or for asserting the crucial value of religious experience. I simply cannot persuade myself that their work might produce the changes they believe desirable: because in order to spread faith, faith is needed, and not an intellectual assertion of the social utility of faith.[23]

Advocates of civil religion must take more seriously than they have to this point the objection that all they have shown is religion's utility, which makes a mean sort of civil faith. Indeed, my own arguments about the role of religion and politics may be open to this kind of objection.

If one of the links between public and private is character and virtue, as I have argued, then religion, again as I have argued, might have a public and political role in forming character. It might even be argued that religion deserves various kinds of public support, whatever kinds would facilitate its performing this job effectively. Yet do all religions make contributions to forming the best kind of character (or at least the kind best fitted to *this* society)? If not, we must judge between religions on political grounds. Is this something advocates of civil religion would welcome? In short, we must go beyond the utility of religion in general to the truth of particular religious claims. Moreover, religion works in mysterious ways. People leave the faiths of their youth and (sometimes) never come back. Their character may be developed in reaction against religion. How can a theory of civil religion take account of character development through rejection of private or civil religion?

Finally, why not cut out the religious middleman and go directly to character formation, or use other middlemen (e.g., the public schools)? Can it really be that only religion can form character? It might be possible to acquire the benefits of religion without its costs, if society could use secular means to accomplish the virtue-forming tasks of religion. This is the solution to the legitimacy problem offered by advocates of the separation of church and state. I shall consider this position in greater detail below.

There is another conundrum at the heart of religion's public role, one that I have not yet confronted. If religion is considered useful rather than true, then civil religion is the result of our analysis. But civil religion is fragile in three ways. First, it easily decays into worship of political society, for reasons I have suggested above. Second, it is rightly viewed as idolatrous and heretical from the perspective of the traditional faiths. Third, civil religion loses (Kolakowski's point) its power to bind loyalty and promote virtue if it is recognized for its utility rather than its truth. The more society is aware of the utility of civil religion, the less effective it becomes. On the other hand, if the public role of religion stresses its truth, then the dangers of dogmatism, coercion, intolerance, and theocracy come to the fore. Public life, especially in liberal democracy, cannot consider the truth-claims of particular religious faiths. The alternative is to look to the truth of religion in general. But there is no such thing. There are only particular religions with particular, historically contingent claims.

Where do these dilemmas leave my position on the public role of religion? First, my position advocates religious interaction with politics from the border of politics, not, as civil religion, from the heartland. My view emphasizes the tensions between religion and politics, not the legitimation religion gives to politics. Religion is freer to criticize and challenge politics from the border than from the capitol. Religion is less likely to be coopted when it remains at arm's length. Second, though I acknowledge particular utilities in religion, my location of it on the border leaves it free to make truth claims from within its own territory and to have them judged on religious grounds. Part of its role as refuge from and challenge to politics depends upon religion being itself, thereby making truth and moral claims different from and alternative to those of politics. Finally, it is up to individual citizens, not political order, to judge the truth claims of specific religions and to find ways to translate them into the language of politics. Religion is justified in entering politics on the basis of its truth, subject to the qualifications already given about its political role, precisely because it enters from its own territory, not from the territory of civil religion.

It is, nevertheless, probably unavoidable that societies develop some qualities of civil religion when particular religions take an active public role. In such circumstances, public morality will take on religious coloring from religion's effect on character and virtue, from religious accounts of sin, evil, and death, and even from the principles from which religion challenges the public order to seek higher ideals. This coloring will inescapably be available for use and abuse by religious and public figures. Despite this inevitable tendency to civil religion, the principal religious-political action should be on the religious-political border, not in civil religion.

Separation of Church and State

Separation of church and state forms a venerable, though contested, American tradition for managing interaction of religion and politics. I have already indicated its affinities to secularization theory, but separation of church and state is more clearly defined than secularization, and it has the advantage of being a familiar institution. Nevertheless, separation of church and state, though valuable in certain contexts, is too limited to serve as a full orientation to religion and politics. Moreover, as we shall see, there is no fixed definition of separation available to establish boundaries for religion and politics. I do not deal in this chapter except in passing with particular constitutional cases or controversies involving separation of church and state. Here I deal only with the general approach and its theoretical justification.

Not surprisingly, Tocqueville furnishes the primary clue to the origin and the contribution of separation of church and state. In the "Author's Preface" to the first volume of *Democracy in America*, he remarks Christianity's natural affinity to equality, but also its historic entanglement with institutions of privilege assailed by democrats. Then he observes:

> By the side of these religious men I discern others whose looks are turned to the earth more than to Heaven; they are the partisans of liberty, not only as the source of the noblest virtues, but more especially as the root of all solid advantages; and they sincerely desire to extend its sway, and to impart its blessings to mankind. It is natural that they should hasten to invoke the assistance of religion, for they must know that liberty cannot be established without morality, nor morality without faith; but they have seen religion in the ranks of their adversaries, and they inquire no further; some of them attack it openly, and the remainder are afraid to defend it.[24]

Given such ambiguous reactions to religion in liberals and democrats, and given, moreover, the dangers of religious passions allied with political power, it seems best to separate church and state. Then we shall be free of any political obligation either to defend or attack religion, and free also to seek secular foundations for moral virtue and character.

Religious groups, too, historically have advocated separation of church and state. As H. Richard Niebuhr argues, the key Protestant idea in America has been the kingdom of God, but the dilemmas of institutionalizing that kingdom have led many Protestants to advocate independence of the church from civil government and, often, withdrawal of believers from the world.[25] Separation protects the church from both political cooptation and persecution. This position, of course, has been most strongly advocated by marginal religious groups—that is, those most likely to suffer if dominant religious groups control the state.

So there are both political and religious grounds for separation of church and state. Separation protects the churches and the political order, especially when combined (this should go without saying in the American context) with freedom of religious exercise. The results have been impressive. America is at the same time modernity's most religious and most secular nation. Religion flourishes in individual hearts and organized religious bodies. But no church is established; religious tests for public office are unconstitutional; there are no religious political parties (three features found in many European democracies); and religious, civil, and political freedom flourish.

The case can be effectively made and is probably true that separation of church and state in America has freed the individual spirit from clerical and political authority and has released the energy of creativity within political and religious institutions. Religion possesses tremendous vitality in the United States because it is free from the burden of defending or attacking an established church. Religion is vital precisely because it is pluralistic and identified neither with the state nor with political ideologies. Compared to Europe and Latin America, the United States lacks pervasive anticlericalism, because clerics have, largely, stayed away from political power and from attempting to have their churches officially recognized and supported by political power.[26] These points are not original; they are the familiar backbone of the defense of separation of church and state in American political thought. They set forth a strong case for the importance of separation.

There is, moreover, one other argument particularly important to recognize in a book accentuating tradition and narrative. Separation of church and state is a fundamental part of the American story, the American tradition of religion and politics. Because, in making practical recommendations and in dealing with specific policy issues it is important to work within society's traditions, separation of church and state must be a significant part of any conception of religion and politics, at least in America. I believe that it should also be part of any theory of religion and politics for the reasons given in the previous three paragraphs.

Separation of church and state, however, can only be part of a theory of religion and politics, for it fails to address a number of vital issues. Moreover, separation of church and state is not itself an unchanging perspective. Its meaning and implications vary over time.

I shall address first the limits of scope. First, separation of church and state is an institutional approach to religion and politics. That is, separation is between church, the most prominent institutional manifestation of religion, and state, the most prominent institution of political life. Church is regarded as an institution of private life and state an institution of public. Separation of church and state is to reflect and exemplify the separation of private from public life characteristic of modern liberal theory. I have argued throughout this book that both religion and politics must be understood as far more than institutions. Separation of church and state fails as a total theory of religion and politics because it focuses only on the institutional, bureaucratic, and private aspects of religion and on the institutional, bureaucratic, and public side of politics. Such a view simply cannot be an adequate account of religion or politics, or of their relationship.

Second, the separation of church and state position attempts to harmonize religion and politics through separation. That is, separation is premised on the hope that social peace and tranquility between politics and religion will prevail if state and church are kept isolated. This assumes that religion will not object to what the state does in its realm, and politics will not object to what the church does in its. Harmony comes through lack of interest or, at most, through each serving as a refuge from the narrowness of the other. I have argued, however, that religion and politics must challenge one another. Indeed, it is inevitable that the issues facing modern society will force such confrontation. Separation of church and state as a surrogate for separation of religion and politics fails to recognize this element of their relationship. Though lip service might be given to the right of religious persons or groups to exercise freedom of speech on public matters, in fact separation of church and state predisposes us to object to the Catholic church's anti- abortion advocacy and to Protestant ministers marching against nuclear weapons. If these are violations of church-state separation, then separation of church and state is too limited. If they are not, then separation of church and state has not covered all of the ground. Moreover, there do come times when the state must intervene in religious life, for example, to protect rights. Separation of church and state covers such intervention only with great difficulty. Separation theory misses the essential tension revealed by the critical function of religion. Third, although separation of church and state might have something to do with the toleration of religious differences in the United States, it cannot be the only explanation. For religious toleration also exists in nations without a tradition of separation of church and state, even in nations with established churches and public aid to parochial schools. Moreover, religious toleration has hardly triumphed in this country. There is a fairly strong propensity for American culture to be least tolerant of religions (different ones at different times) that do not fit the model of individualized, privatized faith.[27]

Public policy is never as neutral with respect to faith as separation of church and state would like to imagine. Certainly the protection afforded by the First Amendment to unusual opinions and behavior in the name of pluralism has unsettled (perhaps appropriately, but unsettled nonetheless) the unofficially privileged place of the early Protestant consensus in American life. Values always conflict, and the state inevitably favors some over others. For example, heterosexuality no longer enjoys quite the privileged place over homosexuality it once had in law. This unsettling of traditional ways and expectations, worked out under the aegis of separation of church and state, itself contributes to possible intolerance. As Michael Sandel observes, "Intolerance flourishes most where forms of life are dislocated, roots unsettled, traditions undone."[28] The neutrality and toleration engendered by separation of church and state have certain blind spots, indeed, must have certain blind spots, for complete toleration and neutrality are impossible.

Finally, separation of church and state cannot handle the experience of civil religion. For reasons given in the previous section, not only is civil religion a reality, it also makes some beneficial contributions to the public realm. Separation of church and state finds it difficult to deal with civil religion, for it can envision religion only in institutional form or in the form of individual belief. Thus, the Supreme Court is forced to decide objections to instances of civil religion, such as nativity scenes in town squares and chaplains in state legislatures, on absurd grounds. In the former case, it rules that a nativity scene is not really a religious symbol; in the latter case, that, in effect, mixing church and state is acceptable if there is a long tradition of doing so.[29]

The second major problem with separation of church and state as a theory of religion and politics is that separation of church and state itself is an ambiguous and changing position. What constitutes a church-state issue is historically conditioned. Separation of church and state has been the general orientation of American constitutional law for two hundred years, but the explosion of novel questions in the last forty years illustrates that it is hardly a fixed and unchanging orientation.

Moreover, it is not even clear that there is a fixed understanding of the general meaning of the term. Both "accommodationists" and "separationists" are often identified within the debates over the meaning of separation of church and state.[30] This is not the place to review the enormous literature on possible claims to the genuine meaning of separation of church and state, but one example of the difficulties might be given. Thomas Robbins identifies a fourfold typology of church-state orientations in the United States.[31] These four types are distinguished by their positions on two large issues: whether separation of church and state permits certain kinds of government support of religion and whether separation of church and state permits government to regulate certain religious practices. "Separationists" answer "no" on both counts. "Statists" answer "yes" on both. "Secularists" would permit government to regulate religion in certain instances, but not to support it. A "Supportive" orientation would allow government support in certain circumstances, but not government regulation. These four are only large-scale orientations; particular issues would certainly produce subsets of the main perspectives. Yet at least three of the four orientations (excluding the statist) have a legitimate claim to being within the tradition of separation of church and state.

Though the separation of church and state position is important and useful, it cannot be a complete theory of religion and politics in any of its forms. All four perspectives considered in the preceding pages—secularization, theocracy, civil religion, and separation of church and state—fail to account for some of the important phenomena of private and public life and of religion and politics. This book's tensional theory, I contend, does have the ability to manage all of the necessary elements of a theory of religion and politics.

Political Action by Religious Groups

Action is the test of the tensional model's superiority to other models. As Eliza Doolittle sings to Freddy, "Don't tell me your love, show me!" What kinds of political activity by religious groups are appropriate to the border area between religion and politics? What kinds contribute to the civil discourse between religion and politics?

It should be clear by now that the entry of religious groups into politics is neither new nor temporary. American movements of radical political reform—public education, women's rights, prison and hospital reform, peace, temperance, and abolition of slavery—are incomprehensible without the evangelistic fervor infused by religious faith.[32] The idea and experience of the kingdom of God as pervading all areas of life runs deeply in the American psyche, attaching itself to all kinds of political crusades.[33] Contemporary religious politics is but the most recent manifestation of that part of our political and religious culture.

Especially because of this tradition, the question of how prudence can operate in a highly charged and pluralistic religious and political environment is pressing. Political activity by religious groups involves them in fundamental tensions. Nevertheless, there are creative sides to this tension, and there are important contributions that religious groups can and do make to political life consistent with the fundamental pluralism of American culture and the kinds of limits to political activity by religious groups entailed in that pluralism and in the tensional model of religion and politics itself.

The public side of religion, including its involvement in distinctly political activity, can range from quite indirect to very direct action. The most indirect is influence on those virtues that link public and private life: integrity, courage, and trust, for example. Moving toward more direct, we pass through support for specific public policy positions, active involvement in electoral politics, interest-group activity, and direct action such as boycotts, civil disobedience, and insurrection. Though few anxieties are created when churches or other religious bodies advance public virtue by promoting the private virtues of their adherents, the farther one moves toward direct action, the greater the tensions.

Direct political activity may be perceived by members of the religious body as conflicting with primary religious activity—prayer, teaching, preaching, administration of sacraments, counseling, proselytizing, and so forth. For example, for the church or its representatives to endorse candidates for public office may be to hinder their ability to minister to the spiritual needs of members who favor other candidates. Lobbying, civil disobedience, and explicit policy stances can have similar effects, sharply dividing local or national churches. Recent conflicts within mainline Protestant denominations over their national offices' public policy stances exemplify these tensions. Withdrawal of Reverend Jerry Falwell from some of his more direct political activities reflects at least in part the tensions and divisions in the fundamentalist community between a more public and a more private religiosity.

Yet to resolve the tension by mandating that religious groups remain within the private sphere, deserting the borderline, is also to have significant and at least potentially divisive effects. To preach, teach, and proselytize only in private terms suggests that religion is irrelevant to public life and, therefore, that public life must live by its own standards—a separation of public and private, of church and state, at odds with the fundamental argument of this book. Moreover, to focus exclusively on the private side of religion is to alienate those members of the faith who wish to integrate its public and private sides. Additionally, as the public implications of religious faith are present willy-nilly, exclusive emphasis on the private side ensures that the public side will burst forth in extreme forms. Witness the emergence of the new religious right.

The tensions within religious groups brought on by entry into the public realm are illustrated in another aspect of the public activity of religious groups. Those groups that have decided to enter the political forum in a regular way are often caught between higher prudence's call to "witness" to the rigor of the principles at stake and the call of lower prudence to cultivate the skills of insider lobbying. Allen D. Hertzke's study of religious lobbies in Washington details this tension. For example, in one interview, "when asked about her lobby effectiveness, the director of the Presbyterian office replied, 'I don't try to evaluate effectiveness. I am more concerned with the biblical basis on which I stand.' "[34] Witnessing faithfully and prophetically to its fundamental principles may be a very satisfying public role for religious groups, but, as Hertzke shows, it is not usually very effective in producing the kind of policy changes those principles specify.

On the other hand, to develop the classic skills of insider lobbying and to strive for attention to detail, to seek reliable access to points of power, and to learn the arts of compromise may well mute the religious message, making it seem just one more voice in the cacophony of interest-group activity. The political system shapes and constrains the way that religious groups witness politically. As Hertzke found,

> It is in the capital, perhaps more than anywhere else, that the "absolutes" of religious faith confront the hard and seductive reality of practical politics. . . . In interviews with congressional staff members the same theme repeatedly emerges: to be effective, religious lobbyists must learn to play the game, to think strategically, and to understand the norms of congressional politics.[35]

In order to play the game, religious lobby groups have to shift from explicitly religious language to secular, political language to make their points. The religious right is now learning the lessons of the religious groups preceding them to Washington.[36] Religious prudence can play the political game. It can survive in the public environment and contribute to that environment, while at the same time learning from it. But it does so at a cost reflected in the strain between witnessing and lobbying.

The story of religious lobbying in Washington illustrates the characteristic tension between religion and politics when religious groups undertake political activity. Such activity generates a struggle within religious groups themselves that may move them to creative reflection on the principles of their faith. Yet, in the political realm itself, the tension between witnessing and insider lobbying means that political realism will be challenged by religious principles and that religious passions will be tamed by the need to learn both religious and political language.

Public officials feel most deeply the tension between religion and politics and the need prudentially to translate religious belief into public terms. Greenawalt's argument demonstrates that it is legitimate for such officials to draw on their religious convictions in prudential policy decisions. The two most recent, in-depth studies of religion in Congress reveal that members of Congress can make this integration in creative and consistent ways. In

addition to Hertzke's study of religious lobbying on Capitol Hill, we have
Peter L. Benson's and Dorothy L. Williams's account of how the deepest
religious experiences, rather than the denominational affiliations, of members of Congress do in fact influence their issue orientations in profound and
coherent ways.[37] For public officials, as for religious lobbyists, the experience
of the transcendent and the demands it places on their lives lead them to
seek ways of reflecting that experience in the public life of a pluralistic and
contingent polity. These officials, by and large, do not see themselves as
representatives of a religious body or a theological position, a role that
would place church at the heart of the political realm. Rather, they view
themselves as representatives of the public, in the various ways they understand that role, who have religious convictions that profoundly affect the
ways they see the world, public and private. Those convictions enter into
their decision making, along with a host of other principled and pragmatic
concerns. It is not the calling of public officials to exhibit the highest forms
of religious prudence, though we hope for at least a few who display the
highest forms of political prudence. But it is reasonable to hope for, and
fortunate to discover, political leaders who appreciate the values of lower
political and religious prudence. Acting from such prudence, they take account of the public significance of religion as well as of specifically political
virtues.

Many politicians who speak of their personal religious faith tend to describe the difficult decisions where different interests conflict, where personal
beliefs clash with each other or with economic or political interests. They
point in such situations to the critical importance of respect for political
opponents and for their political positions. At the same time, and for the
same reasons, they express exasperation with religious interest groups that
assault them on all sides of the issues and in self-serving ways, who naively
assert that there is only one truly religious perspective on the issues at hand.
Such groups hurt religion itself and frustrate political action.[38] Prudent
politicians realize the fundamental value of respect in civil discourse.

Religious activity in public life can make another contribution to that life.
Modern democracy attenuates the participation that is so vital for cultivating
the values of public life. The dominance of policy by interest-group liberalism
and of electoral politics by the same interest groups and the mass media's
attention to popularity make it difficult for civic concern about fundamental
principles to be heard by candidates or public officials. Moreover, ordinary
citizens have limited opportunities to participate publicly in meaningful
ways. Because, in America at least, church membership and religious belief
are so pronounced, religious life provides alternate vehicles for representation, civic education, and participation.[39]

Religious movements often provide representation for ethical perspectives
otherwise minimally acknowledged in ordinary politics. Moreover, the

churches and evangelistic groups provide opportunities for ordinary citizens to participate in causes as diverse as fighting for the abolition of slavery or the prohibition of alcoholic beverages, advocacy of prison reform and of female suffrage. In the 1960s the base of the civil rights movement in the churches opened opportunities for church members to enter public life in ways that profoundly linked their deepest beliefs with the most serious political issues. In the 1980s hitherto apolitical members of society have begun to become citizens by participating in electoral campaigns under the auspices of the new religious right and in policy debates over abortion, pornography, nuclear weapons policy, the Middle East, and public education. Whether one agrees with the goals or tactics of the civil rights movement or of the new religious right is beside the point here. What I wish to emphasize is that, through them and through politically active religion throughout American history, religious convictions entered public life, motivating passive subjects to become active citizens.[40] Specifically religious phenomena, in other words, stimulated healthy political involvement by ordinary persons.

Activity by religious interest groups is the most difficult test for the model of church-state relations outlined here. Such activity seems to cross the border and enter directly into the life of the state, violating the basic principles of the model. It is certainly not the most desirable form of public activity. Yet, given the conditions of American politics in the late twentieth century, some interest-group activity seems necessary if the voice of religion is to be heard at all in the public sphere. To a large extent, that is, religious groups with a public message must employ the particular forms of public access available. Regrettably, public life has become impoverished enough to make interest groups the dominant mode of influence. This being the case, much depends on the language and the forms of prudence employed by religious interest groups. Because such groups are the most direct entry of religion into public life, they must be judged by their ability to learn and use political language and by their willingness to learn to compromise.

There is a delicate balance here between the role of religion in facilitating citizen participation and its role in challenging easy political compromise. The more readily religious groups learn the art of compromise and the language of politics, the less likely they are to challenge politics in fundamental ways. The more ready to challenge, the less likely the compromise. This dilemma has no fixed solution, only the prudential guidelines elaborated in earlier chapters. The dilemma reveals the tension between higher and lower prudence, the tension involved in learning to translate religious principle into public policy without losing the distinctive idiom of one's particular language.

We must be careful, however, not to fall into the trap of regarding political participation as the whole of public life. The value of citizenship is also served when believers participate in the life of their own religious communities. Issues of justice, freedom, decency, and respect appear there too. For the political participation of religious groups to be authentic, it must also challenge religious institutions to live up to the ideals they espouse. Churches cannot legitimately promote minimum-wage laws and just treatment of employees if they do not themselves pay just wages or allow their workers to organize. Indeed, an effective public role for religion is often not in direct political involvement, but in public witness to what equality, solidarity, and mutual respect look like in specific institutional forms.

Stanley Hauerwas dramatically expresses the truth that politics must move beyond power and interests to be fully itself:

> The most basic task of any polity is to offer its people a sense of participation in an adventure. For finally what we seek is not power, or security, or equality, or even dignity, but a sense of worth gained from participation and contribution to a common adventure. Indeed, our "dignity" derives exactly from our sense of having played a part in such a story.[41]

Religious groups have a vital part to play in cultivating this sense of adventure, for they foster participation in two ways. First, the believer participates in the story of the religious community itself. The religious community is itself a polity,with politics, policy, and authority. Second, the story of his faith community can draw him into the story of the political community. A polity of religious and political pluralism most especially needs a border area in which the lives of all citizens are enriched by the conversation and exchange and, yes, conflict and tension among the variety of voices and stories. Religion in public and private life is the continual experience of this variety.

Notes

Chapter 1

1. Michael Walzer, "Liberalism and the Art of Separation," *Political Theory*, 12 (August 1984), p. 315.

2. John Gray's little summary of the central meaning of liberalism stresses the core of liberal values within a diversity of emphases. John Gray, *Liberalism* (Minneapolis, MN: University of Minnesota Press, 1986), esp. the introduction and chap. 7. More profound accounts of the impact of these elements in liberalism may be found in John H. Hallowell, *The Decline of Liberalism as an Ideology* (Berkeley, CA: University of California Press, 1943), and Thomas A. Spragens, Jr., *The Irony of Liberal Reason* (Chicago: University of Chicago Press, 1981).

3. Christopher Lasch, *The Culture of Narcissism: American Life in an Age of Diminishing Expectations* (New York: Warner Books, 1979), and *The Minimal Self: Psychic Survival in Troubled Times* (New York: W. W. Norton & Company, 1984); Philip Rieff, *The Triumph of the Therapeutic: Uses of Faith After Freud* (New York: Harper Torchbooks, 1968).

4. Robert N. Bellah *et al.*, *Habits of the Heart: Individualism and Commitment in American Life* (Berkeley, CA: University of California Press, 1985).

5. Robert Booth Fowler makes this case in *Religion and Politics in America* (Metuchen, NJ: The Scarecrow Press, 1985), pp. 37–42, and more fully in *Unconventional Partners: Religion and Liberal Culture in the United States* (Grand Rapids, MI: Eerdmanns, 1988). The public activity of Jews, liberal Protestants, and (increasingly) liberal Catholics might be thought an exception to this generalization. And it partly is. Religious groups do take public stances challenging established policies. This public activity, however, supports my contention that the conventional public-private dichotomy, especially as it relates to religion, is flawed. Moreover, although these groups do challenge policies, they tend to do so *within* the confines of the liberal consensus, including the consensus on public and private.

6. Richard John Neuhaus, *The Naked Public Square: Religion and Democracy in America* (Grand Rapids, MI: Eerdmans, 1984), pp. 14ff.

7. See John Murray Cuddihy, *No Offense: Civil Religion and Protestant Taste* (New York: Seabury, 1978); see also Will Herberg, *Protestant-Catholic-Jew: An Essay in American Religious Sociology* (Garden City, NY: Doubleday Anchor, 1960).

8. Peter L. Benson and Dorothy L. Williams, *Religion on Capitol Hill: Myths and Realities* (New York: Oxford University Press, 1986), pp. 9–14.

9. Benson and Williams, *Religion on Capitol Hill*, pp. 12–13.

10. See, for example, H. Paul Chalfant, Robert E. Beckley, and C. Eddie Palmer, *Religion in Contemporary Society*, 2d ed. (Palo Alto, CA: Mayfield, 1987), esp. pp. 12–18, 27–39, and 59–73. On some of the dangers of institutional, substantive, and exclusive definitions of religion, see Thomas Luckmann, *The Invisible Religion: The Problem of Religion in Modern Society* (New York: Macmillan, 1967), esp. pp. 22–27.

11. The phrase is Cuddihy's; see *No Offense*, esp. chap. 1.

12. See Cushing Strout, *The New Heavens and the New Earth: Political Religion in America* (New York: Harper Torchbooks, 1975), chap. 3.

13. Neuhaus, *Naked Public Square*, p. 36.

14. Deane William Ferm, *Contemporary American Theologies: A Critical Survey* (New York: Seabury, 1981), esp. chaps. 7 and 8.

15. Alexis de Tocqueville, *Democracy in America*, trans. Henry Reeve (New Rochelle, NY: Arlington House, n.d.), vol. 1, p. 294.

16. Strout (*New Heavens*, chap. 8) points out that in the mid-nineteenth century similar battles raged over family and schooling, but the focus was on the challenge of Mormon and Catholic communalism and hierarchy to traditional Protestant individualistic and egalitarian values.

17. Wilson Carey McWilliams, "In Good Faith: On the Foundations of American Politics," *Humanities in Society*, 6 (Winter 1983), 19–40; Stanley I. Benn and Gerald F. Gaus, "The Liberal Conception of the Public and the Private," in *Public and Private in Social Life*, ed. S. I. Benn and G. F. Gaus (New York: St. Martin's Press, 1983), pp. 31–65.

18. Sandel, *Liberalism and the Limits of Justice*; Michael Walzer, *Spheres of Justice: A Defense of Pluralism and Equality* (New York: Basic Books, 1983); Walzer, *Exodus and Revolution* (New York: Basic Books, 1985); Wildavsky, *The Nursing Father: Moses as a Political Leader* (University, AL: University of Alabama Press, 1984); MacIntyre, *After Virtue: A Study in Moral Theory* (Notre Dame, IN: University of Notre Dame Press, 1981); Hadley Arkes, *First Things: An Inquiry into the First Principles of Morals and Justice* (Princeton, NJ: Princeton University Press, 1986); and J. Budziszewski, *The Resurrection of Nature: Political Theory and the Human Character* (Ithaca, NY: Cornell University Press, 1986). I have considered some of these developments in "Political Science Confronts the Book: Recent Work on Scripture and Politics," *Journal of Politics*, 50 (February 1988), 219–34; see also "The Thin Theory of Community: The Communitarians and their Critics," *Political Studies*, 32 (September 1989), 422–35, and Y. K. Hui and Clarke E. Cochran, "Virtue Ethics and Natural Law," paper presented at the November 1988 Annual Meeting of the Southern Political Science Association, Atlanta, Georgia.

19. See Thomas A. Spragens, Jr., "Reconstructing Liberal Theory: Reason and Liberal Culture," in *Liberals on Liberalism*, ed. Alfonso J. Damico (Totowa, NJ: Rowman & Littlefield, 1986), pp. 34–53. See also Gerald F. Gaus, *The Modern Liberal Theory of Man* (New York: St. Martin's, 1983), and Nancy L. Rosenblum, *Another Liberalism: Romanticism and the Reconstruction of Liberal Thought* (Cambridge, MA: Harvard University Press, 1987).

20. Tocqueville, *Democracy in America*, vol. 1, pp. 291–305; vol. 2, p. 154.

Chapter 2

1. Stanley I. Benn and Gerald F. Gaus, "The Public and the Private: Concepts and Action," in *Public and Private in Social Life*, ed. S. I. Benn and G. F. Gaus (New York: St. Martin's Press, 1983), pp. 3–27, esp. pp. 3–11. See also W. T. Jones, "Public Roles, Private Roles, and Differential Moral Assessments of Role Performances," *Ethics*, 94 (July 1984), 603–20, for criteria of distinction.

2. Barrington Moore, *Privacy: Studies in Social and Cultural History* (Armonk, NY: M. E. Sharpe, Inc., 1984), pp. ix, and 267–88. John M. Roberts and Thomas Gregor, "Privacy: A Cultural View," in *Nomos XIII: Privacy*, ed. J. Roland Pennock and John W. Chapman (New York: Atherton Press, 1971), 199–225. See also Leslie K. Haviland and John B. Haviland,

"Privacy in a Mexican Indian Village," in Benn and Gaus, eds., *Public and Private*, pp. 341–61; Robert F. Murphy, "Social Distance and the Veil," in *Philosophical Dimensions of Privacy: An Anthology*, ed. Ferdinand David Schoeman (Cambridge: Cambridge University Press, 1984), pp. 34–55; and Alan Westin, "The Origin of Modern Claims to Privacy," in Schoeman, ed., *Philosophical Dimensions of Privacy*, pp. 56–74.

3. Martin Krygier, "Publicness, Privateness and 'Primitive Law,' " in Benn and Gaus, eds., *Public and Private*, pp. 307–40.

4. That not only primitive and classical cultures embody the need for privacy in variant cultural forms related to public life is evident also from how modern, developed cultures handle the concepts. Herbert J. Spiro has described the very different ways in which privacy has developed in the United States, Britain, and continental Europe. See Herbert J. Spiro, "Privacy in Comparative Perspective," in Pennock and Chapman, eds., *Nomos XIII: Privacy*, pp. 121–48.

5. Classification of definitions and a long bibliography may be found in W. A. Parent, "Recent Work on the Concept of Privacy," *American Philosophical Quarterly*, 20 (October 1983), 341–55. Valuable collections of articles on privacy, ones that indicate the range of research and disagreements on the concept are: William C. Bier, S.J., ed., *Privacy: A Vanishing Value?* (New York: Fordham University Press, 1980); Pennock and Chapman, eds., *Nomos XIII: Privacy*; and Schoeman, ed., *Philosophical Dimensions of Privacy*. Steven Lukes's valuable *Individualism* (Oxford: Basil Blackwell, 1973) situates privacy and related concepts within the tradition of individualism. The strength of individualism in American culture certainly accounts for some of the passion associated with privacy issues.

6. Michael Walzer, *Spheres of Justice: A Defense of Pluralism and Equality* (New York: Basic Books, 1983), p. 87. See Tracy B. Strong, "The Practical Unity of Community and Privacy," *Humanitas*, 11 (February 1975), 85–97.

7. The discussion in this paragraph is based on the *Oxford English Dictionary* (hereafter *OED*) and its *Supplement*, s.v. "Private."

8. This meaning is most striking in a quotation from the *OED Supplement* (p. 799) that refers to the "private parts of a modest woman, and the public parts of a prostitute."

9. Herman van Gunsteren, "Public and Private," *Social Research*, 46 (Summer 1979), 255–71.

10. Michael A. Weinstein, "The Uses of Privacy in the Good Life," in Pennock and Chapman, eds., *Nomos XIII: Privacy*, p. 94.

11. J. Roland Pennock, "Introduction," in Pennock and Chapman, eds., *Nomos XIII: Privacy*, pp. xi–xvi.

12. I have argued this case in *Character, Community, and Politics* (University, AL: University of Alabama Press, 1982), chap. 6. I shall not repeat the argument here.

13. Jean Bethke Elshtain describes this development perceptively in *Public Man, Private Woman* (Princeton, NJ: Princeton University Press, 1981), pp. 56ff.

14. Hannah Arendt, *The Human Condition* (Garden City, NY: Doubleday Anchor, 1959), esp. pp. 65–69, 217–23, and 287f.

15. Gilbert Meilaender, approaching this from a Christian perspective, points to the miraculous appearance of virtue. He sees limits to the public inculcation of virtue, limits marked by the gift of grace. "Virtue in Contemporary Religious Thought," in *Virtue—Public and Private*, ed. Richard John Neuhaus (Grand Rapids, MI: Eerdmans, 1986), pp. 26–29.

16. Particularly revealing is the practice of self-criticism in totalitarian ideologies. It mocks

the form of confession in religion, but the lack of a private, intimate context (among other things) reveals its emptiness, its parody of religion.

17. John R. Silber, "Masks and Fig Leaves," in Pennock and Chapman, eds., *Nomos XIII: Privacy*, p. 232.

18. See Carl J. Friedrich, "Secrecy versus Privacy: The Democratic Dilemma," in Pennock and Chapman, eds., *Nomos XIII: Privacy*, pp. 105–20.

19. Ferdinand Schoeman, "Privacy: Philosophical Dimensions of the Literature," in Schoeman, ed., *Philosophical Dimensions of Privacy*, p. 1.

20. Judith Martin, *Miss Manners' Guide to Rearing Perfect Children*, illustrated by Gloria Kamen (New York: Penguin Books, 1985), p. 161.

21. See, for example, Elshtain, *Public Man, Private Woman*, passim, esp. pp. 8–9.

22. This idea is suggested by Weinstein, "Uses of Privacy," p. 103.

23. Henri J. M. Nouwen, *Reaching Out: The Three Movements of the Spiritual Life* (Garden City, NY: Doubleday, 1975), p. 20.

24. Jeffrey H. Reiman, "Privacy, Intimacy, and Personhood," *Philosophy and Public Affairs*, 6 (Fall 1976), 26–44. See also Constance T. Fischer, "Privacy as a Profile of Authentic Consciousness," *Humanitas*, 11 (February 1975), 27–43.

25. James M. Glass, *Delusion: Internal Dimensions of Political Life* (Chicago: University of Chicago Press, 1985).

26. Glass, *Delusion*, p. 36.

27. On the importance of an inclusive, integrating faith, see H. Richard Niebuhr, *Radical Monotheism and Western Culture* (New York: Harper Torchbooks, 1970), esp. pp. 30–31. Some of my comments about the significance of religious faith draw on the discussion of the functions and dysfunctions of religion in H. Paul Chalfant, et al., *Religion in Contemporary Society*, 2d ed. (Palo Alto, CA: Mayfield, 1987), pp. 27–39.

28. Simone Weil, *The Simone Weil Reader*, ed. George A. Panichas (New York: David McKay, 1977), esp. pp. 313–20.

29. J. S. Mill, *On Liberty*, ed. David Spitz (New York: W. W. Norton, 1975), p. 57.

30. For a fine discussion of conscience, see James F. Childress, "Appeals to Conscience," *Ethics*, 89 (July 1979), 315–35.

31. This argument is similar to Isaiah Berlin's criticism of positive notions of liberty and his defense of negative liberty, "Two Concepts of Liberty," in *Four Essays on Liberty* (London: Oxford University Press, 1969), pp. 118–72. It is open to the same criticisms as an exclusively negative conception of freedom. See Cochran, *Character, Community, and Politics*, chap. 6.

32. Annette Baier, "Trust and Antitrust," *Ethics*, 96 (January 1986), p. 234. Baier's discussion is seminal, and I have drawn upon it throughout this section.

33. Baier, "Trust," pp. 241–42.

34. Sissela Bok, *Lying: Moral Choice in Public and Private Life* (New York: Pantheon Books, 1978), p. 31. Emphasis in original. Note what Bok says on that same page: "*Whatever* matters to human beings, trust is the atmosphere in which it thrives."

35. Thus Arendt is wrong to see privacy's protection of intimacy as a function of *modern* privacy. Arendt, *Human Condition*, p. 35. Rather, intimacy is an essential quality of private life. Note that Arendt does give grudging recognition to the value of intimate relations (pp. 46 and 64).

36. Robert S. Gerstein, "Intimacy and Privacy," in Schoeman, ed., *Philosophical Dimen-*

sions of Privacy, pp. 265–71. See also, in the same volume, Richard A. Wasserstrom, "Privacy: Some Arguments and Assumptions," pp. 317–32, and Ferdinand Schoeman, "Privacy and Intimate Information," pp. 403–18. On observation and privacy, see also Stanley I. Benn, "Privacy, Freedom, and Respect for Persons," in Pennock and Chapman, eds., *Nomos XIII: Privacy*, pp. 3–13.

37. Charles Fried, "Privacy [A Moral Analysis]," in Schoeman, ed., *Philosophical Dimensions of Privacy*, p. 211. Emphasis in original.

38. Walzer, *Spheres of Justice*, p. 227. Though Walzer emphasizes keeping spheres of life as distinct as possible, he recognizes that private life and public life have many fundamental and necessary connections and analogies.

39. Thomas Luckmann, *The Invisible Religion* (New York: Macmillan, 1967). I shall summarize the broad outlines of Luckmann's argument and extract their more specific implications for my account of the private and public sides of religion. Page and chapter references appear in parentheses in the text.

Chapter 3

1. Charles Taylor, "Hegel, History, and Politics," in *Liberalism and its Critics*, ed. Michael Sandel (New York: New York University Press, 1984), p. 183.

2. *OED*, s.v. "public," p. 1558.

3. The typology below was developed by Manfred Stanley, "The Mystery of the Commons: On the Indispensability of Civic Rhetoric," *Social Research*, 50 (Winter 1983), 851–83.

4. Even Kant has been recast in the context of advocacy of an active public realm. See John Christian Laursen, "The Subversive Kant: The Vocabulary of 'Public' and 'Publicity,' " *Political Theory*, 14 (November 1986), 584–603. For my own analysis of some of the new communitarian literature, see Clarke E. Cochran, "The Thin Theory of Community: The Communitarians and their Critics," *Political Studies*, 32 (September 1989), 219–34.

5. Stanley I. Benn and Gerald F. Gaus, "The Public and the Private: Concepts and Action," in *Public and Private in Social Life*, ed. S. I. Benn and G. F. Gaus (New York: St. Martin's Press, 1983), pp. 3–27.

6. Peter L. Berger and Thomas Luckmann, *The Social Construction of Reality: A Treatise in the Sociology of Knowledge* (New York: Doubleday, 1967), p. 37. For development of these ideas, see Peter Winch, *The Idea of a Social Science and its Relation to Philosophy* (London: Routledge and Kegan Paul, 1958); Leslie White, *The Science of Culture: A Study of Man and Civilization* (New York: Grove Press, 1949), chap. 2; and Ernst Cassier, *An Essay on Man* (New Haven, CT: Yale University Press, 1944), chaps. 2 and 8.

7. Hannah Arendt, *The Human Condition* (Garden City, NY: Doubleday Anchor Books, 1959), esp. pp. 178ff. While Arendt had important things to say about the private world, her conviction that the loss of the public world was the most pressing dilemma of the modern world kept her from recognizing and appreciating the elements of private life discussed in the previous chapter. Labor, work, contemplation, and love are certainly vital parts of private life, but so are integrity, intimacy, exclusion, and mystery. Moreover, my account of private life should indicate why Arendt was wrong to see the public world as uniquely related to development of the self and of freedom. In private life the person appears in a different light, but he does appear, and he discovers and shapes identity. Moreover, political freedom finds support in private life as well as in public.

8. This account of public life in Arendt is indebted to Margaret Canavan, "Politics as Culture: Hannah Arendt and the Public Realm," *History of Political Thought*, 6 (Winter 1985),

617–42. Canavan argues that for Arendt the world of high culture is also a public world. Yet Canavan acknowledges that the attribution of public to high culture was only implicit in Arendt and that politics for her often seems to bear all public burdens and responsibilities.

9. Arendt, *Human Condition*, pp. 45–53 and chap. 5.

10. Arendt, *Human Condition*, pp. 159–60, 170–83, 205, and 222–23.

11. See Richard J. Bernstein's defense against this objection to Arendt's account of public life. "The Meaning of Public Life," in *Religion and American Public Life: Interpretations and Explorations*, ed. Robin W. Lovin (Mahwah, NJ: Paulist Press, 1986), pp. 37–40.

12. See Patricia Boling, "Why Public v. Private is Wrong," paper presented at the September 1985 Annual Meeting of the American Political Science Association, New Orleans, Louisiana. Even Canavan and Bernstein (see notes 8 and 11 above) object to this separation as they defend her.

13. Hanna Fenichel Pitkin, "Justice: On Relating Private and Public," *Political Theory*, 9 (August 1981), 327–52.

14. Carole Pateman, *Participation and Democratic Theory* (Cambridge: Cambridge University Press, 1970). I have discussed the value of participation in community in *Character, Community, and Politics* (University, AL: University of Alabama Press, 1982), pp. 156–59. My comments on Pateman draw on this previous discussion.

15. See Michael Walzer, *Spheres of Justice: A Defense of Pluralism and Equality* (New York: Basic Books, 1983), chap. 12.

16. Walzer, *Spheres of Justice*, pp. 52–63.

17. Benjamin R. Barber, *Strong Democracy: Participatory Politics for a New Age* (Berkeley, CA: University of California Press, 1984).

18. Barber, *Strong Democracy*, p. xv.

19. Barber, *Strong Democracy*, pp. 133–34, 197–98, and 209–12.

20. Barber, *Strong Democracy*, pp. 158, and 198–209.

21. Barber, *Strong Democracy*, pp. 208–9, and 224.

22. Arendt, *Human Condition*, p. 33.

23. Michael Harrington, *The Politics at God's Funeral: The Spiritual Crisis of Western Civilization* (New York: Penguin, 1983), pp. 206–7. Not only atheists want religion to play a public role! Harrington's Marxist attack on privatized religion parallels the arguments, for example, of Robert Bellah and his colleagues and of the Christian ethicist, Stanley Hauerwas. See Robert H. Bellah et al., *Habits of the Heart* (Berkeley, CA: University of California Press, 1985), chap. 9; and Hauerwas, *The Peaceable Kingdom* (Notre Dame, IN: University of Notre Dame Press, 1983), pp. 12–15.

24. Eldon J. Eisenach, *The Two Worlds of Liberalism: Religion and Politics in Hobbes, Locke, and Mill* (Chicago: University of Chicago Press, 1981).

25. See esp. John H. Hallowell, *The Decline of Liberalism as an Ideology* (Berkeley, CA: University of California Press, 1943), and *Main Currents in Modern Political Thought* (New York: Holt, 1950).

26. See Wilson Carey McWilliams, "The Bible in the American Political Tradition," in *Political Anthropology, III: Religion and Politics*, ed. by Myron J. Aronoff (New Brunswick, NJ: Transaction, 1984), pp. 11–45.

27. See H. Richard Niebuhr, *Christ and Culture* (New York: Harper Colophon, 1975), pp.

245ff. See also Clyde A. Holbrook, *Faith and Community: A Christian Existential Approach* (New York: Harper & Brothers, 1959).

28. Alexis de Tocqueville, *Democracy in America*, trans. Henry Reeve (New Rochelle, NY: Arlington House, n.d.), vol. 1, p. 294. See also, vol. 2, book 1, chap. 5. For discussion of these elements of Tocqueville's thought, see Stephen Baron, "Morality and Politics in Modern Life: Tocqueville and Solzhenitsyn on the Importance of Religion to Liberty," *Polity*, 14 (Spring 1982), 395–413; Peter Dennis Bathory, "Tocqueville on Citizenship and Faith: A Response to Cushing Strout," *Political Theory*, 8 (February 1980), 27–38; and Catherine Zuckert, "Not by Preaching: Tocqueville on the Role of Religion in American Democracy," *Review of Politics*, 43 (April 1981), 259–80. Deanna H. Greisen argues that empirical studies of the political attitudes and behavior of American active church members confirm Tocqueville's thesis that religion in America promotes civic action and counteracts individualism. "The Civic Role of Religion in a Democracy," paper presented at the March 1989 Annual Meeting of the South-western Political Science Association, Little Rock, AR.

29. On the Founders, see Jean Yarbrough, "The Constitution and Character: The Missing Critical Principle?" Paper presented at the Annual Conference of the United States Capitol Historical Society, Washington, D.C., March 26–27, 1987.

30. Tocqueville, *Democracy in America*, e.g., vol. 1, pp. 50–53, 83–88, 166–74, 177–83, 261–76, and 291–305; vol. 2, pp. 109–28. Phillip E. Hammond, "Another Great Awakening?" in *The New Christian Right: Mobilization and Legitimation*, ed. Robert C. Liebman and Robert Wuthnow (New York: Aldine Publishing Company, 1983), pp. 207–25, provides a particularly insightful account of this side of Tocqueville's argument.

31. Bernstein, "The Meaning of Public Life," p. 47.

32. I have discussed the importance of roles for the development of character in *Character, Community, and Politics*, esp. pp. 18- 20, 63, and 71.

33. Eisenach, *Two Worlds of Liberalism*, p. 9. On the significance of loyalty see, John H. Schaar, *Loyalty in America* (Berkeley, CA: University of California Press, 1957), and "The Case for Patriotism," in *Legitimacy in the Modern State* (New Brunswick, NJ: Transaction Books, 1981), pp. 285–311.

34. Walzer, *Spheres of Justice*, p. 8.

35. See Walker Percy, *Lost in the Cosmos* (New York: Farrar, Straus and Giroux, 1983), pp. 35, and 85–126, and Paul Tournier, *The Meaning of Persons*, trans. Edwin Hudson (New York: Harper, 1957), pp. 67ff, and 123–40.

36. Aristotle, *Politics*, trans. Ernest Barker (New York: Oxford University Press, 1962), p. 6 (1253a10).

37. In Cochran, *Character, Community, and Politics* (esp. chap. 7) I argued that the political realm cannot be community. Attempts to make it so create what I called "pseudo-community." While the political realm, even the nation, does have legitimate community-like features, it cannot be community without corrupting the essential nature of community. What the political realm can be, and what public life can be, is a community of communities. That is, public life is community only in so far as it facilitates and promotes smaller, genuine communities. This argument is presupposed and not repeated here.

38. Schaar discusses the difference between loyalty and conformity in *Loyalty in America*, esp. pp. 120–29, and 178–79.

39. On *philia* in early political thought, see Eric Voegelin, *Order and History, Volume III: Plato and Aristotle* (Baton Rouge, LA: Louisiana State University Press, 1957), pp. 36, 189, 217, 223, 235, 249–50, 320–21, and 339.

40. Barber, *Strong Democracy*, p. 229. I have discussed the relation between public and private goods in "Yves R. Simon and 'The Common Good': A Note on the Concept," *Ethics*, 88 (April 1978), 229–39; see also *Character, Community, and Politics*, pp. 135–41.

41. Note also that various modern political ideologies can be more dangerous in this respect than religion, for such ideologies lack any reference to transcendent limits on state power.

42. See Thomas Luckmann, *The Invisible Religion* (New York: Macmillan, 1967), pp. 96–97. H. Paul Chalfant, Robert E. Beckley, and C. Eddie Palmer refer to the related danger of "religiocentrism" in *Religion in Contemporary Society*, 2d ed. (Palo Alto, CA: Mayfield Publishing Company, 1987), pp. 37–39. Religiocentrism refers to feelings of rightness and superiority resulting from religious affiliation. It produces intrareligious squabbles and schisms, group separation from the rest of the world, and, not infrequently, interreligious conflict, bloodshed, and warfare.

43. George M. Marsden, "Are Secularists the Threat? Is Religion the Solution?" in *Unsecular America*, ed. by Richard John Neuhaus (Grand Rapids, MI: Eerdmans, 1986), p. 48.

44. Robert Booth Fowler, *Religion and Politics in America* (ATLA Monograph Series, no. 21) (Metuchen, NJ: Scarecrow Press, 1985), p. 39. For elaboration, see Fowler, *Unconventional Partners: Religion and Liberal Culture in the United States* (Grand Rapids, MI: Eerdmanns, 1988). See also Bellah et al., *Habits of the Heart*, chap. 9, esp. pp. 219–25, and W. Carey McWilliams, *The Idea of Fraternity in America* (Berkeley, CA: University of California Press, 1974), pp. 384–85. McWilliams's view combines both functions of religion, though he does not entirely approve of religion as a refuge. He believes that religion, more specifically the Bible, has served in American history as both retreat from and challenge to prevailing liberal political assumptions and practices. See his "Bible in the American Political Tradition," pp. 11–45.

45. See George Armstrong Kelly, *Politics and Religious Consciousness in America* (New Brunswick, NJ: Transaction, 1984), pp. 25–27.

46. See David Little, "Legislating Morality," in *Christianity and Politics*, ed. Carol Friedley Griffith (Washington, DC: Ethics and Public Policy Center, 1981), pp. 39–53.

47. This seems to be the primary form of challenge and confrontation outlined in Hauerwas's social ethic. See Stanley Hauerwas, *A Community of Character* (Notre Dame, IN: University of Notre Dame Press, 1981), esp. chaps. 4 and 5, and *Peaceable Kingdom*, esp. chap. 6. Hauerwas's first commandment for Christian social ethics is for the church to be itself. Fowler, *Unconventional Partners*, esp. chaps. 6–8, is skeptical of the degree to which religion in America radically challenges liberal culture.

48. The eighteenth and nineteenth centuries demonstrated that intensely personal, "private" religious experience can have profound and valuable public consequences. The Great Awakenings, the clerical support for the American Revolution, and the abolition movement are just a few examples.

Chapter 4

1. These headings are suggested by S. I. Benn, "Privacy, Freedom, and Respect for Persons," pp. 15–26. I have integrated with Benn's perspective some ideas of J. Roland Pennock, "Introduction," and Michael A. Weinstein, "The Uses of Privacy in the Good Life," esp. pp. 100–104. These are all to be found in *Nomos XIII: Privacy*, ed. J. Roland Pennock and John W. Chapman (New York: Atherton Press, 1971).

2. See Paul A. Freund, "Privacy: One Concept or Many," in Pennock and Chapman, eds., *Privacy*, pp. 182–98, esp. 195–96. Rosabeth Moss Kanter, in her famous study of successful utopian communities, discovered that even those emphasizing group cohesion provided fairly

well-defined occasions for privacy. See *Commitment and Community: Communes and Utopias in Sociological Perspective* (Cambridge, MA: Harvard University Press, 1972), esp. pp. 98–99, 110–11, and 132–33.

3.   The now nearly standard critique is Theodore J. Lowi, *The End of Liberalism: The Second Republic of the United States*, 2d ed. (New York: Norton, 1979). For my own critique of private interest as the basis of political theory, see Clarke E. Cochran, "The Politics of Interest: Philosophy and the Limitations of the Science of Politics," *American Journal of Political Science*, 17 (November 1973), 745–66; "Political Science and 'The Public Interest,' " *Journal of Politics*, 36 (May 1974), 327–55; and *Character, Community, and Politics* (University, AL: University of Alabama Press, 1982), chap. 1.

4.   Sissela Bok, *Lying: Moral Choice in Public and Private Life* (New York: Pantheon Books, 1978), p. 92; for elaboration, see pp. 91–103.

5.   Eric Josephson, "Notes on the Sociology of Privacy," *Humanitas*, 11 (February 1975), 15–25.

6.   Walker Percy, *Lost in the Cosmos: The Last Self-Help Book* (New York: Farrar, Straus and Giroux, 1983); see also his *The Thanatos Syndrome* (New York: Farrar, Straus and Giroux, 1987).

7.   Percy, *Lost in the Cosmos*, p. 21.

8.   Marvin Zetterbaum, "Self and Subjectivity in Political Theory," *Review of Politics*, 44 (January 1982), pp. 59 and 81. See also Peter L. Berger, Brigitte Berger, and Hansfried Kellner, *The Homeless Mind* (New York: Vintage Books, 1974).

9.   See, for example, Alasdair MacIntyre, *After Virtue* (Notre Dame, IN: University of Notre Dame Press, 1981; 2d ed., 1984); Michael Walzer, *Spheres of Justice: A Defense of Pluralism and Equality* (New York: Basic Books, Inc., 1983); and J. Budziszewski, *The Resurrection of Nature: Political Theory and the Human Character* (Ithaca, NY: Cornell University Press, 1986).

10.   The best history is Jean Bethke Elshtain, *Public Man, Private Woman* (Princeton, NJ: Princeton University Press, 1981).

11.   Etienne Gilson, *The Spirit of Medieval Philosophy* (New York: Charles Scribner's Sons, 1940), p. 399.

12.   W. L. Weinstein, "The Private and the Free: A Conceptual Inquiry," in Pennock and Chapman, eds., *Privacy*, p. 53.

Chapter 5

1.   James M. Glass, *Delusion* (Chicago: University of Chicago Press, 1985).

2.   See Gabriel Marcel, *Homo Viator*, trans. Emma Craufurd (New York: Harper & Row, 1962), esp. pp. 18–22. Contemporary American culture makes the task specially difficult. See Christopher Lasch, *The Culture of Narcissism* (New York: Warner, 1979), and *The Minimal Self* (New York: Norton, 1984).

3.   Alasdair MacIntyre, *After Virtue: A Study in Moral Theory* (Notre Dame, IN: University of Notre Dame Press, 1981), p. 200.

4.   Mary P. Nichols has shown how, for Aristotle, political rhetoric bridges the gap between public and private, reason and passion, individual interest and common good. Mary P. Nichols, "Aristotle's Defense of Rhetoric," *Journal of Politics*, 49 (August 1987), 657–77.

The rarity of politics in human history is another reason for contending that it is not an absolutely necessary link between public and private and for arguing that other forms of public life are essential. The absence of all forms of public life is indeed uncommon, signaling something terribly wrong in society. Participation in public life is indeed critical for human well-being, but public life is, historically speaking, most often not political.

One possible implication of politics's rarity is that the obligation of political participation when possible is even stronger than the obligation to participate in other forms of public life. This ramification might seem to contradict my earlier contention that political participation is optional. Preserving a rarity of such importance, it could be argued, is hardly optional.

This contention possesses considerable merit. Yes, political participation where possible must never be taken for granted. Devotion to the political order and some minimal level of attention to and participation in politics is obligatory. Nevertheless, human beings are limited creatures. They cannot perform all that it might be good, valuable, and praiseworthy. Therefore, one may legitimately opt for minimal political participation and for maximal participation in some other public realm.

5. Michael Walzer, *Spheres of Justice* (New York: Basic, 1983). The structure of Walzer's argument appears throughout the book, but chaps. 11 and 12 are particularly important.

6. See Herman van Gunsteren, "Public and Private," *Social Research*, 46 (Summer 1979), esp. pp. 260–65.

7. Roberto Mangabeira Unger, *Knowledge and Politics* (New York: Free Press, 1975), p. 235.

8. Stanley Hauerwas, *Community of Character* (Notre Dame, IN: Notre Dame University Press, 1981), p. 85.

9. Kent Greenawalt, *Religious Convictions and Political Choice* (New York: Oxford University Press, 1988). Guido Calabresi, from the unusual perspective of tort law, also arrives at the position that we must find ways to allow "deeply held convictions to survive in tension with one another." Guido Calabresi, *Ideals, Beliefs, Attitudes and the Law: Private Law Perspectives on a Public Law Problem* (Syracuse, NY: Syracuse University Press, 1985), p. 117. Christopher F. Mooney, S.J., also argues that there is an important function served in liberal democracy by the entry of the "public church" into political dialogue. Christopher F. Mooney, *Public Virtue: Law and the Social Character of Religion* (Notre Dame, IN: University of Notre Dame Press, 1986), esp. Chap. 1. Neither Calabresi nor Mooney, though they suggest similar conclusions, discusses the issues with the same depth, scope, and theoretical subtlety as Greenawalt.

10. Greenawalt, *Religious Convictions*, pp. 16–21.

11. Greenawalt, *Religious Convictions*, p. 23.

12. Greenawalt, *Religious Convictions*, p. 12.

13. Greenawalt, *Religious Convictions*, chap. 5.

14. Greenawalt, *Religious Convictions*, p. 113. See chaps. 6–8.

15. Greenawalt, *Religious Convictions*, chaps. 9–10.

16. Greenawalt, *Religious Convictions*, pp. 145, 155.

17. Greenawalt, *Religious Convictions*, pp. 216–17.

18. Greenawalt, *Religious Convictions*, pp. 225–27. These conclusions about the appropriate scope of political action by religious groups and institutions are not without controversy. I shall discuss these topics in later chapters.

19. The following arguments were stimulated by James Skillen's reaction to earlier formulations of my ideas on this topic. I am very grateful for his prodding. Robert Audi argues that Greenawalt gives too much scope to religious views in secular discourse. See Robert Audi, "Religion and the Ethics of Political Participation," *Ethics*, 100 (January 1990), 386–97.

20. Greenawalt, *Religious Convictions*, pp. 217–18.

21. Greenawalt, *Religious Convictions*, pp. 219–20. For an account of such use of religious imagery in America, see Wilson Carey McWilliams, "The Bible in the American Political Tradition," in *Political Anthropology, III: Religion and Politics*, ed. Myron J. Aronoff (New Brunswick, NJ: Transaction Books, 1984), pp. 11–45.

22. George M. Marsden, "Are Secularists the Threat? Is Religion the Solution?" in *Unsecular America*, ed. Richard John Neuhaus (Grand Rapids, MI: Eerdmans, 1986), pp. 50–55. Robin W. Lovin, "Religion and American Public Life," in *Religion and American Public Life*, ed. Robin W. Lovin (New York: Paulist Press, 1986), esp. p. 24. See also, in the same collection, Franklin I. Gamwell, "Religion and Reason in American Politics," pp. 97–100.

Chapter 6

1. Alasdair MacIntyre, *After Virtue* (Notre Dame, IN: University of Notre Dame Press, 1981), pp. 236–37.

2. Of course, growing consensus on virtue and character in education does not descend to the precise *meaning* of the virtues to be inculcated or to the *methods* appropriate to doing so. I do not take a position on this consensus here, but only point to it as indicative of openness to virtue language.

3. I have discussed character at length in Clarke E. Cochran, *Character, Community, and Politics* (University, AL: University of Alabama Press, 1982), esp. chap. 2.

4. Some of the most significant works are MacIntyre, *After Virtue*; Yves R. Simon, *The Definition of Moral Virtue*, ed. Vukan Kuic (New York: Fordham University Press, 1986) (Simon never completed his work on virtue, and Professor Kuic produced this book from transcripts of Simon's 1957 lectures on "Virtues"); James D. Wallace, *Virtues and Vices* (Ithaca, NY: Cornell University Press, 1978); J. Budziszewski, *The Resurrection of Nature: Political Theory and the Human Character* (Ithaca, NY: Cornell University Press, 1986); Stanley Hauerwas, *A Community of Character: Toward a Constructive Christian Social Ethic* (Notre Dame, IN: University of Notre Dame Press, 1981); and Hauerwas, *The Peaceable Kingdom: A Primer in Christian Ethics* (Notre Dame, IN: University of Notre Dame Press, 1983). Many of the philosophical issues are discussed in Peter A. French, Theodore E. Uehling, Jr., and Howard K. Wettstein, eds., *Midwest Studies in Philosophy, Vol. XIII: Ethical Theory: Character and Virtue* (Notre Dame, IN: University of Notre Dame Press, 1988).

5. See the discussion in *Virtue—Public and Private*, ed. Richard John Neuhaus (Grand Rapids, MI: Eerdmanns, 1986), pp. 61–62.

6. See, for example, Hauerwas, *Community of Character*, p. 121.

7. Wallace, *Virtues and Vices*, chaps. 3–4.

8. Budziszewski, *Resurrection of Nature*, pp. 95–103.

9. Simon, *Moral Virtue*, p. 47. Cf. Philip Rieff's contention that the emerging Western culture based on the "dialectic of fulfillment" is destroying the Western culture of character based on deprivation of desire. *The Triumph of the Therapeutic* (New York: Harper & Row, 1968), pp. 49–50.

10. Wallace, *Virtues and Vices*, p. 99.

11. See Stuart Hampshire, "Morality and Pessimism" and "Public and Private Morality," both in *Public and Private Morality*, ed. Stuart Hampshire (Cambridge: Cambridge University Press, 1978), 1–22 and 23–53.

12. Hampshire, "Public and Private Morality," pp. 50–52.

13. Michael J. Sandel, *Liberalism and the Limits of Justice* (Cambridge: Cambridge University Press, 1982). William A. Galston, "Public Morality and Religion in the Liberal State," *PS*, 19 (Fall 1986), esp. 822–24. It was, indeed, one of the functions of Christian religion in the West to open the public realm more fully to such virtues, for Christianity regarded political justice as a secondary virtue, thus providing space for other public virtues to emerge. I owe this suggestion to Carey McWilliams.

14. Budziszewski, *Resurrection of Nature*, pp. 103–15 and chap. 4. Wallace, *Virtues and Vices*, chaps. 3 and 5.

15. See Glenn Tinder, *Tolerance: Toward a New Civility* (Amherst, MA: University of Massachusetts Press, 1976).

16. Wallace, *Virtues and Vices*, pp. 152–58.

17. Bernard Williams, "Politics and Moral Character," in Hampshire, ed., *Public and Private Morality*, p. 64.

18. See, for example, MacIntyre, *After Virtue*, chap. 16 and two papers delivered at the Annual Conference of the United States Capitol Historical Society, March 26–27, 1987, Washington, D.C.: Isaac Kramnick, "The Constitution and Its Critics on Individualism, Community, and the State," and Jean Yarbrough, "The Constitution and Character: The Missing Critical Principle?" For a defense of the centrality of virtue in the Founding period and an emphasis on its religious roots, see Richard Vetterli and Gary Bryner, *In Search of the Republic: Public Virtue and the Roots of American Government* (Totowa, NJ: Rowman & Littlefield, 1987).

19. Annie Dillard, *Teaching a Stone to Talk* (New York: Harper Colophon, 1983), p. 121.

20. See esp. MacIntyre, *After Virtue*, chap. 15. Cf. Budziszewski, *Resurrection of Nature*, "Mezzalogue" and chap. 3; Simon, *Moral Virtue*, p. 102 and chap. 6; and Wallace, *Virtues and Vices*, pp. 121–27.

21. MacIntyre, *After Virtue*, p. 205.

22. Simon, *Moral Virtue*, chap. 6.

23. Gilbert Keith Chesterton, *Orthodoxy* (Chicago: Thomas More Press, 1985), pp. 37–38.

24. In Neuhaus, ed., *Virtue—Public and Private*, p. 63.

25. Jean Bethke Elshtain, *Public Man, Private Woman* (Princeton, NJ: Princeton University Press, 1981), p. 321. Emphasis in original.

26. Tinder, *Tolerance*, p. 69.

27. On judgment and prudence, see for example, such different authors as MacIntyre, *After Virtue*, pp. 140–47; Budziszewski, *Resurrection of Nature*, pp. 81–94; Benjamin R. Barber, *Strong Democracy* (Berkeley, CA: University of California Press, 1984), pp. 158 and 198–209; and Lasch, *Minimal Self*, pp. 253–54.

28. For similar conclusions, see Gerald M. Mara, "Virtue and Pluralism: The Problem of the One and the Many," paper presented at the Georgetown University Colloquium in Social and Political Theory, Washington, D.C., February 1987. An extended defense of the politics of virtue is made by J. Budziszewski in *The Nearest Coast of Darkness: A Vindication of the Politics of Virtues* (Ithaca, NY: Cornell University Press, 1988).

29. Budziszewski, *Resurrection of Nature*, pp. 112–15. MacIntyre also calls attention to the importance of conflict in a theory of the virtues and faults Aristotle for not recognizing it; see *After Virtue*, esp. pp. 152–53, 160, and 167.

30. See Philip Hallie, *Lest Innocent Blood Be Shed* (New York: Harper & Row, 1979).

31. See Martha Nussbaum, "Aeschylus and Practical Conflict," *Ethics*, 95 (January 1985),

233–67. Some theorists of virtue have incorporated the tragic dimension of life. See MacIntyre, *After Virtue*, pp. 152–53 and 167 and Hauerwas, *Community of Character*, pp. 106–8.

32. Remarks at a conference on "The Public Turn in Philosophy," Center for Philosophy and Public Policy, University of Maryland, College Park, Maryland, December 1986.

33. Religious thinkers have come explicitly to recognize that judgment, not dogma, is the most important component of policy discourse. See Hauerwas, *Community of Character*, pp. 220–22 and Arthur Simon, *Christian Faith and Public Policy: No Grounds for Divorce* (Grand Rapids, MI: Eerdmans, 1987). (Simon is Director of the Christian lobby group, Bread for the World.) H. Richard Niebuhr argued that attention to the relative values of persons, places, and things does not mean Christian relativism. Concern for absolute truth does not mean dogmatism, but the ability to see each person and situation as it is, in relation to the absolute and to other persons and situations in all their contingency. H. Richard Niebuhr, *Christ and Culture* (New York: Harper Colophon, 1975), pp. 234–41.

34. Budziszewski, *Resurrection of Nature*, chap. 4.

35. These claims may conveniently be found in *A Reader in Political Theology*, ed. Alistair Kee (Philadelphia: Westminster Press, 1974). For a relatively uncritical acceptance of them, see Richard J. Cassidy, *Jesus, Politics, and Society* (Maryknoll, NY: Orbis Books, 1978). For an uncritical rejection, see Ernest W. Lefever, *Amsterdam to Nairobi* (Washington, DC: Ethics and Public Policy Center, 1979).

36. All Scripture quotations are from the Revised Standard Version, as published in *The New Oxford Annotated Bible with the Apocrypha* (New York: Oxford University Press, 1977).

37. See John H. Yoder, *The Politics of Jesus* (Grand Rapids, MI: Eerdmans, 1972). I am grateful to my former student, Rob Swanton, for suggesting some of these ways.

38. Niebuhr, *Christ and Culture*, esp. chaps. 2 and 6.

39. See *Baker's Dictionary of Theology* (Grand Rapids, MI: Baker Book House, 1960), s.v. "prudence," and *Interpreter's Dictionary of the Bible* (New York: Abingdon, 1962), s.v. "discretion and prudence."

40. Niebuhr, *Christ and Culture*, esp. chaps. 4 and 5.

41. Aquinas considers prudence especially in *Summa Theologica*, IIa-IIae, q. 47–56.

42. For an extended exploration of prophetic politics, see Neal Riemer, *The Future of the Democratic Revolution: Toward a More Prophetic Politics* (New York: Praeger Publishers, 1984).

43. St. Thomas Aquinas, *Philosophical Texts*, selected and translated by Thomas Gilby (New York: Oxford University Press, 1951), p. 357.

44. Peter H. Davids, "God and Caesar, II," *Sojourners*, May 1981, pp. 24–26.

Chapter 7

1. Alasdair MacIntyre, *After Virtue* (Notre Dame, IN: University of Notre Dame Press, 1981), p. 153; for the ideas expressed in the text see esp. pp. 133–36 and 190–209.

2. J. Budziszewski, *The Resurrection of Nature* (Ithaca, NY: Cornell University Press, 1986), pp. 53–62.

3. William H. Poteat, *Polanyian Meditations* (Durham, NC: Duke University Press, 1985), p. 175. I cannot hope to sustain this claim here. It depends upon the general epistemological approach of Michael Polanyi, which I have summarized briefly in "Authority and Community: The Contributions of Carl Friedrich, Yves R. Simon, and Michael Polanyi," *American Political Science Review*, 71 (June 1977), 546–58.

4. MacIntyre, *After Virtue*, p. 163. For a similar narrative account of self, virtue, and character, see Stanley Hauerwas, *The Peaceable Kingdom* (Notre Dame, IN: University of Notre Dame Press, 1983), esp. chap. 3. My discussion of failure, contingency, history, and tradition reflects Hauerwas's three essential features of the narrative character of life (contingency, history, and sin). See Hauerwas, *Peaceable Kingdom*, pp. 28–29.

5. Stories are not always straightforward. Sometimes stories become myths whose public, explicit meaning is not identical to the hidden (perhaps unconscious) meaning for the same public or for private persons. Stories sometimes conceal truths too horrible to display explicitly. For example, Moses' punishment, not being allowed to enter the Promised Land, hardly seems to fit his crime. Perhaps the simple story in Num. 20: 1–12 conceals a darker story. I am indebted to James Glass for this point.

6. See Aaron Wildavsky on memory and renewal in the Book of Deuteronomy in *The Nursing Father: Moses as a Political Leader* (University, AL: University of Alabama Press, 1984), pp. 153–54. Michael Walzer builds a theory of social criticism as interpretation from within a living cultural controversy. See *Interpretation and Social Criticism* (Cambridge, MA: Harvard University Press, 1987).

7. For such stories from a number of religious traditions, see John Stratton Hawley, ed., *Saints and Virtues* (Berkeley, CA: University of California Press, 1987).

8. See Robert K. Fullinwider, "Learning Morality," *QQ: Report from the Institute for Philosophy and Public Policy*, 8 (Spring 1988), 12–15.

9. See Christopher Lasch, *The Culture of Narcissism* (New York: Warner Books, 1979), pp. 23–25.

10. Sydney E. Ahlstrom, *A Religious History of the American People* (Garden City, NY: Doubleday Image Books, 1975), vol. 1, p. 15.

11. See Stanley Hauerwas, *A Community of Character* (Notre Dame, IN: University of Notre Dame Press, 1981), p. 14, and Walzer, *Interpretation and Social Criticism*.

12. Wilson Carey McWilliams, "The Bible in the American Political Tradition," in *Political Anthropology III: Religion and Politics*, ed. Myron J. Aronoff (New Brunswick, NJ: Transaction Books, 1984), pp. 11–45, and Michael Walzer, *Exodus and Revolution* (New York: Basic Books, 1985).

13. Budziszewski, *Resurrection of Nature*, p. 128. Emphasis in original.

14. MacIntyre, *After Virtue*, pp. 199–203; Budziszewski, *Resurrection of Nature*, p. 54.

15. Hadley Arkes, *First Things: An Inquiry into the First Principles of Morals and Justice* (Princeton, NJ: Princeton University Press, 1986).

16. Budziszewski, *Resurrection of Nature*, p. 106.

17. I have already indicated Budziszewski's awareness. MacIntyre's discussion of the unity of life as a quest for the good is an implicit response to the charge of relativism. See *After Virtue*, pp. 203–4 and, esp., *After Virtue*, 2d ed. (Notre Dame, IN: University of Notre Dame Press, 1984), pp. 272–78. Stanley Hauerwas responds to the relativistic objection in *Community of Character*, chap. 5. See also Martha C. Nussbaum, "Non-Relative Virtues: An Aristotelian Approach," in *Midwest Studies in Philosophy, XIII: Ethical Theory: Character and Virtue*, ed. Peter A. French, Theodore E. Uehling, Jr., and Howard K. Wettstein (Notre Dame, IN: University of Notre Dame Press, 1988), pp. 32–53.

18. See Aristotle, *Politics*, book 4, esp. chaps. 11–16. I am indebted to Gerald Mara for this point.

19. Robert A. Nisbet, *The Quest for Community* (New York: Oxford University Press, 1953), esp. chaps. 4–8. Emil Oestereicher speaks similarly of the "privatized self" in the modern

world. He says, "As long as the self remains the product of clear and traditional social definitions, self-experience remains virtually inseparable from the experience of society, nature, and the divine. It is only when traditional social definitions are removed that there develops a bifurcation between the experience of the self and the experience of the world, and between a private and a public self." "The Privatization of the Self in Modern Society," *Social Research*, 46 (Autumn 1979), 613. Robert Wuthnow and Clifford Nass provide some cautious empirical support for the "civil privatism" thesis that government expansion has weakened voluntary associations, in this case church membership in relation to other memberships and to political activity. "Government Activity and Civil Privatism: Evidence from Voluntary Church Membership," *Journal for the Scientific Study of Religion*, 27 (June 1988), 157–74.

20.   See Robert A. Nisbet, *The Social Bond* (New York: Knopf, 1970), pp. 148–49 and 154–55. I have discussed the relation of roles to character in *Character, Community, and Politics* (University, AL: University of Alabama Press, 1982), chap. 2.

21.   Saul Bellow, *Mr. Sammler's Planet* (Greenwich, CT: Fawcett, 1970), esp. pp. 134–37 and 206ff.

22.   Yves R. Simon, *The Definition of Moral Virtue*, ed. Vukan Kuic (New York: Fordham University Press, 1986), pp. 35–44. Sissela Bok's observation that neither "white lies" nor excuses can be evaluated without attention to the social practices in which they are situated reinforces the connection of right and wrong with roles and institutions. See *Lying* (New York: Pantheon, 1978), chap. 5 and pp. 99–104.

23.   I cannot hope to prove this contention here. For insight into the relation of these institutions to public and private life in other cultures see, for example, Barrington Moore, Jr., *Privacy: Studies in Social and Cultural History* (Armonk, NY: M.E. Sharpe, 1984); articles by Herbert J. Spiro and by John M. Roberts and Thomas Gregor in *Nomos XIII: Privacy*, ed. J. Roland Pennock and John W. Chapman (New York: Atherton Press, 1971); articles by Martin Krygier and by Leslie K. Haviland and John B. Haviland in *Public and Private in Social Life*, ed. S.I. Benn and G.F. Gaus (New York: St. Martin's, 1983); and articles by Robert F. Murphy and by Alan Westin in *Philosophical Dimensions of Privacy: An Anthology*, ed. Ferdinand David Schoeman (Cambridge: Cambridge University Press, 1984).

24.   Though I emphasize the public side of the family here and stress its integrating functions, I recognize, of course, its private side, its inclusive and exclusive dimensions, which I have discussed previously. Moreover, I recognize as well that families are often destructive, that their inclusive and exclusive characteristics can take the form of physical and emotional violence. Travis Billings reminded me to acknowledge these.

25.   For examples, see Sarah Ban Breathnach, "Tradition, the Tie That Defines," *The Washington Post*, March 3, 1987, p. D5.

26.   See Jean Bethke Elshtain, *Public Man, Private Woman* (Princeton, NJ: Princeton University Press, 1981), esp. chap. 2–3 and 6. See also Elshtain, ed., *The Family in Political Thought* (Amherst, MA: University of Massachusetts Press, 1982), and her "Feminism, Family, & Community," *Dissent*, 29 (Fall 1982), 442–49.

27.   See Virginia Sapiro, "Private Costs of Public Commitments or Public Costs of Private Commitments? Family Roles Versus Political Ambition," *American Journal of Political Science*, 26 (May 1982), 265–79.

28.   See, for example, Karl Zinsmeister, "Are We Demanding More Than Day Care Can Deliver?" *The Washington Post National Weekly Edition*, October 3–9, 1988, pp. 28–29; also the remarks by Mary Stewart VanLeeuwen and Ronald J. Sider at the conference on "Christian Perspectives: Issues Facing the New Administration," Pepperdine University, Malibu, CA, January 26–28, 1989.

29.   I have framed this argument in terms of intimate relations with others. The same points apply, *mutatis mutandis*, within the person. There is a tension between the inclusive and exclusive sides of the self, an attraction to and repulsion from introspection and contemplation.

30.   Arkes, *First Things*. This perspective runs throughout Arkes's moral theory. I shall not, however, comment on or criticize his general moral theory, but only its applications to and implications for private and public.

31.   Arkes, *First Things*, p. 173.

32.   For these contentions, see Arkes, *First Things*, esp. pp. 28, 179, 182, and 238, and chaps. 9 and 15.

33.   Roberto Mangabeira Unger, *Knowledge and Politics* (New York: Free Press, 1975), p. 274.

34.   Arkes, *First Things*, pp. 280–282, 301, and 302.

35.   See Eldon J. Eisenach, *The Two Worlds of Liberalism* (Chicago: University of Chicago Press, 1981), pp. 117–18. Sissela Bok, who like Arkes places considerable weight on the idea of public justification, does a far better job than he of treating public and private. She recognizes that both public and private morality have the same justificatory requirement of public reason, but she recognizes at the same time the differences between public and private life that affect the significance of lying in each realm. See Bok, *Lying*, esp. chaps. 7, 11, 12, and 14.

36.   Thomas Luckmann, *The Invisible Religion: The Problem of Religion in Modern Society* (New York: Macmillan, 1967), p. 117.

Chapter 8

1.   The perspective of this paragraph was suggested by H. Richard Niebuhr's discussion of the tension between Christ and culture; *Christ and Culture* (New York: Harper Colophon, 1975), esp. chap. 1.

2.   Martin E. Marty, "Foreword," in *Religion in American Public Life*, ed. Robin W. Lovin (New York: Paulist, 1986), p. 1.

3.   Michael Walzer, *Spheres of Justice* (New York: Basic, 1983), chap. 10.

4.   Peter Berger, "Religious Liberty and the Paradox of Relevance," *The Religion & Society Report*, 5 (January 1988), 1–2.

5.   Wilson Carey McWilliams, "The Bible in the American Political Tradition," in *Political Anthropology, III: Religion and Politics*, ed. Myron J. Aronoff (New Brunswick, NJ: Transaction, 1984), p. 19. On the political not being the whole of public life, see H. M. Kuitert, *Everything is Political, But Politics is not Everything: A Theological Perspective on Faith and Politics*, trans. John Bowden (London: SCM, 1986). On the biblical tension between religious prophets and political values, see H. Mark Roelofs, "Church and State: Biblical Antecedents," in *Religion and Politics*, ed. Thomas E. Scism (mimeo) (Charleston, IL: Eastern Illinois University, 1987), pp. 18–26.

6.   Philip Rieff, *The Triumph of the Therapeutic* (New York: Harper Torchbooks, 1968).

7.   Religions have more than didactic teachings on these subjects. The exemplary lives of saints in many religious traditions provide models of outstanding lives, often in tension with ordinary cultural norms and expectations. See John Stratton Hawley, ed., *Saints and Virtues* (Berkeley, CA: University of California Press, 1987). John A. Coleman, S.J., points out how saints represent religion as a whole in being liminal figures, pointing "beyond the threshold they occupy to a larger, transcendent whole. They represent the primary locus for the human

experience of the religious." "Conclusion: After Sainthood?" in Hawley, ed., *Saints and Virtues*, p. 221.

8. Though we try in many subtle ways. See the profound meditations of Ernest Becker, *The Denial of Death* (New York: Free Press, 1973). Becker's account of how repression of the knowledge of death distorts life suggests the necessity of considering how the public denial of death distorts public life.

9. To take this matter to its *n*th degree, witness the news item in July 1987 that grave robbers broke into the coffin of Juan Peron (secured with twelve combination locks), cut off his hands, and held them for $8 million ransom.

10. See the discussion with Cephalus in Book 1 and the Myth of Er in Book 10. George Armstrong Kelly is an exception to my generalization about political theorists ignoring the importance of death and religion. See George Armstrong Kelly, *Politics and Religious Consciousness in America* (New Brunswick, NJ: Transaction, 1984), e.g., pp. 11–13.

11. See Eldon J. Eisenach, *The Two Worlds of Liberalism* (Chicago: University of Chicago Press, 1981), esp. pp. 13–17, 47ff, and 57. To accept this Hobbesian insight, of course, is not to accept his resolution of the problem. For other reflections on Hobbes, death, and politics, see James M. Glass, *Delusion* (Chicago: University of Chicago Press, 1985), esp. pp. 100–102 and 148–49. In some delusional patients, death is the only escape from a private tyranny analogous to public despotism.

12. Philosophy, of course, may do so. Nothing in my discussion of religion rules out philosophy, and I have explicitly not assimilated philosophy to religion. Although politics could itself never perform the special functions of religion considered in this chapter, philosophy might. Hence the tension between Athens and Jerusalem. Nevertheless, historically speaking, philosophy, though it motivated individuals such as Socrates and, perhaps, Seneca to die, seems unlikely to play a significant public role in regard to death. Ideology is another matter, and I address it below.

Finally, this thought. We would like to imagine and to live in a world where there was nothing to kill for, but what about a world, *pace* John Lennon's song "Imagine," with nothing to die for?

13. See Stanley Hauerwas, *A Community of Character* (Notre Dame, IN: University of Notre Dame Press, 1981), pp. 85–86.

14. See Becker, *Denial of Death*. On the idea of religion as an antidote to liberal individualism, see Robert Booth Fowler, *Unconventional Partners* (Grand Rapids, MI: Eerdmanns, 1989), and his "Religion and the Escape from Liberal Individualism," in *Religion in American Politics*, ed. Charles W. Dunn (Washington, DC: CQ Press, 1989), pp. 39–49; also Robert N. Bellah et al., *Habits of the Heart* (Berkeley, CA: University of California Press, 1985).

15. Hannah Arendt, *The Human Condition* (Garden City, NY: Doubleday Anchor, 1959), pp. 212–23.

16. William H. Poteat stresses the important difference between the Greek and Hebrew languages relating to the meaning of "word." The Hebrew, as distinct from the Greek, stresses the person of the speaker of the word. For Hebrew, God is the paradigmatic speaker of words, and his faithfulness to his word becomes a paradigm of what it means to be a person, which is to be faithful to promises explicit and implicit in one's words. *Polanyian Meditations* (Durham, NC: Duke University Press, 1985), pp. 104–32.

17. Remarks summarized in *Virtue—Public and Private*, ed. by Richard John Neuhaus (Grand Rapids, MI: Eerdmans, 1986), p. 73. On some of the pains of public life and the role of religion in coping with them, see Parker J. Palmer, *The Company of Strangers: Christians and the Renewal of America's Public Life* (New York: Crossroad, 1981), chap. 6.

18.   Roland Robertson, "Church-State Relations and the World System," in *Church-State Relations: Tensions and Transitions*, ed. Thomas Robbins and Roland Robertson (New Brunswick, NJ: Transaction, 1987), p. 50.

19.   I do not contend that religious groups alone keep substantive, principled issues before the public. Nor do I contend that religious groups are the most important actors in this respect. Rather, my point is that religion can and should contribute by pushing politics to confront such principled issues, even though a democratic politics oriented toward compromise finds them disturbing.

20.   I am indebted to Jim Skillen for these points.

21.   For a religious "pro-life" argument grounded in principles similar to these, see Ronald J. Sider, *Completely Pro-Life: Building a Consistent Stance* (Downers Grove, IL: InterVarsity Press, 1987).

22.   United States Catholic Conference, *Economic Justice for All: Pastoral Letter on Catholic Social Teaching and the U.S. Economy* (Washington, DC: United States Catholic Conference, 1986). Gerald M. Mara, "Poverty and Justice: The Bishops and Contemporary Liberalism," in *The Deeper Meaning of Economic Life: Critical Essays on the U.S. Catholic Bishops' Pastoral Letter on the Economy*, ed. R. Bruce Douglass (Washington, DC: Georgetown University Press, 1986), pp. 157–78.

23.   See Glenn Tinder, "Christianity and the Welfare State," unpublished paper.

24.   Stanley Milgram, *Obedience to Authority* (New York: Harper, 1974). W. Carey McWilliams has reminded me that Milgram's experiments dealt with the authority of science and scientists, the exception to the rule in liberal society.

25.   This perspective is similar to that advanced by Stanley Hauerwas, *Community of Character* and *A Peaceable Kingdom* (Notre Dame, IN: University of Notre Dame Press, 1983). David Walsh makes similar points in "The Role of the Church in the Modern World," *Journal of Church and State*, 29 (Winter 1987), 63–77.

26.   Kelly, *Politics*, p. 186. Fowler argues that the challenge that religion has offered in the American liberal context has not been genuinely radical—that is, it has not posed an alternative social and political ideology, nor has it acted to institute alternative basic institutions. See his *Unconventional Partners*, pp. 83–84.

27.   On public life as the realm of strangers and its significance for religion, see Palmer, *Company of Strangers*. That religion can be liberating without decaying into fanaticism is one of the lessons of the Exodus story, according to Michael Walzer. See his *Exodus and Revolution* (New York: Basic Books, 1985), esp. the conclusion.

28.   On God as stranger, see Palmer, *Company of Strangers*. I do not argue that humility and moderation are learned only in politics, but that in regimes with a genuine public and political life politics is a readily available teacher. Tocqueville saw that religion makes a contribution to democracy, but he also realized that democracy in America tames religious passion.

29.   Aaron Wildavsky argues, from a perspective analogous to this one, that God needs Moses as much as Moses needs God, for the implacable divine law needs a mediator when it encounters human weakness. See his *The Nursing Father: Moses as a Political Leader* (University, AL: University of Alabama Press, 1984), esp. p. 89.

30.   J. Budziszewski, *The Resurrection of Nature* (Ithaca, NY: Cornell University Press, 1986), p. 153.

31.   With respect to the idea of politics welcoming the sharp advocacy of religious views, I am indebted to the remarks of Senator John Danforth and Representative Lindy Boggs during

an interreligious forum on religion and politics at St. Alban's Church, Washington, D.C., March 17, 1987.

This point is analogous to the recommendation in the religious world that the Christian churches stop trying to advance ecumenical unity by becoming like each other. Rather, ecumenism is best advanced when Catholics strive to become the best Catholics they can be, and Lutherans strive to become the best Lutherans they can be.

On the creative power of compromise witness this amusing, but telling, example. In the United States Capitol there is a prayer room for members and staff. In it there is an open Bible. The story goes that, when the room was designed, Jewish members objected to having a Bible in it, for the Bible would include both Testaments. A compromise was reached: A Bible would be placed in the room, but it had always to be open to the Old Testament. I do not think it matters whether the story is apocryphal.

32.   For criticism along these lines, see Henry Briefs, "The Limits of Scripture: Theological Imperatives and Economic Reality," in Douglass, ed., *Deeper Meaning of Economic Life*, pp. 57–96.

33.   These points are difficult to prove conclusively, but the actual political behavior of American religion suggests their truth. Religious groups rise and fall in influence, and the virulence of their expression wanes as it breaks against the hard rock of competing interests and the labyrinthine ways of law-making. See especially Allen D. Hertzke's study of religious groups on the Washington scene, *Representing God in Washington* (Knoxville, TN: University of Tennessee Press, 1988), as well as Matthew C. Moen, *The Christian Right and Congress* (Tuscaloosa, AL: University of Alabama Press, 1989).

34.   See Budziszewski's account of these devices in *Resurrection*, Chap. 5.

35.   The temptations of Christ, especially the third, are instructive in this respect. See Matt. 4:1–11. (In Luke 4:1–13 the most political temptation is the second.)

Chapter 9

1.   Secularization—which urges the decreasing influence of religion in social life—is the mirror image of H. Richard Niebuhr's famous first position in the history of Christian interpretation of culture, "Christ Against Culture." See H. Richard Niebuhr, *Christ and Culture* (New York: Harper Colophon, 1975), chap. 2. Secularization often amounts to culture against religion. For a convenient summary of different patterns of religious-political interaction, see Roland Robertson, "Church-State Relations in Comparative Perspective," in *Church-State Relations: Tensions and Transitions*, ed. Thomas Robbins and Roland Robertson (New Brunswick, NJ: Transaction Books, 1987), pp. 153–60.

2.   These positions are analogous to Niebuhr's "Christ Of Culture" position. See Niebuhr, *Christ and Culture*, chap. 3.

3.   Kenneth D. Wald, *Religion and Politics in the United States* (New York: St. Martin's, 1987), p. 136.

4.   I have mentioned two of Niebuhr's models. My tensional model may seem closest to his "Christ And Culture In Paradox," and that may be so. Certainly, my focus on tension owes a good deal to his account of the paradox model. Nevertheless, I reject the separation of the worlds of faith and culture that often goes with this model. I find appealing also the importance of the continuity between religion and culture (with the transcendence of the former) in the "Christ Above Culture" model and the challenge religion makes to politics in the "Christ Transforming Culture" model. See Niebuhr, *Christ and Culture*, chaps. 4–6. A healthy theory of religion and politics must have a place for transcendence, tension, and challenge. These models have analogies in religions other than Christianity.

5. H. Mark Roelofs, *The Tensions of Citizenship: Private Man and Public Duty* (New York: Rinehart & Co., 1957), p. 155. David Walsh frames well the issue of the tension between the public and private roles of religion as it addresses public policy. See David Walsh, "The Role of the Church in the Modern World," *Journal of Church and State*, 29 (Winter 1987), 63–77.

6. Thomas Luckmann, *The Invisible Religion* (New York: Macmillan, 1967), p. 67.

7. Meredith McGuire, *Religion: The Social Context* (Belmont, CA: Wadsworth, 1981), pp. 215–45.

8. See George M. Marsden, "Are Secularists the Threat? Is Religion the Solution?" in *Unsecular America*, ed. Richard John Neuhaus (Grand Rapids, MI: Eerdmans, 1986), pp. 31–51.

9. Bryan Wilson, "Secularization: The Inherited Model," in *The Sacred in a Secular Age: Toward Revision in the Scientific Study of Religion*, ed. Phillip E. Hammond (Berkeley, CA: University of California Press, 1985), p. 18. This volume as a whole is a good introduction to the debate and to doubts within sociology about secularization theory as received wisdom.

10. See, for example, Luckmann, *Invisible Religion*, pp. 35ff, and James A. Beckford, "Religious Organization," in Hammond, ed., *Sacred in a Secular Age*, pp. 125–38.

11. Sydney E. Ahlstrom, *A Religious History of the American People* (Garden City, NY: Doubleday Image, 1975), vol. 1, pp. 54ff.

12. Rodney Stark, "Church and Sect," in Hammond, ed., *Sacred in a Secular Age*, pp. 139–49. See also Jeffrey K. Hadden, "Religious Broadcasting and the Mobilization of the New Christian Right," *Journal for the Scientific Study of Religion*, 26 (March 1987), 1–24. In addition to being an excellent account of the mobilization of the new religious right, Hadden provides a good summary critique of secularization theories. On the distinctions between church, denomination, and sect and how some are strongly acculturated (secularized) and others critical of culture, see H. Paul Chalfant, et al., *Religion in Contemporary Society*, 2d ed. (Palo Alto, CA: Mayfield, 1987), pp. 84–99.

13. For good discussions of American exceptionalism, see Neuhaus, ed., *Unsecular America*; and Wald, *Religion and Politics in the United States*, esp. chap. 1.

14. On Israel see, for example, Manfred H. Vogel, "The State as Essential Expression of the Faith of Judaism," and Mitchell Cohen, "Pluralism and Theocracy: The Conflict Between Religion and State in Israel," both in *Cities of Gods: Faith, Politics, and Pluralism in Judaism, Christianity, and Islam*, ed. Nigel Biggar, Jamie S. Scott, and William Schweiker (Westport, CT: Greenwood, 1986), pp. 11–20 and 35–54. On theocratic tendencies inherent in Islam, see Fazlur Rahman, "Islam and Political Action: Politics in the Service of Religion," in Biggar, et al., eds., *Cities of Gods*, pp. 153–65. Solzhenitsyn's ideas are described in Stephen Baron, "Morality and Politics in Modern Life: Tocqueville and Solzhenitsyn on the Importance of Religion to Liberty," *Polity*, 14 (Spring 1982), 395–413. The Reconstructionist program is described and criticized in Kevin L. Clausen, "The Intellectual Elite of the Christian Right: The Political Theory of the 'Reconstructionist' Movement," *Journal of Political Science*, 16 (Spring 1988), 24–32, and in *The Religion and Society Report* (May 1987), 2–3. On theocratic tendencies within Protestantism, see Martin E. Marty, "The Protestant Principle: Between Theocracy and Propheticism," in Biggar, et al., eds., *Cities of Gods*, pp.101–17.

15. Thomas Hobbes, *Leviathan*, ed. Michael Oakeshott (New York: Collier Books, 1962), chap. 31, pp. 268 and 269.

16. The civil religion literature, like the secularization literature, is massive. I shall not review it or supply a bibliography. My interests will be served by representative cases. The best

brief introduction to the debates is still Russell E. Richey and Donald G. Jones, eds., *American Civil Religion* (New York: Harper, 1974).

17.   Jean-Jacques Rousseau, *The Social Contract*, trans. Maurice Cranston (Baltimore, MD: Penguin Books, 1968), book 4, chap. 8; Bellah, "Civil Religion in America," in Richey and Jones, eds., *American Civil Religion*, pp. 21–44; Peter Berger, *The Sacred Canopy* (New York: Doubleday, 1967). For the crisis of legitimacy in contemporary politics, see esp. John H. Schaar, "Legitimacy in the Modern State," in *Power and Community*, ed. Philip Green and Sanford Levinson (New York: Vintage, 1970), pp. 276–327. For different expressions of the legitimacy need, see George Armstrong Kelly, *Politics and Religious Consciousness in America* (New Brunswick, NJ: Transaction, 1984), pp. 27–28, and Michael Harrington, *The Politics at God's Funeral* (New York: Penguin, 1985).

18.   Richard John Neuhaus, *The Naked Public Square: Religion and Democracy in America* (Grand Rapids, MI: Eerdmans, 1984). References to this work appear in the text. Although Neuhaus does not call his perspective civil religion, his advocacy of religion's clothing the naked public realm takes the form of civil religion's concern with the sacred legitimation of public life.

For a similar perspective on the need for a religious legitimation of democratic public life, see A. James Reichley, *Religion in American Public Life* (Washington, DC: Brookings Institution, 1985), esp. chaps. 1, 2, and 7. It is curious to note how the argument for civil religion parallels Lord Devlin's argument for the necessity of a shared moral consensus to ground the law. The entire debate over that thesis is relevant to the debate over civil religion. The main arguments are expressed in Patrick Devlin, *The Enforcement of Morals* (London: Oxford University Press, 1965, H. L. A. Hart, *Law, Liberty, and Morality* (New York: Vintage Books, 1963); and Ronald Dworkin, "Lord Devlin and the Enforcement of Morals," in *Political and Social Philosophy*, ed. J. Charles King and James A. McGilvray (New York: McGraw-Hill, 1973), pp. 348–62.

One of the most creative, but iconoclastic, accounts of civil religion with a good deal to say about the tension between private and public expression of faith is John Murray Cuddihy's *No Offense: Civil Religion and Protestant Taste* (New York: Seabury, 1978). What is most offensive about the new religious right, if we follow Cuddihy's version of civil religion, is that it disturbs liberals and mainstream religionists because it violates the style more than the substance of American civil religion, namely, the tolerant, pluralistic, private, inoffensive "religion of civility."

Some of the paradoxes of the new religious right as it simultaneously condemns and exalts American society may be explained by the Reformation, especially Lutheran, separation of public and private life. It is the "outer man" that is subject to the powers that be. The freedom of the "inner man" to remain uncorrupted by outer behavior and to serve as a source of redemption is not compromised by what the powers require of the "outer man." On this distinction in the Reformation, see Jean Bethke Elshtain, *Public Man, Private Woman* (Princeton, NJ: Princeton University Press, 1981), p. 83.

19.   Alasdair MacIntyre, *After Virtue* (Notre Dame, IN: University of Notre Dame Press, 1981), p. 48.

20.   The image of legal aspiration is taken from the "jurisprudence of aspirations" advocated by Robert E. Rodes, Jr., "On Law and Virtue," in Neuhaus, ed., *Virtue—Public and Private*, pp. 30–42. The image of the "republican banquet" is borrowed from William James by Martin E. Marty, "A Sort of Republican Banquet," in Lovin, ed., *Religion in American Public Life*, pp. 146–80.

21.   Quoted in Ahlstrom, *Religious History*, vol. 2, p. 450. See chaps. 43, 52, and 56 for religious accommodation in the periods mentioned. Other examples are frequent throughout American religious history. The Vietnam War, of course, was an exception in many ways to

religion's accommodation to politics; indeed, religious criticism of American conduct of the war actually signaled the breakdown of American civil religion. For a criticism of civil religion similar to mine, see Neal Riemer, "The Civil Religion in America and Prophetic Politics." *The Drew Gateway*, 44 (Fall 1973), 20–32.

22. Stanley Hauerwas, *The Peaceable Kingdom* (Notre Dame, IN: University of Notre Dame Press, 1983), p. 15. Compare Werner Dannhauser's excellent dissection of the utility of religion, "Religion and the Conservatives," *Commentary* (December 1985), 51–55. I am not contending that the advocates of civil religion are indifferent to the truth of religion, only that they have not taken seriously enough the difference between truth and utility claims. Tocqueville, indeed, could be charged with originating the advocacy of religion simply for its utility to democratic society. For discussion of this charge, see Catherine Zuckert, "Not by Preaching: Tocqueville on the Role of Religion in American Democracy," *Review of Politics*, 43 (April 1981), 259–80.

23. Leszek Kolakowski, "Modernity on Endless Trial," *Encounter* (March 1986), p. 11. Kelly argues (*Politics and Religious Consciousness*, chap. 7) that in its historical context the civil religion debate says more about contemporary religious and political decline than about the reality of civil faith.

24. Alexis de Tocqueville, *Democracy in America*, trans. Henry Reeve (New Rochelle, NY: Arlington House, n.d.), vol. 1, pp. xliv–xlv.

25. H. Richard Niebuhr, *The Kingdom of God in America* (New York: Harper Torchbooks, 1959), esp. chap. 2 and 3.

26. For the contentions of this paragraph, see, for example, Wald, *Religion and Politics*, chap. 1; Paul Seabury, "Caesar and the Religious Domain in America," *Teaching Political Science*, 10 (Fall 1982), 20–29; and Ralph Lerner, "Facing Up to the Founding," paper presented at the Annual Conference of the United States Capitol Historical Society, March 26–27, 1987, Washington, D.C.

27. On continued intolerance between and even within religious groups in the United States, see Robert N. Bellah and Frederick E. Greenspahn, eds., *Uncivil Religion: Interreligious Hostility in America* (New York: Crossroad, 1987).

28. Michael J. Sandel, "Morality and the Liberal Ideal," *The New Republic*, May 7, 1984, p. 17. For rather intemperate statements of the unsettling of moral traditions, see James Hitchcock, "Church, State, and Moral Values: The Limits of American Pluralism," and Francis Canavan, "The Pluralist Game," both in *Law and Contemporary Problems*, 44 (Spring 1981), 3–21 and 23–37. To agree that the state inevitably promotes some values over others is not to agree with the argument of the religious right that it thereby promotes a "religion of secularism."

29. *Lynch v. Donnelly* 465 U.S. 668 (1984); *Marsh v. Chambers* 463 U.S. 783 (1983).

30. See, for example, Richard H. Jones, "Accommodationist and Separationist Ideals in Supreme Court Establishment Clause Decisions," *Journal of Church and State*, 28 (Spring 1986), 193–223.

31. Thomas Robbins, "Church-State Tensions in the United States," in Robbins and Robertson, eds., *Church-State Relations*, pp. 67–75.

32. "If the collective conscience of evangelical America is left out, the movement as a whole is incomprehensible." Ahlstrom, *Religious History*, vol. 2, p. 83.

33. H. Richard Niebuhr, *Kingdom of God*.

34. Allen D. Hertzke, *Representing God in Washington: The Role of Religious Lobbies in the American Polity* (Knoxville, TN: University of Tennessee Press, 1988), p. 75.

35. Hertzke, *Representing God*, p. 3. I encountered a clear example of this learning in a

discussion with Jack Smalligan of JustLife, a religiously oriented PAC supporting candidates who advocate policies representing a "consistent life ethic." To my question about whether giving and withholding money for candidates might not taint the motives of politicians on this fundamentally moral position, Smalligan argued that money is necessarily connected to politics and so is cynicism, especially in the American political structure. He only asks that once the—perhaps partially cynical—deal is struck both sides hold to it with "integrity." I was struck by how very political this response was, how it reflected specifically political values, but in the service of a principle. It simultaneously and integrally united high ideals and political compromise. The remarks were made at a Capitol Hill breakfast sponsored by the Association for Public Justice, April 9, 1987, Washington, D.C.

36.   Hertzke, *Representing God*, pp. 88–93, 195–98. See also Matthew C. Moen, *The Christian Right and Congress* (Tuscaloosa, AL: University of Alabama Press, 1989).

37.   Peter L. Benson and Dorothy L. Williams, *Religion on Capitol Hill: Myths and Realities* (New York: Oxford University Press, 1986).

38.   Such remarks were frequent, for example, among the politicians participating in a conference at Pepperdine University on "Christian Perspectives: Issues Facing the New Administration," Malibu, CA, January 26–28, 1989.

39.   Hertzke, *Representing God*, esp. pp. 119, 132, and 154–58, finds that religious lobbies in Washington, D.C., play a very important role in representing broad, diffuse public sentiment on a variety of issues, especially those in foreign policy. He believes that they make the American system more representative on the whole, especially relative to fundamental values, than it would be without them. This role of religious bodies engaged in political activity is an example of the "mediating structures" that Peter L. Berger and Richard John Neuhaus advocated in the middle 1970s. See *To Empower People: The Role of Mediating Structures in Public Policy* (Washington, DC: American Enterprise Institute for Public Policy Research, 1977). Mediating structures help overcome the alienation between public and private life in an impersonal, pluralistic society.

40.   Phillip E. Hammond, "Another Great Awakening?" in *The New Christian Right: Mobilization and Legitimation*, ed. by Robert C. Liebman and Robert Wuthnow (New York: Aldine Publishing Company, 1983), pp. 207–23, argues that Tocqueville recognized the public participatory effects of previous religious awakenings. Hammond describes how the activity of religious groups in an awakening can stimulate public life—though he argues that the new religious right is not doing so, because its concerns remain too private.

41.   Stanley Hauerwas, *A Community of Character* (Notre Dame, IN: University of Notre Dame Press, 1981), p. 13.

Bibliography

Ahlstrom, Sydney E. *A Religious History of the American People*. Garden City, NY: Doubleday Image, 1975.

Aquinas, Thomas. *Philosophical Texts*. Selected and translated by Thomas Gilby. New York: Oxford University Press, 1951.

Arblaster, Anthony. *The Rise and Decline of Western Liberalism*. Oxford: Basil Blackwell, 1984.

Arendt, Hannah. *The Human Condition*. Garden City, NY: Doubleday Anchor, 1959.

Aristotle. *Politics*. Translated by Ernest Barker. New York: Oxford University Press, 1962.

Arkes, Hadley. *First Things: An Inquiry into the First Principles of Morals and Justice*. Princeton, NJ: Princeton University Press, 1986.

Audi, Robert. "Religion and the Ethics of Political Participation." *Ethics*, 100 (January 1990), 386–97.

Baier, Annette. "Trust and Antitrust." *Ethics*, 96 (January 1986), 231–60.

Barber, Benjamin. *Strong Democracy: Participatory Politics for a New Age*. Berkeley, CA: University of California Press, 1984.

Baron, Stephen. "Morality and Politics in Modern Life: Tocqueville and Solzhenitsyn on the Importance of Religion to Liberty." *Polity*, 14 (Spring 1982), 395–413.

Bathory, Peter Dennis. "Tocqueville on Citizenship and Faith: A Response to Cushing Strout." *Political Theory*, 8 (February 1980), 27–38.

Becker, Ernest. *The Denial of Death*. New York: Free Press, 1973.

Bellah, Robert N. and Frederick E. Greenspahn, eds. *Uncivil Religion: Interreligious Hostility in America*. New York: Crossroad, 1987.

Bellah, Robert N., Richard Madsen, William M. Sullivan, Ann Swidler, and Steven M. Tipton, *Habits of the Heart: Individualism and Commitment in American Life*. Berkeley, CA: University of California Press, 1985.

Bellow, Saul. *Mr. Sammler's Planet*. Greenwich, CT: Fawcett, 1970.

——. *A Theft*. New York: Penguin Books, 1989.

Benn, S. I., and G.F. Gaus, eds. *Public and Private in Social Life*. New York: St. Martin's Press, 1983.

Benson, Peter L. and Dorothy L. Williams. *Religion on Capitol Hill: Myths and Realities*. New York: Oxford University Press, 1986.

Berger, Peter. "Religious Liberty and the Paradox of Relevance." *The Religion & Society Report*, 5 (January 1988), 1–2.

——. *The Sacred Canopy*. NY: Doubleday, 1967.

Berger, Peter, Brigitte Berger, and Hansfried Kellner. *The Homeless Mind*. New York: Vintage Books, 1974.

Berger, Peter, and Thomas Luckmann. *The Social Construction of Reality: A Treatise in the Sociology of Knowledge*. New York: Doubleday, 1967.

Berger, Peter, and Richard John Neuhaus. *To Empower People: The Role of Mediating Structures in Public Policy*. Washington, DC: American Enterprise Institute for Public Policy Research, 1977.

Berlin, Isaiah. "Two Concepts of Liberty." In *idem, Four Essays on Liberty*, pp. 118–72. London: Oxford University Press, 1969.

Bier, William C., S.J., ed. *Privacy: A Vanishing Value?* New York: Fordham University Press, 1980.

Biggar, Nigel, Jamie S. Scott, and William Schweiker, eds. *Cities of Gods: Faith, Politics, and Pluralism in Judaism, Christianity, and Islam*. Westport, CT: Greenwood, 1986.

Bok, Sissela. *Lying: Moral Choice in Public and Private Life*. New York: Pantheon Books, 1978.

Boling, Patricia. "Why Public v. Private is Wrong." Paper presented at the September 1985 Annual Meeting of the American Political Science Association, New Orleans. Louisiana.

Budziszewski, J. *The Nearest Coast of Darkness: A Vindication of The Politics of Virtues*. Ithaca, NY: Cornell University Press, 1988.

_____. *The Resurrection of Nature: Political Theory and the Human Character*. Ithaca, NY: Cornell University Press, 1986.

Calabresi, Guido. *Ideals, Beliefs, Attitudes and the Law: Private Law Perspectives on a Public Law Problem*. Syracuse, NY: Syracuse University Press, 1985.

Canavan, Francis. "The Pluralist Game." *Law and Contemporary Problems*, 44 (Spring 1981), 23–37.

Canavan, Margaret. "Politics as Culture: Hannah Arendt and the Public Realm." *History of Political Thought*, 6 (Winter 1985), 617–42.

Cassidy, Richard J. *Jesus, Politics, and Society*. Maryknoll, NY: Orbis Books, 1978.

Cassirer, Ernst. *An Essay on Man*. New Haven, CT: Yale University Press, 1944.

Chalfant, H. Paul, Robert E. Beckley, and C. Eddie Palmer. *Religion in Contemporary Society*. 2d ed. Palo Alto, CA: Mayfield, 1987.

Chesterton, Gilbert Keith. *Orthodoxy*. Chicago: Thomas More Press, 1985.

Childress, James F. "Appeals to Conscience." *Ethics*, 89 (July 1979), 315–35.

Clausen, Kevin L. "The Intellectual Elite of the Christian Right: The Political Theory of the 'Reconstructionist' Movement." *Journal of Political Science*, 16 (Spring 1988), 24–32.

Cochran, Clarke E. "Authority and Community: The Contributions of Carl Friedrich, Yves R. Simon, and Michael Polanyi." *American Political Science Review*, 71 (June 1977), 546–58.

_____. *Character, Community, and Politics*. University, AL: University of Alabama Press, 1982.

_____. "Political Science Confronts the Book: Recent Work on Scripture and Politics." *Journal of Politics*, 50 (February 1988), 219–34.

_____. "Political Science and 'The Public Interest.' " *Journal of Politics*, 36 (May 1974), 327–55.

———. "The Politics of Interest: Philosophy and the Limitations of the Science of Politics." *American Journal of Political Science*, 17 (November 1973), 745–66.

———. "The Thin Theory of Community: The Communitarians and their Critics." *Political Studies*, 32 (September 1989), 422–35.

———. "Yves R. Simon and 'The Common Good': A Note on the Concept." *Ethics*, 88 (April 1978), 229–39.

Cuddihy, John Murray. *No Offense: Civil Religion and Protestant Taste*. New York: Seabury, 1978.

Dannhauser, Werner. "Religion and the Conservatives." *Commentary* (December 1985), 51–55.

Devlin, Patrick. *The Enforcement of Morals*. London: Oxford University Press, 1965.

Dillard, Annie. *Teaching a Stone to Talk*. New York: Harper Colophon, 1983.

Douglass, R. Bruce, ed. *The Deeper Meaning of Economic Life: Critical Essays on the U.S. Catholic Bishops' Pastoral Letter on the Economy*. Washington, DC: Georgetown University Press, 1986.

Dunn, Charles W., ed. *Religion in American Politics*. Washington, DC: CQ Press, 1989.

Dworkin, Ronald. "Lord Devlin and the Enforcement of Morals." In *Political and Social Philosophy*, edited by J. Charles King and James A. McGilvray, pp. 348–62. New York: McGraw-Hill, 1973.

Eisenach, Eldon J. *The Two Worlds of Liberalism: Religion and Politics in Hobbes, Locke, and Mill*. Chicago: University of Chicago Press, 1981.

Elshtain, Jean Bethke. "Feminism, Family, & Community." *Dissent*, 29 (Fall 1982), 442–49.

———. *Public Man, Private Woman: Women in Social and Political Thought*. Princeton, NJ: Princeton University Press, 1981.

———, ed. *The Family in Political Thought*. Amherst, MA: University of Massachusetts Press, 1982.

Ferm, Deane William. *Contemporary American Theologies: A Critical Survey*. New York: Seabury, 1981.

Fischer, Constance T. "Privacy as a Profile of Authentic Consciousness." *Humanitas*, 11 (February 1975), 27–43.

Fowler, Robert Booth. *Religion and Politics in America*. Metuchen, NJ: The Scarecrow Press, 1985.

———. *Unconventional Partners: Religion and Liberal Culture in the United States*. Grand Rapids, MI: Eerdmanns, 1989.

French, Peter A., Theodore E. Uehling, Jr., and Howard K. Wettstein, eds. *Midwest Studies in Philosophy, Vol. XIII: Ethical Theory: Character and Virtue*. Notre Dame, IN: University of Notre Dame Press, 1988.

Fullinwider, Robert K. "Learning Morality." *QQ: Report from the Institute for Philosophy and Public Policy*, 8 (Spring 1988), 12–15.

Galston, William A. "Public Morality and Religion in the Liberal State." *PS*, 19 (Fall 1986), 807–24.

Gaus, Gerald F. *The Modern Liberal Theory of Man*. New York: St. Martin's, 1983.

Gilson, Etienne. *The Spirit of Medieval Philosophy*. New York: Charles Scribner's Sons, 1940.

Glass, James M. *Delusion: Internal Dimensions of Political Life*. Chicago: University of Chicago Press, 1985.

Gray, John. *Liberalism*. Minneapolis, MN: University of Minnesota Press, 1986.

Greenawalt, Kent. *Religious Convictions and Political Choice*. New York: Oxford University Press, 1988.

Greisen, Deanna H. "The Civic Role of Religion in a Democracy." Paper presented at the March 1989 Annual Meeting of the Southwestern Political Science Association, Little Rock, Arkansas..

Gunsteren, Herman van. "Public and Private." *Social Research*, 46 (Summer 1979), 255–71.

Hadden, Jeffrey K. "Religious Broadcasting and the Mobilization of the New Christian Right." *Journal for the Scientific Study of Religion*, 26 (March 1987), 1–24.

Hallie, Philip. *Lest Innocent Blood Be Shed*. New York: Harper & Row, 1979.

Hallowell, John H. *The Decline of Liberalism as an Ideology*. Berkeley, CA: University of California Press, 1943.

———. *Main Currents in Modern Political Thought*. New York: Holt, 1950.

Hammond, Phillip E. "Another Great Awakening?" In *The New Christian Right: Mobilization and Legitimation*, edited by Robert C. Liebman and Robert Wuthnow, pp. 207–23. New York: Aldine Publishing Company, 1983.

———, ed. *The Sacred in a Secular Age: Toward Revision in the Scientific Study of Religion*. Berkeley, CA: University of California Press, 1985.

Hampshire, Stuart, ed. *Public and Private Morality*. Cambridge: Cambridge University Press, 1978.

Harrington, Michael. *The Politics at God's Funeral: The Spiritual Crisis of Western Civilization*. New York: Penguin, 1983.

Hart, H. L. A. *Law, Liberty, and Morality*. New York: Vintage Books, 1963.

Hauerwas, Stanley. *A Community of Character*. Notre Dame, IN: University of Notre Dame Press, 1981.

———. *The Peaceable Kingdom*. Notre Dame, IN: University of Notre Dame Press, 1983.

Hawley, John Stratton, ed. *Saints and Virtues*. Berkeley, CA: University of California Press, 1987.

Herberg, Will. *Protestant-Catholic-Jew: An Essay in American Religious Sociology*. Garden City, NY: Doubleday Anchor, 1960.

Hertzke, Allen D. *Representing God in Washington*. Knoxville, TN: University of Tennessee Press, 1988.

Hitchcock, James. "Church, State, and Moral Values: The Limits of American Pluralism." *Law and Contemporary Problems*, 44 (Spring 1981), 3–21.

Hobbes, Thomas. *Leviathan*. edited by Michael Oakeshott. New York: Collier Books, 1962.

Holbrook, Clyde A. *Faith and Community: A Christian Existential Approach*. New York: Harper & Brothers, 1959.

Hui, Y. K. and Clarke E. Cochran. "Virtue Ethics and Natural Law." Paper presented at the 1988 Annual Meeting of the Southern Political Science Association, Atlanta, Georgia.

Jones, Richard H. "Accommodationist and Separationist Ideals in Supreme Court Establishment Clause Decisions." *Journal of Church and State*, 28 (Spring 1986), 193–223.

Jones, W. T. "Public Roles, Private Roles, and Differential Moral Assessments of Role Performances." *Ethics*, 94 (July 1984), 603–20.

Josephson, Eric. "Notes on the Sociology of Privacy." *Humanitas*, 11 (February 1975), 15–25.

Kanter, Rosabeth Moss. *Commitment and Community: Communes and Utopias in Sociological Perspective*. Cambridge, MA: Harvard University Press, 1972.

Kee, Alistair, ed. *A Reader in Political Theology*. Philadelphia: Westminster Press, 1974.

Kelly, George Armstrong. *Politics and Religious Consciousness in America*. New Brunswick, NJ: Transaction, 1984.

Kramnick, Isaac. "The Constitution and Its Critics on Individualism, Community, and the State." Paper delivered at the Annual Conference of the United States Capitol Historical Society, March 26–27, 1987, Washington, D.C.

Kuitert, H. M. *Everything is Political, But Politics is not Everything: A Theological Perspective on Faith and Politics*. Translated by John Bowden. London: SCM, 1986.

Lasch, Christopher. *The Culture of Narcissism: American Life in an Age of Diminishing Expectations*. New York: Warner Books, 1979.

————. *The Minimal Self: Psychic Survival in Troubled Times*. New York: W. W. Norton & Company, 1984.

Laursen, John Christian. "The Subversive Kant: The Vocabulary of 'Public' and 'Publicity.' " *Political Theory*, 14 (November 1986), 584–603.

Lefever, Ernest W. *Amsterdam to Nairobi*. Washington, DC: Ethics and Public Policy Center, 1979.

Lerner, Ralph. "Facing Up to the Founding." Paper presented at the Annual Conference of the United States Capitol Historical Society, March 26–27, 1987, Washington, D.C.

Little, David. "Legislating Morality." In *Christianity and Politics*, edited by Carol Friedley Griffith, pp. 39–53. Washington, DC: Ethics and Public Policy Center, 1981.

Lovin, Robin W., ed. *Religion and American Public Life: Interpretations and Explorations*. Mahwah, NJ: Paulist Press, 1986.

Lowi, Theodore J. *The End of Liberalism: The Second Republic of the United States*. 2d ed. New York: Norton, 1979.

Luckmann, Thomas. *The Invisible Religion: The Problem of Religion in Modern Society*. New York: Macmillan, 1967.

Lukes, Steven. *Individualism*. Oxford: Basil Blackwell, 1973.

MacIntyre, Alasdair. *After Virtue*. Notre Dame, IN: University of Notre Dame Press, 1981; 2d ed., 1984.

Mara, Gerald M. "Virtue and Pluralism: The Problem of the One and the Many." Paper presented at the Georgetown University Colloquium in Social and Political Theory, February 1987, Washington, D.C.

Marcel, Gabriel. *Homo Viator*. Translated by Emma Craufurd. New York: Harper & Row, 1962.

Martin, Judith. *Miss Manners' Guide to Rearing Perfect Children*. Illustrated by Gloria Kamen. New York: Penguin Books, 1985.

McGuire, Meredith. *Religion: The Social Context*. Belmont, CA: Wadsworth, 1981.

McWilliams, Wilson Carey. "The Bible in the American Political Tradition." In *Political Anthropology, III: Religion and Politics*, edited by Myron J. Aronoff, pp. 11–45. New Brunswick: Transaction, 1984.

_____. *The Idea of Fraternity in America*. Berkeley: University of California Press, 1974.

_____. "In Good Faith: On the Foundations of American Politics," *Humanities in Society*, 6 (Winter 1983), 19–40.

Milgram, Stanley. *Obedience to Authority*. New York: Harper, 1974.

Mill, John Stuart. *On Liberty*, edited by David Spitz. New York: W. W. Norton, 1975.

Moen, Matthew C. *The Christian Right and Congress*. Tuscaloosa, AL: University of Alabama Press, 1989.

Mooney, Christopher F., S.J. *Public Virtue: Law and the Social Character of Religion*. Notre Dame, IN: University of Notre Dame Press, 1986.

Moore, Barrington. *Privacy: Studies in Social and Cultural History*. Armonk, NY: M. E. Sharpe, Inc., 1984.

Neuhaus, Richard John. *The Naked Public Square: Religion and Democracy in America*. Grand Rapids, MI: Eerdmans, 1984.

_____, ed. *Unsecular America*. Grand Rapids, MI: Eerdmans,1986.

_____, ed. *Virtue—Public and Private*. Grand Rapids, MI: Eerdmans, 1986.

Nichols, Mary P. "Aristotle's Defense of Rhetoric." *Journal of Politics*, 49 (August 1987), 657–77.

Niebuhr, H. Richard. *Christ and Culture*. New York: Harper Colophon, 1975.

_____. *The Kingdom of God in America*. New York: Harper Torchbooks, 1959.

_____. *Radical Monotheism and Western Culture*. New York: Harper Torchbooks, 1970.

Nisbet, Robert A. *The Quest for Community*. New York: Oxford University Press, 1953.

_____. *The Social Bond*. New York: Knopf, 1970.

Nouwen, Henri J. M. *Reaching Out: The Three Movements of the Spiritual Life*. Garden City, NY: Doubleday, 1975.

Nussbaum, Martha. "Aeschylus and Practical Conflict." *Ethics*, 95 (January 1985), 233–67.

Oestereicher, Emil. "The Privatization of the Self in Modern Society." *Social Research*, 46 (Autumn 1979), 600–615.

Palmer, Parker J. *The Company of Strangers: Christians and the Renewal of America's Public Life*. New York: Crossroad, 1981.

Parent, W. A. "Recent Work on the Concept of Privacy." *American Philosophical Quarterly*, 20 (October 1983), 341–55.

Pateman, Carole. *Participation and Democratic Theory*. Cambridge: Cambridge University Press, 1970.

Pennock, J. Roland, and John W. Chapman. *Nomos XIII: Privacy*. New York: Atherton Press, 1971.

Percy, Walker. *Lost in the Cosmos: The Last Self-Help Book*. New York: Farrar, Straus and Giroux, 1983.

_____. *The Thanatos Syndrome*. New York: Farrar Straus and Giroux, 1987.

Pitkin, Hanna Fenichel. "Justice: On Relating Private and Public." *Political Theory*, 9 (August 1981), 327–52.

Poteat, William H. *Polanyian Meditations*. Durham, NC: Duke University Press, 1985.

Reichley, A. James. *Religion in American Public Life*. Washington, DC: Brookings Institution, 1985.

Reiman, Jeffrey H. "Privacy, Intimacy, and Personhood." *Philosophy and Public Affairs*, 6 (Fall 1976), 26–44.

Richey, Russell E. and Donald G. Jones, eds. *American Civil Religion*. New York: Harper, 1974.

Rieff, Philip. *The Triumph of the Therapeutic: Uses of Faith After Freud*. New York: Harper Torchbooks, 1968.

Riemer, Neal. *The Future of the Democratic Revolution: Toward a More Prophetic Politics*. New York: Praeger Publishers, 1984.

Robbins, Thomas and Roland Robertson, ed. *Church-State Relations: Tensions and Transitions*. New Brunswick, NJ: Transaction, 1987.

Roelofs, H. Mark. *The Tensions of Citizenship: Private Man and Public Duty*. New York: Rinehart & Co., 1957.

Rosenblum, Nancy L. *Another Liberalism: Romanticism and the Reconstruction of Liberal Thought*. Cambridge, MA: Harvard University Press, 1987.

Rousseau, Jean-Jacques. *The Social Contract*. Translated by Maurice Cranston. Baltimore, MD: Penguin Books, 1968.

Sandel, Michael J. *Liberalism and the Limits of Justice*. Cambridge: Cambridge University Press, 1982.

———. "Morality and the Liberal Ideal." *The New Republic*, May 7, 1984, pp. 15–17.

Sapiro, Virginia. "Private Costs of Public Commitments or Public Costs of Private Commitments? Family Roles Versus Political Ambition." *American Journal of Political Science*, 26 (May 1982), 265–79.

Schaar, John H. "The Case for Patriotism." In *idem, Legitimacy in the Modern State*, pp. 285–311. New Brunswick, NJ: Transaction Books, 1981.

———. "Legitimacy in the Modern State." In *Power and Community*, edited by Philip Green and Sanford Levinson, pp. 276–327. New York: Vintage, 1970.

———. *Loyalty in America*. Berkeley, CA: University of California Press, 1957.

Schoeman, Ferdinand David, ed. *Philosophical Dimensions of Privacy: An Anthology*. Cambridge: Cambridge University Press, 1984.

Seabury, Paul. "Caesar and the Religious Domain in America." *Teaching Political Science*, 10 (Fall 1982), 20–29.

Sider, Ronald J. *Completely Pro-Life: Building a Consistent Stance*. Downers Grove, IL: InterVarsity Press, 1987.

Simon, Arthur. *Christian Faith and Public Policy: No Grounds for Divorce*. Grand Rapids, MI: Eerdmans, 1987.

Simon, Yves R. *The Definition of Moral Virtue*, edited by Vukan Kuic. New York: Fordham University Press, 1986.

Spragens, Thomas A., Jr. *The Irony of Liberal Reason*. Chicago: University of Chicago Press, 1981.

———. "Reconstructing Liberal Theory: Reason and Liberal Culture," in *Liberals on Liberalism*, edited by Alfonso J. Damico, pp. 34–53. Totowa, NJ: Rowman & Littlefield, 1986.

Stanley, Manfred. "The Mystery of the Commons: On the Indispensability of Civic Rhetoric." *Social Research*, 50 (Winter 1983), 851–83.

Strong, Tracy B. "The Practical Unity of Community and Privacy." *Humanitas*, 11 (February 1975), 85–97.

Strout, Cushing. *The New Heavens and the New Earth: Political Religion in America.* New York: Harper Torchbooks, 1975.

Taylor, Charles. "Hegel, History, and Politics," in *Liberalism and its Critics*, edited by Michael Sandel, pp. 177–99. New York: New York University Press, 1984.

Tinder, Glenn. *Tolerance: Toward a New Civility.* Amherst, MA: University of Massachusetts Press, 1976.

Tocqueville, Alexis de. *Democracy in America.* Translated by Henry Reeve. New Rochelle, NY: Arlington House, n.d.

Tournier, Paul. *The Meaning of Persons.* Translated by Edwin Hudson. New York: Harper, 1957.

Unger, Roberto Mangabeira. *Knowledge and Politics.* New York: Free Press, 1975.

United States Catholic Conference. *Economic Justice for All: Pastoral Letter on Catholic Social Teaching and the U.S. Economy.* Washington, DC: United States Catholic Conference, 1986.

Vetterli, Richard, and Gary Bryner. *In Search of the Republic: Public Virtue and the Roots of American Government.* Totowa, NJ: Rowman & Littlefield, 1987.

Voegelin, Eric. *Order and History, Volume III: Plato and Aristotle.* Baton Rouge, LA: Louisiana State University Press, 1957.

Wald, Kenneth D. *Religion and Politics in the United States.* New York: St. Martin's, 1987.

Wallace, James D. *Virtues and Vices.* Ithaca, NY: Cornell University Press, 1978.

Walsh, David. "The Role of the Church in the Modern World." *Journal of Church and State*, 29 (Winter 1987), 63–77.

Walzer, Michael. *Exodus and Revolution.* New York: Basic Books, 1985.

——. *Interpretation and Social Criticism.* Cambridge, MA: Harvard University Press, 1987.

——. "Liberalism and the Art of Separation." *Political Theory*, 12 (August 1984), 315–30.

——. *Spheres of Justice: A Defense of Pluralism and Equality.* New York: Basic Books, Inc., 1983.

Weil, Simone. *The Simone Weil Reader*, edited by George A. Panichas. New York: David McKay, 1977.

White, Leslie. *The Science of Culture: A Study of Man and Civilization.* New York: Grove Press, 1949.

Wildavsky, Aaron. *The Nursing Father: Moses as a Political Leader.* University, AL: University of Alabama Press, 1984.

Winch, Peter. *The Idea of a Social Science and its Relation to Philosophy.* London: Routledge and Kegan Paul, 1958.

Wuthnow, Robert and Clifford Nass. "Government Activity and Civil Privatism: Evidence from Voluntary Church Membership." *Journal for the Scientific Study of Religion*, 27 (June 1988), 157–74.

Yarbrough, Jean. "The Constitution and Character: The Missing Critical Principle?" Paper presented at the Annual Conference of the United States Capitol Historical Society, March 26–27, 1987, Washington, D.C.

Yoder, John H. *The Politics of Jesus*. Grand Rapids, MI: Eerdmans, 1972.

Zetterbaum, Marvin. "Self and Subjectivity in Political Theory." *Review of Politics*, 44 (January 1982), 59–82.

Zuckert, Catherine. "Not by Preaching: Tocqueville on the Role of Religion in American Democracy." *Review of Politics*, 43 (April 1981), 259–80.

Index